Manager's Guide to Operations Management

Other titles in the Briefcase Books series include:

To learn more about titles in the Briefcase Books series go to
www.briefcasebooks.com

Manager's Guide to Operations Management

John Kamauff

New York Chicago San Francisco Lisbon
London Madrid Mexico City Milan New Delhi
San Juan Seoul Singapore Sydney Toronto

1 2 3 4 5 6 7 8 9 0 DOC/DOC 0 1 0 9

ISBN 978-0-07-162799-3
MHID   0-07-162799-5

This is a CWL Publishing Enterprises book developed for McGraw-Hill by CWL Publishing Enterprises, Inc., Madison, Wisconsin, www.cwlpub.com.

McGraw-Hill books are available at special quantity discounts to use as premiums and sales promotions, or for use in corporate training programs. To contact a representative please e-mail us at bulksales@mcgraw-hill.com.

Contents

Preface

Operations management is all around us, and when you become enamored of it, you schedule your vacations around manufacturing plant tours, you cannot eat in a buffet line without approaching the manager about the food service operations, and you practice queuing theory when you are trying to merge into traffic … but I digress.

Traditionally, "operations" was closely identified with what occurs within the four walls of a manufacturing facility, but service-related roles now account for 80 percent of all jobs in North America, competition is global, and individual companies no longer compete—rather virtual end-to-end organizations known as supply chains do!

Companies like Amazon, Dell, Southwest Airlines, Cintas, and Google have figured out the true ramifications of operational synergies, and they have exploited discontinuities in the marketplace to develop entrepreneurial service delivery models that continue to yield sustainable competitive advantages. The good news is that we understand these operations techniques and, more importantly, we can learn and readily apply them in a variety of situations from our kitchens to NASA.

Being an operations manager is one of the most rewarding jobs in the world. You get to realize your vision by making things happen—often by actually creating something or delivering a service, and you have the opportunity to help and mentor those around you along the way.

Operations management starts with strategy and develops through the realm of processes. A *process* is simply a series of actions, changes, transformations, or functions designed to achieve a specified result. And that's what operations does—it brings about results, preferably results that are desired, preferably efficiently and effectively.

What we need to understand about operations is what levers we need to pull to achieve the desired results. Once we understand the process orientation of operations, we need to be able to apply the principles of quality and of lean thinking. How can we do more with less? How can we get the most from our plant and equipment, our people, our technology, and our leadership, given the ever-present constraint on resources?

What we learned in kindergarten really does apply—we have to play well with others (in this case suppliers, buyers, and even competitors) in order to provide what our customers really want and need. And we have to share—most importantly, information—to become supply chain champions, not bullies, to leverage our core competencies and those of our partners.

Operations entails the best side of project management and necessarily requires an ability to forecast and understand the demands of the marketplace as well as an ability to plan, budget, and schedule how we will satisfy those needs. And although we ostensibly would like to make everything ourselves, the reality is that we will need to buy things from others, move those things (and other things as well), and possibly even rely on others to do a variety of tasks for us. These activities all fall under the purview of the operations manager.

Inventory (what you have and hold) and throughput (how fast you move it through the system) also matter when we are trying to do more with less, so your ability to manage them is directly correlated with success.

And then there's the issue of technology. Technology is not a panacea, but neither can it be ignored. Operations managers must be able to use technology as an enabler to get the job done.

And just as important is your ability to make a difference in the world. Operations managers have a unique position of influence and accountability for what we do when we are transforming inputs into our products and services. Our ability to integrate the basic tenets of corporate social responsibility (CSR) into our daily operations is becoming increasingly important, and, just as significantly, CSR is good business!

This book will cover the basics. It will also illuminate light bulbs and yield some "aha's" along the way. But be ready for moments—many moments, probably—when you'll say to yourself, "I've always known that. That's common sense." And also remember: common sense is not so common. Even if you know it, are you applying it? After all, as you'll discover, much of the practice of operations management is about recommitting to what you already know.

The principles of operations management that can be scientifically adopted across manufacturing can also often be creatively applied in service operations and across the extended links of the supply chain.

Operations managers learn "by walking around," observing, sharing information, working with others, and acting accordingly. Throughout this book we suggest that operations managers must exercise a significant role in developing a firm's competitive advantage, particularly with regard to customer satisfaction, quality, and total systems cost. The strategic firm must include operations and operational considerations in its planning, development, and execution across the extended enterprise.

This book describes how these changes apply to making operations work and offers insights into how operations management across the extended enterprise is likely to be affected. In addition, this book addresses an array of suitable responses for operations professionals, so you can continue to add value over time.

Chapter 1 provides an overview of operations management. Chapter 2 discusses product design and process development. The next three chapters are about operations improvement: Chapter 3 explains how to improve production processes, Chapter 4 presents the basics of improving quality using the Six Sigma approach, and Chapter 5 introduces lean thinking and lean principles. Chapter 6 moves beyond the walls of the organization to extended supply chain. Chapters 7 through 11 cover forecasting, planning, scheduling, sourcing, procurement, outsourcing, logistics, inventory management, and operations technology. Chapter 12 goes above and beyond operations management to discuss an area of growing importance—corporate social responsibility. The book concludes with a short overview on the role of operations managers and the challenges they face.

Special Features

The idea behind the books in the Briefcase Books series is to give you practical information written in a friendly, person-to-person style. The chapters deal with both strategic and tactical issues and include lots of examples and how-to information. They also feature numerous sidebars designed to give you specific types of information you can use. Here are descriptions of the boxes you'll find in this book.

KEY TERM Every subject has some special jargon, especially this one, dealing with operations management. These boxes provide definitions of these terms and concepts.

SMART MANAGING These boxes do just what their name implies: give you tips and tactics for using the ideas in this book to intelligently manage and encourage effective operations management practices in your organization.

TRICKS OF THE TRADE These boxes give you how-to hints on techniques insiders use to manage and execute the strategies and tactics described in this book.

FOR EXAMPLE It's always useful to have examples that show how the principles in the book are applied. These boxes provide descriptions of how managers and organizations have implemented the techniques in this book.

CAUTION These boxes provide warnings for where things could go wrong in the operations management process.

How can you make sure you won't make a mistake when you're trying to implement the techniques the book describes? You can't, but these boxes will give you practical advice on how to minimize the possibility of an error.

This icon identifies boxes where you'll find specific procedures or techniques you can follow as well as additional resources you can use to take advantage of the book's advice.

TOOLS

Acknowledgments

Every author needs a reason to get started, if not a muse. For this book, it was my son, Ryan. Not only did he serve his country with distinction in Iraq, he returned a more focused young man, quickly finished his undergraduate degree, and embarked on a promising career as a business technology consultant with Crucial Point LLC. In addition, he helped me to get started with the *Manager's Guide to Operations Management* by helping me to understand and articulate how operations management, which has meant so much to me in my personal and professional life, should be shared with others. He even convinced his mother, Susan, to proofread the chapter on corporate social responsibility—a cause that she supports passionately. Thanks, Ryan, for getting the character "Jessica" off the ground and into her role in the book as the epitome of an operations manager.

Additionally, this book would never have gotten anywhere without Bob Magnan. A gifted author in his own right, Bob used his many talents to keep the process moving and contributed immeasurably to the final product. His insight, due diligence, creativity, and work ethic are embedded within the book. And the project would never have taken flight were it not for the instincts, perseverance, and patience of John Woods of CWL Publishing Enterprises, the instigator of this project.

I was also aided in my thinking, before and during this effort, by my good friends, Geoff Peters, Peter Dowling, and Mark Simmons, who are preeminent strategy and operations consultants (from North America,

Australia, and Europe, respectively). Over the past five years, Archstone Consulting has been my home—a place that has allowed me to work with outstanding and dedicated consultants and even better clients. I continue to be impressed with the quality of results we provide across strategy, operations, and other critical business areas such as financial advisory services. Throughout this time, I have been able to rely on the insight, technical knowledge, and support of colleagues, including those at Archstone Consulting. A special thanks to Diana Bersohn and Ryan Reeser for their editing and proofreading assistance. I also had the great fortune to learn about teaching and mentoring as well as the theoretical and pragmatic precepts of operations management from Robert Spekman, Ed Davis, and Bob Landel from the Darden Graduate School of Business (University of Virginia); Mike Leenders and Paul Beamish from the Richard Ivey School of Business (University of Western Ontario); and Bob Collins from IMD (Lausanne, Switzerland).

But most of all, a special thanks to the clients I've been able to serve during my career—many of whom have become close friends—from whom I have learned so much, and yet with whom I have been able to ply my trade. These include Lawrence Aldridge, Jeff Miller, Bill Segil, Valerie Szabo, Tiffany Kolchins, Steve Miller, Bill Patrizio, Carmen Bauza, Bill Shannon, Randy MacDonald, Henri Steenkamp, Mark Fiebert, Steve Kass, Avram Kornberg, Ken Going, Harold Karp, Brent Buckner, Jim Simpson, Pat Keating, Steve Golliher, Marc Latney, Ryan Aytay, Bob Barnes, Aris Melissaratos, Sean Eveland, and John Carr. You all have played a part in making this book a reality.

Operations Management:
Combining Art, Science, and Good Shoes

I n all walks of life, you will find operations managers. They don't fit into any one category, and they do not have all the same responsibilities, but one thing is the same—they make everything happen.

Operations management is both an art and a science. It involves working with things and with people, with certainties and with possibilities and probabilities. The science includes understanding the processes, tools, and techniques. The art is in applying them effectively within the context of the people who provide the inputs, the people who process the inputs into outputs, the people who deliver the outputs, and the people who buy those outputs.

Operations management
The direction and control of the processes that transform inputs into outputs **KEY TERM** for customers—finished goods or services. It entails the design and control of systems responsible for the productive use of raw materials, human resources, equipment, and facilities in developing goods and/or services. Operations management encompasses planning, sourcing and purchasing, inventory management, production management, marketing, sales, distribution, supply chain management, quality management, management information systems, and more.

Process In an organization, any activity that transforms inputs into outputs, with **KEY TERM** the intention that the output will be of greater value than the input.

We Are All Operations Managers

A plant supervisor, a quick-service restaurant manager, a mother of four planning meals for the week—each of these people is an operations manager. The operations manager takes charge of the processes that take inputs, raw materials (in our three examples, truckloads of iron ore, cases of ground beef, and loaves of bread), and makes them into outputs (steel I-beams, hamburger dinners, and peanut butter sandwiches).

Input Raw material that is turned into a final product. Inputs consist of things like **KEY TERMS** wood, metal, nails, and even labor. Inputs can determine the success of the final product, so sourcing them must be taken seriously.

Output The final product. Outputs are what is sold to (or, in the case of services, consumed by) the customer. This can be a service (consulting), food (a hamburger), or something that will become the input for another product (2x4 lumber). Outputs are what your company makes and sells.

How does all this occur? How does a plant turn iron ore into steel? Well, I won't bore you with the details, but it requires three things. The operations manager must *plan, implement* the plan, and *monitor* the processes. These three steps are also the same for the restaurant manager and the mother. In order for operations managers to succeed, they must make the most of the assets they possess—financial, material, and human.

The first step of this process is *planning*. An operations manager must plan for procuring the inputs; plan the path they will follow through the warehouse and factory, the restaurant, or the home; and plan for how those inputs will be turned into the final products, how long that will take, and when they will be sold.

For the planning process to be a success, the operations manager will want to include all the stakeholders or their representatives in the planning process. Stakeholders include anyone who contributes to or is affected by these decisions.

After the planning process ends, the operations manager must _implement_ the plans. Implementation or execution simply means going through the processes that turn the inputs into the outputs. This series of processes can be as simple as making a sandwich or as complex as creating silicon wafers. Whatever the situation, the operations manager needs to know which processes are involved and what occurs in each process.

Finally, the operations

> **Stakeholder** Any person or group likely to be affected by a decision. Stakeholders can include **KEY TERM** shareholders, the people creating the product or service, and the people in logistics and supply who move your product or deliver your service.

> **QUALIFY THE STAKEHOLDERS** **SMART**
> The circles of stakeholders can extend pretty far, so be careful to include only the stakeholders who really matter and to **MANAGING** whom the discussion really matters and involve them only to the degree that seems appropriate for each person or group.

manager _monitors_ the processes. That means keeping track of what's happening and supervising the employees involved in the processes. A good manager intervenes only when necessary.

So now you know what operations managers do, but how do they do it? What are the steps a good operations manager takes? What are the actions a good operations manager avoids?

To fully flesh out operations management, we will take the example of a mother of four, Jessica, preparing meals for her family. How is Jessica an operations manager? She plans for the meals she cooks, she buys all the food, and she ensures the food gets prepared properly and provided to the end customer, her family. To prepare meals in the least time and with the least effort, it's essential that she make the best use of the available assets.

Those assets are facilities (the kitchen, with a refrigerator, a stove, an oven, counters, etc.), equipment (pots, pans, implements, dishes, silverware, etc.), raw materials (foods), and human resources—her four children: Dave, 15, Stephanie, 12, Amanda, 8, and Danny, 4.

Each of her children has his or her strengths and weaknesses in the kitchen. Dave is good at preparing any vegetable, but not very capable with the oven. Stephanie loves to bake and will cook all types of treats, yet she cannot figure out how to boil water. Amanda is great at washing dishes and she always helps Jessica clean up, but doesn't much like to help with any of the cooking, preferring to help at the end. Danny is great at setting the table and that's about it. So Jessica uses what she knows of her children's strengths and weaknesses in planning for each meal. How does she determine what food to make?

Planning

Every Sunday, Jessica gets together with the members of her family and asks them what they want to eat that week. From this list of meals, she compiles a list of needs, her shopping list. These items—the bread, meat, cheese, peanut butter, jelly, pastas, and so on—are all her inputs. An operations manager would typically shop around, trying to find sources for the least expensive inputs possible. Jessica looks for the lowest prices at the grocery store, sometimes buys generics rather than name brands, uses coupons, and buys in larger quantities when appropriate. She tries to get the foods she knows her family likes, but she will look at the ingredients and make sure the proper nutrients are all there.

SMART MANAGING

COST VS. QUALITY

This is a central tenet of operations management: everyone wants a product that's great...and cheap! But you can't always make a product of high quality inexpensively. So what do you do?

It depends on your customers—what do they really want or need? Do they prefer quality over cost or cost over quality? A plugged-in operations manager should work with his or her marketing or sales team to garner this information and work to create the product or service most likely to succeed. When you find the proper balance between cost and quality, your product should do well!

Few operations managers ever deal with any unrefined products; most likely they will receive a product from another company and add as much value to it as they can. Here we see the <u>first of many trade-offs central to operations management: cost vs. quality</u>.

Jessica will also make a list of chores and assign them to the children. She makes sure that she assigns the right chore to the right person. By delegating the activities to the members of her work force according to their strengths, she achieves efficiency in her operations.

Assigning Workloads

Every person has a certain set of skills. As an operations manager, it is your job to keep people doing work that they are capable of doing and feel comfortable doing. You will find employees doing jobs that don't match their strengths. Sometimes you'll have to make tough decisions in assigning roles.

Something to remember here is to not alienate the employees who aren't always the most accomplished or capable—not every team has all "A" players, and it is the operations manager's responsibility to make the best use of his or her resources while helping them to get better. You can work to include all your employees in decisions. You can stress that all positions, however menial they may seem, are integral to success. You can create Gantt charts (we'll learn about those later) and other performance diagrams to show the contributions of each employee. People will work harder and better if they can see regular improvement or action from their work.

When allocating tasks, be sure to leave some for yourself. People don't want to work for someone whom they don't see working as well. It's essential for you to work, even if you're just helping someone else finish his or her work. When the manager and employees work as a team, they can create solutions that weren't previously imagined and maybe even speed up completion of projects.

WHY IS MY WORK NOT THAT IMPORTANT?   CAUTION

As previously stated, it is essential to keep all of your employees working toward a goal. This is because one asset that will always be in short supply is your employees and the number of hours they can work. Keep your employees happy and they will do their best for you. Don't minimize any aspect of any process or any employee working in it!

It's important that Jessica not give too much work to any of her kids; obviously they have lives outside the kitchen. If anyone gets saddled with more than he or she feels able to handle, that worker will start to feel overused and unappreciated. So what does Jessica do? She asks Dave to cook veggies every night. She tasks Stephanie to cook desserts twice a week, making enough to supply the family all week. Amanda helps Jessica with dishes a few nights a week. Every evening Jessica helps Danny set the table. With this division of labor, Jessica doesn't have to do all the cooking; most evenings she can focus on just the main course. Then, Jessica and the kids get to eat as a family and talk about things, including their kitchen processes and workloads.

Jessica's family members get together every evening as a team. It's a good idea for your team as well. We'd suggest meeting at least once a week to talk about the processes and workloads (like Jessica does with her Sunday planning session). This way, you keep members of the working group informed regarding each other's projects, which can lead to unexpected instances of the "Eureka!" moment, when someone suggests a solution out of nowhere—sometimes for a problem you didn't even know existed.

Creating Timelines

Timelines will drive your processes from start to end. As you and your working group keep to task, the work should be manageable and easily completed. If not, you will probably find it necessary to have employees work overtime and/or miss your deadline. Timelines give you a benchmark by which you can measure and document progress.

At the end of every project, it's necessary to look back and see when you reached your benchmarks, when you made it earlier than planned, and when you missed your benchmarks. Knowing these facts will help you when you need to plan for other projects and assign workloads.

SET ACHIEVABLE BENCHMARKS

A benchmark is an intermediary goal to help measure progress on a project. Make sure your benchmarks can actually be achieved. It's great to shoot high, but if you consistently shoot high and rarely or never hit your mark, it can lower morale and hurt your reputation as a manager. Keeping benchmarks and expectations achievable will give your employees a morale boost and allow them to achieve their goals.

Supply Chain and Logistics

Properly managing the supply chain can make or break your production. If your inputs don't reach the right people in time for them to add their value, you can slow down everything, creating delays that will cost lots of money.

Supply chain The series of processes by which inputs are transformed into outputs and delivered to customers. In addition to the processes within the organization, the chain includes suppliers and distributors. The processes are linked by logistics.   **KEY TERMS**

Logistics The management of assets (inputs/outputs) from one place to another. It requires a high level of knowledge of timetables and work allocation to properly move the right assets at the right times.

Here is an example of a simple supply chain:

supplier ➝ production processes ➝ distributor ➝
retail outlets ➝ customers ➝ supplier ➝ Web site

For Jessica, the supply chain and logistics are simple. The supply chain consists of purchasing food and any equipment necessary (stores), preparation (refrigerator and counters) and cooking (stove and oven), and delivery (table). In terms of logistics, she must make sure that she has purchased the necessary foods and stored them where Dave can find the vegetables to cook, Stephanie can find the ingredients for making desserts, and she can find what she needs to prepare the rest of each meal. Jessica must also make sure that she and Amanda have cleaned the dishes, silverware, pots, pans, and utensils, and put them away properly so Dave and Stephanie can find what they need for cooking and baking and Danny can find what he needs for setting the table. Finally, Jessica must coordinate use of the kitchen facilities and equipment so that Dave can use the stove, Stephanie can use the oven, she can use the stove and/or oven at the same time, and Danny can access the dishes and silverware for the table.

Implementing the Plans

Once the planning stage is completed, the real fun can begin. An operations manager will move from planning to implementing the plans. At this point he or she needs to be sure that all members of the team understand what they are responsible for doing, when, and how. A review of the planning stage is key, because it can help in future planning stages and in identifying current and potential problems.

Implementation or execution moves the business forward. It requires you to find sources for all the inputs and purchase them. It requires staffing the processes and assigning the work. It is also necessary that you, as the manager, make sure the processes are completed correctly. We will discuss implementation as starting with purchasing. Most often, sourcing occurs prior to implementation, but we will discuss sourcing and purchasing together due to their connection.

Sourcing and Purchasing

Jessica sources primarily from the local grocery store, occasionally from several specialty food stores, and, if necessary, from the nearby convenience store; she researches the nutritional values and food trends, and she tracks price trends and sales at other grocery stores in the area.

She makes many purchasing decisions, trying to keep her costs low while buying the best food for her family. When she's at the store, she tries to maximize the value for her money. She compares prices between or among items, considering also whether to use coupons from the free local newspaper and whether to buy in larger quantities to get a lower price. As she compares products, she'll determine what is more important to her family: cost or quality.

These little decisions that she makes, often instinctively, almost without thinking, are those of an operations manager. Her choices—between name brands and generics, between margarine and butter, between cow's milk and soy milk—will affect not only the quality of the food, but also the budget. For example, if she buys the more expensive cereal every week for a whole year, at an additional cost of $1.50, she'll wind up spending an extra $78 a year just on cereal. Should she stock up on a few staples now or wait until there's a sale—and hope the family doesn't run out of something

KEY TERMS

Sourcing Determining how and where to buy inputs. The sourcing part of the purchasing equation has become so essential to maintaining or achieving competitive advantage that it must be examined in great detail. With the advent of the Internet, even small businesses can source from overseas.

Purchasing Buying inputs. This means materials, supplies, and services—whatever the company needs to produce and deliver outputs.

vital, a situation that might require a quick trip to the nearby convenience store, where the prices are always higher?

These little costs add up, and it is up to the operations manager to determine if they are worth it or not! Every operations manager faces similar decisions in sourcing and purchasing. Each operations manager considers factors such as cost, quality, discounts, quantities, and timing.

Processing

This is the heart of operations—the processes by which goods are produced and services are delivered. The processes vary almost infinitely among organizations, from manufacturing to service, from huge to tiny, and even within the same sector or niche. They are beyond discussion and even defy generalizations.

When you plan properly, by developing timetables, delegating work, and sourcing properly, you will find that the implementation phase can be both simple and easily managed.

Monitoring the Processes

A good operations manager will have a good attitude, good shoes, and a small desk. Always on the move and desperate to get and share information, a good manager will monitor processes and supervise groups of employees. This means anticipating potential problems and putting out fires.

For Jessica, it's relatively easy to monitor the processes. She may need to remind her four children to do their tasks and deal with occasional complaints and arguments. But since Amanda does her work only after the family has eaten dinner, and Stephanie makes desserts only twice a week, there are usually only two children in the kitchen with her—Dave cooking vegetables at the stove and Danny moving between the kitchen and the dining room as he sets the table. However, occasionally the kitchen gets a little crowded, so Jessica may need to intervene. She may also need to put out a fire from time to time, literally as well as figuratively, but she can monitor the processes without much effort while doing her tasks. Generally, all goes well, but if there's a problem, it means only that the family will be eating overcooked broccoli or scorched apple pie—no big deal.

Operations Management: The Big Picture

Operations management in organizations is more complicated, of course, than turning food into meals. The purpose of operations management is to make the best use of productive resources. It entails the design and control of systems for the productive use of raw materials, human resources, equipment, and facilities to develop and deliver products and/or services. How we manage productive resources is critical to making profits, growing, and competing.

At the start of this chapter, we said of operations managers that "they make everything happen." That's only a slight exaggeration.

Operations management is a functional area, like finance, marketing, and human resources in most organizations. It is responsible for making strategic (long-term) decisions that affect the entire organization. Those decisions must support the mission and the overall strategy of the organization. The operations strategy is basically a plan for using production resources to support the long-term competitive strategy of the organization.

Operations Strategy

The operations strategy of an organization depends on the mission—central purpose, core values, and goals—and the overall strategy of the organization. However, operations strategies generally involve plans for improving processes and creating shareholder value, by doing the following:

- Decreasing total costs.
- Decreasing working capital.
- Increasing the return on assets—doing more with less.
- Leveraging the value chain for tax advantages.
- Growing revenue—using our operations portfolio to uncover latent requirements (features or capabilities that customers do not expect or maybe even imagine).

Developing an operations strategy requires a solid working knowledge of the processes and the factors that we call *competitive dimensions*. These are the specific factors that a company uses to compete within its industry—quality (actual or perceived), price, target customers, geographical scope, size of target market, number of products, distribution network, and so on. Good operations management maximizes competitive dimensions as part of a strategic approach that creates growth and promotes that rarest of assets—competitive advantage.

> **Competitive dimensions** **KEY TERM**
> The specific factors that a company uses to compete within its industry, such as quality (actual or perceived), price, target customers, geographical scope, size of target market, number of products, and distribution network. Competitive dimensions are more specific than the generic competitive strategies of the industry.

Competitive Dimensions

Operations management entails *optimizing the flow of products, information, and cash across the extended enterprise.* Success in operations is related to competitiveness across core competencies and often includes multiple dimensions: cost, product

> **Extended enterprise** A **KEY TERM**
> loosely connected network of companies that work together to provide goods or services to a market, also known as a supply chain or a value chain. Exhibit 1-1 illustrates the concerns of the operations manager and the flows involved in operations management.

quality, reliability, delivery speed, delivery reliability, demand changes, flexibility, and support.

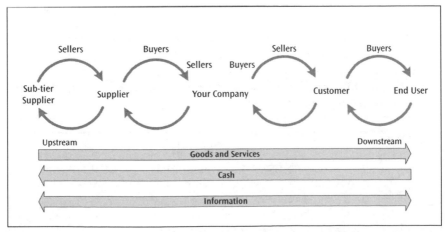

Exhibit 1-1. The flow of products, information, and cash.

- *Cost* is the total cost that each product or service will incur across the entire extended enterprise.
- *Product quality* is how customers perceive a product or service in terms of something they want in that product or service, such as reliability, convenience and ease of use, safety, and durability.
- *Reliability* is how sure you are that a process will work consistently and produce the same results.
- *Delivery speed* is how long it takes to provide customers with a finished product or a service.
- *Delivery reliability* is how likely a delivery is to happen as expected and when scheduled.
- *Demand changes* are market changes that affect the aggregate demand for a product or service.
- *Flexibility* is how easily the company can react to demand changes.
- *Support* is composed of four additional key dimensions: technical liaison and support, meeting launch dates, supplier after-sale support, and other dimensions.

While it would be wonderful to succeed in all these competitive dimensions simultaneously, it is unlikely that you will do so and you do

---

GREEN COMPETITIVE ADVANTAGE

TRICKS OF THE TRADE

Savvy managers are always looking for new competitive advantages. Two trends that have developed in recent decades are "environmentally friendly processes and products" and "the use of information," as Mark M. Davis, Nicholas J. Aquilano, and Richard B. Chase pointed out in the 1990s in *Fundamentals of Operations Management* (McGraw-Hill, 2003).

We could also add the whole area usually labeled "corporate social responsibility"—social, natural (e.g., no product testing on animals), health (e.g., support of campaigns against heart disease and breast cancer), and political causes as well as charities of all kinds.

PROVE IT!

CAUTION

If a cause really matters to your organization, don't just express it in words. Show it with facts, if possible, and/or with real support for the cause.

Talk is cheap. If you don't back up your words with actions, the effect on potential customers is like breaking a promise.

BEN & JERRY'S HOMEMADE, INC.

This company has long supported causes. On its Web site (www.benjerry.com), the company posts a yearly report on its "social and environmental performance." There's also a "Social & Environmental Assessment" that states, "We believe it's our duty to use our business to improve social, economic and environmental conditions around us. And around the world." In 1992, the company signed on to the CERES Principles, "which state a business has a responsibility to the environment and should uphold a set of aspirational principles."

In 1985 the company donated stock to establish Ben & Jerry's Foundation, "which supports community groups seeking solutions to social, economic and environmental injustice." Also, the company "makes yearly donations at its board's discretion of over $1.1 million dollars, adjusted upward annually for sales growth and inflation."

DON'T ASSUME

CAUTION

Operations managers must stay on top of the game and be aware of changes in their markets, their industry, and the world around them.

A senior executive from BellSouth once shared an interesting fact of life: "For the last 20 years we have chosen our suppliers; over the next 20 years they will choose us."

Recent changes in the automobile industry have provided another example. General Motors was once the largest corporation in the world. As recently as 2000, its market capitalization was $52.4 billion and its stock price was at $93. By June 2009 its market cap was below $700 million, its stock was at 75 cents, and GM filed for Chapter 11 bankruptcy.

---

not need to do so. It is properly managing the tradeoffs between them that will lead to success or failure for an operations manager.

It is up to operations managers to find creative, innovative ways to integrate strengths and weaknesses into a more cohesive, more distinctive competitive force. The essence of operations management, then, is based on developing strategies, managing projects, executing processes, managing people, and leading change.

Development of an Operations Strategy

The first step toward more effective operations is developing a consistent and congruent operations strategy—one that is consistent across its key elements while being congruent with other business strategies, such as marketing or finance. In the absence of a clearly articulated operations strategy, the plans, policies, and procedures that are in place, in essence, form the operations strategy and can be a good starting point. In any case, an operations strategy typically consists of the broad totality of decisions that shape the long-term capabilities of any type of operations and their contribution to the overall strategy by reconciling downstream needs and requirements of the markets to be served with upstream operational resources and abilities of the extended enterprise.

To develop an operations strategy, it is important to take four steps:

1. Segment the market according to the product or the service.
   - What parts of the market can you easily reach?
   - What parts of the market are most profitable?
   - What parts of the market are most open or closed to entry?

2. Identify the product or service requirement, demand patterns, and profit margins for each segment.
   - What makes your product or service salable?
   - When is demand greatest? When is demand least?
   - What parts of the market are most profitable?

3. Determine the *order winners* and *order qualifiers* for each grouping.
   - What separates a product or service that customers want from one that they don't want?
   - What level of performance for a product or service is the minimum acceptable to customers?

4. Convert order winners into specific performance requirements.
   - How can we relate what we know customers want to what we can produce?
   - It is necessary to ensure that order winners are our benchmarks for success.

An operations strategy is the key roadmap to success. An operations strategy must consider all the processes involved as well as all of the supply chain across the extended enterprise.

ORDER QUALIFIES AND ORDER WINNERS   SMART

The concept of *order qualifiers* and *order winners* was established by Terry Hill in *Manufacturing Strategy* (Macmillan, 1993). Order qualifiers are criteria that a company must meet just to be considered by customers as a potential source, but meeting those criteria is not likely to be enough to help a company get orders. To do that, a company must meet order-winner criteria.

MANAGING

Operations Manager's Checklist for Chapter 1

☑ Operations management is the direction and control of the processes that transform inputs into outputs for customers—finished goods or services. It entails the design and control of systems responsible for the productive use of raw materials, human resources, equipment, and facilities in developing goods and/or services.

☑ The fundamental work of operations management consists of three steps: *plan, implement* the plan, and *monitor* the processes.

☑ Operations management is both an art and a science. The science includes understanding the processes, tools, and techniques. The art is in applying them effectively within the context of the people involved in those processes and the people who buy the goods and services generated by those processes.

☑ Operations management is responsible for making strategic (long-term) decisions that affect the entire organization. Those decisions must support the mission and the overall strategy of the organization. The operations strategy is basically a plan for fulfilling the mission and pursuing the organization's strategy through operations.

☑ All operating managers should be very well versed in the science of operations management. Instinct alone will not suffice: you cannot survive without knowledge.

Product Design and Process Development:
Build It Right and They Will Come

After developing an operations strategy, the operations manager has to decide what to produce and how, where, and when to produce it. These activities include designing the product or service and designing the implementation or execution processes. In this context, a *product* is anything—goods or services—that can be offered to people who might need or want it. A *process*, as defined in Chapter 1, is any part of an organization or enterprise that transforms inputs into outputs, with the implicit contention that the output will be of greater value than the input.

Four basic product/process tenets must be kept in mind:

- Decisions about product and process design are strategic—product characteristics and features must support the organization's competitive strategy.
- Product or service development decisions and process selection decisions are dependent upon one another—even if they occur in different organizations.
- Decisions about product design naturally determine the process selected to produce the product—facilities, equipment, skills required, and so forth.
- Decisions about product design must be made in consideration of the organization's current processes.

Designing a product—whether goods or services—consists of deciding on the purposes, characteristics, materials, customer benefits, and performance standards of that product. Decisions about the product or process design necessary to produce that product are typically made at the same time, together. They both determine product quality, product cost, and customer satisfaction.

Operations Management and the Team

The operations manager must work with representatives of stakeholder functions to make decisions. Operations managers ultimately broker and share information with a variety of key people across the extended enterprise and coordinate cross-functional and cross-organizational activities to deliver the products or services being developed.

Marketing plays an important role in product design decisions for two important reasons. First, the marketers are responsible for knowing what the customers want and need and are likely to buy, what the competitors are offering, and any trends that should influence product design decisions. Second, the marketers must know the full implications of what it can and cannot do in order to meet customers' needs and uncover latent demand.

Finance must be involved in decisions about both product design and process selection, because these decisions require substantial financial investment. Finance must evaluate the potential impact on the organization and the risks-rewards equation.

Human resources is involved in product and process selection decisions to the extent that the results will require special skills, reassignment of employees, and hiring.

Sourcing and purchasing must be part of product design and process selection because they are responsible for finding and procuring any materials, equipment, and services needed for the product. Purchasers are responsible for ensuring supply and knowing about availability, prices, and possible alternatives.

Engineering plays a vital role in process selection and product design decisions because engineers know about equipment and about materials and their characteristics. The best ideas are worth nothing if they can't work.

Information technology must be involved in process selection decisions to the extent that the processes being considered require technology and the functional areas rely on technology—market analysis and forecasting, purchasing, inventory control, scheduling, and so on, depending on the organization.

DON'T DO IT THE OLD WAY

CAUTION This approach to product design and process development, using a team whose members represent various functional areas, is an improvement over the old approach. Traditionally, people would develop a product idea, design the product, and determine the characteristics. Then, they would pass the design on to people in operations, who would subsequently design the process to produce the product. The old approach was inefficient, costly, and time-consuming and brought to mind the notion of tossing the idea over the wall. It also reinforced the functional silos in companies that hindered teamwork and fostered "blame games."

Goods vs. Services

People have long distinguished between businesses that produce goods and businesses that provide services. This distinction between producing goods and providing services seems simple and logical, based on two basic differences:

- Goods are tangible and services are intangible. You can touch goods. They are products. They have a physical form. You cannot touch services. They are activities. They have no physical form.
- Providing services involves more customer contact than producing goods.

This distinction between goods and services is simple and logical. However, it's also more and more problematic. The Navy has the adage that if it moves, salute it, and if it doesn't, paint it. Such a simple notion for distinguishing between products and services no longer exists. Companies that produce goods—manufacturers—often also provide services. Companies that provide services may also produce goods. For example, restaurants are included in the services sector even though they produce meals from raw and processed materials.

Goods and services are not two separate worlds, because the degree of customer contact varies greatly.

Many types of companies in the services sectors come to mind when we think "services": restaurants, retail stores, hospitals and other health care facilities, barber shops, beauty salons, health clubs, day-care centers, schools, etc. Such businesses have been labeled *pure services*— although these companies may vary greatly in the extent and nature of customer contact and the standardization of their processes.

Other companies that provide services involve less customer contact (and often the contact is by phone, letter, or e-mail rather than in person) and less standardization. Such businesses as banks, credit unions, insurance agencies, accounting firms, equipment repair shops, etc., are considered *mixed services*.

In other services companies, little direct customer contact occurs, and a high degree of standardization exists. For these reasons, such businesses as warehouses and distribution centers and the back-office operations of virtually all companies—administration, accounting, clerical and data entry, information technology, inventory, etc.—can be categorized as *quasi-manufacturing*.

So, what's the point? The point is that, in selecting processes, an operations manager should focus on the purpose of the process and not be influenced by labels of "goods" and "services." And in our discussion of product design, keep in mind the more general use of the word "product,"

SERVICE DESIGN: KNOW WHAT YOU'RE DESIGNING   SMART

Service design consists of both the service and the service concept. Design considerations must include not only the actual service provided but also aesthetic and psychological benefits, such as image, ambiance, friendliness or professionalism, and anything else MANAGING that causes customers to feel good choosing one brand of service over another. The service and the concept together constitute the *service package*, and operations managers must strive for *service breakthroughs*.

Here again, services and goods may not be all that different. Goods can often be satisfying aesthetic and psychological needs, especially if the product bears a brand name or the company is liked for its social, environmental, and/or political positions and actions.

as it is used in marketing circles. A product is anything—goods or services—that can be offered to people who might need or want it.

Product Design

Whatever the product and the particular circumstances, the design process generally consists of four phases:

1. Idea development or generation
2. Screening of ideas
3. Preliminary design testing
4. Final design

Idea Development of Generation

Design ideas might come from various sources, within and outside the organization:

- product managers
- marketers
- engineers
- customer service representatives
- other employees
- senior managers
- customers
- suppliers
- distributors

CREATE THE PACKAGE

When developing or improving the design of a service, you must identify every aspect of the package. It's a mistake to think only about the service, whether it's coffee, a haircut, a hamburger, or auto repair. With the proliferations of services, what causes customers to choose one company over others are often the aesthetic and psychological benefits mentioned earlier. A key distinction of service offerings is that the service package typically integrates the consumer of those services as part of the service itself. Southwest Airlines operations strategy inherently incorporates the flying passenger as part of its seat selection and baggage handling operations. You must design the entire service package to provide what your target customers expect—and you must develop a process that will deliver that service consistently.

- competitors—or rather their products and services
- other companies, not in competition

The smart operations manager is open to all ideas from all sources. Always take note of any product design ideas that come to mind or that others mention to you. An idea is a terrible thing to waste.

The operations manager meets with product managers, marketers, customer service reps and other employees in contact with customers, R&D staff, and any other people who could offer ideas. The point here is to generate possibilities; the probabilities of success come later.

Screening of Ideas

To evaluate the ideas developed during idea development, the operations manager meets with representatives from marketing, finance, purchasing, engineering, information technology, and any other functional area that could provide important input at this point. They all bring to the table different perspectives, different experiences, different interests, and different concerns, and they look at the world through different glasses; operations has the incumbent responsibility to align those views and perspectives in order to get something done. Some of the basic questions that would likely arise for any idea under consideration include:

Operations

- What would be required to produce this product?
- Should we make this product or buy it?
- Could we produce it with our current facilities and equipment?
- Would our employees have the skills to produce it? Would we need to provide training? Would we need to hire people with the required skills?

Sourcing/Purchasing

- Could we obtain the materials necessary to produce this product? What quantities would we need? What suppliers could we use? What would the materials cost?

Marketing

- What would be the market potential for this product?
- How would we reach potential customers?
- How would we develop the market for this product?

Finance

- What would be the financial potential of this product?
- What would it cost to produce it?
- What return on investment could we expect?

The focus of this discussion should be the bottom line. The participants in this discussion can disagree on the merits of a product idea from all perspectives, but what matters is the potential for profit. To marketing and sales, all dollars, euros, pounds, yen, and remnimbi are created equally; the operations manager knows that they are not. To evaluate the *cost-to-serve*, one can start with a *break-even analysis*.

Break-Even Analysis. *Break-even analysis* is a calculation that uses expenses and revenues to determine how many units of a product you would need to sell to generate enough revenues to cover the expenses incurred in producing it. The formula is easy to use; the only thing difficult about calculating the break-even point is forecasting your expenses and revenues (sales) accurately.

$$\text{Break-even point (number of sales)} =$$
$$\text{Fixed costs/(Unit selling price} - \text{Variable costs)}$$

You can also start by projecting the number of units you expect to sell and using that figure to calculate the price you would need to charge for each unit in order to break even for that number of sales:

$$\text{Break-even price} = \text{Variable costs per unit} + (\text{Fixed costs/Sales})$$

KEY TERMS

Break-even analysis Calculation that determines the break-even point, the level of sales at which total (gross) revenues equal total costs.

Unit contribution margin Difference between the sales revenue (price) of a product or service and the variable costs of the product or service.

Variable costs Costs that vary in total in direct proportion to the quantity of activity (products produced or services provided). Variable costs include direct materials, labor, packaging, shipping, etc.

Fixed costs Costs that remain constant in total regardless of changes in the quantity of activity (products produced or services provided). Fixed costs include overhead (rent, utilities, administrative expenses), insurance, etc.

Above the break-even point, each unit sold increases profit by the unit contribution margin, the amount by which revenues for a unit surpass the variable costs incurred to produce, deliver, and sell it.

Unit contribution margin = Price of unit − Variable costs for unit

The cost of producing a product or providing a service is the sum of its fixed and variable costs.

Profit = Quantity sold (Selling price −
Variable costs per unit) − Fixed Costs

Preliminary Design Testing

If a product idea passes through the screening phase of the product design process, the next step is to develop a preliminary design and put it to the test.

Design engineers convert performance and functional requirements and expectations into technical specifications for a preliminary design. This design is then tested. How? By simulating real-world conditions as accurately as possible. For a product, this generally means creating a prototype. For a service, this might mean offering the test product on a small scale, in selected markets for a limited time. Testing would probably involve surveying potential customers and possibly holding focus groups. The surveys and discussions should test reactions to the product or service, the design, and the price.

Depending on the testing results, the design is dropped, modified, or passed on to the final design phase. A gated product development process with enforceable go/no-go decisions is critical to affording operations managers the opportunity to focus on the critical few products and processes that will yield a sustainable competitive advantage. This testing phase may last a long time, depending on the extent of the testing, the number of preliminary designs necessary, and the complexity of the product or service.

This phase may also be expensive, but the expense should always be considered in terms of the amount that would be invested in launching the new product or service and the importance of reducing the risk of failure. Operations often use the rule of thumb that a flaw corrected in design costs a dollar to fix, whereas a flaw uncovered during implementation or execution costs $10, and one that the customer finds costs $100.

Final Design

After the product design passes the testing, the design engineers draw up the final specifications. From these specifications the operations manager derives processing instructions, selects the equipment, identifies the materials needed, creates job descriptions as necessary, decides on the suppliers (with the purchasing manager), and attends to any other aspects of preparing for producing the product or providing the service.

Although the focus in product design should be the customer, of course, we must also consider realities such as complexity and costs. A product that could sell very well might be impossible or too expensive to produce or deliver.

> **KEY TERM**
>
> **Design for manufacture and assembly (DFMA)** Guidelines that focus on two aspects of producing a product—*simplification* and *standardization*. Also considered separately, as *design for manufacture* and *design for assembly*.

Design for manufacture and assembly (DFMA) is a general term for guidelines that focus on two aspects of producing a product:

- *Simplification*—reducing the number of features and parts. A simpler product is easier to make, costs less, and enables us to produce it with greater consistency and higher quality.
- *Standardization*—using common and interchangeable parts. With standardization we can make a greater variety of products with greater flexibility, maintain lower inventories, and significantly lower costs.

Specific applications of these general guidelines will vary widely, according to the products or services. Although DFMA has been developed primarily for goods, the principles behind the guidelines can be applied to services.

> **FOR EXAMPLE**
>
> **PRODUCTION LINE THINKING IN SERVICES 1**
>
> Production-line approaches are being used more and more for services. Technology is replacing human labor wherever possible, to ensure consistency and simplify processes, and reduce the need for employees to use their discretion. Procedures are structured to simplify human effort, both physical and mental. We're all familiar with the consistency and speed of delivery that make fast-food restaurants popular and the production-line thinking behind it that minimizes costs.

PRODUCTION LINE THINKING IN SERVICES 2

Simplifying or eliminating human intervention is a growing trend in services. Service stations are almost all self-service, which reduces labor and the possibility of error; most allow for credit card payment at the pump, which reduces labor, time, and cash on hand. Automated teller machines (ATMs) enable us to do our banking 24/7 without any human interaction, and automated processes, despite the frequently evidenced frustration of not having human contact, are inherently more consistent, especially when the service offerings incorporate the potential customers into the design phase.

In fast-food restaurants, condiment stations let us customize our hamburgers, burritos, coffee, and other edible commodities and pour our soft drinks. Buffet tables allow us to choose our food "live," rather than from words and pictures on a menu, and the restaurant reduces the need for humans to help us. We can get snacks and even meals from vending machines. Grocery stores have been adding "express checkout lanes"—do-it-yourself stations where customers can scan items and pay through a machine. This is the thinking behind *design for manufacture and assembly*, adding *delivery* to the equation.

Some basic DFMA guidelines include:

- Simplify the design.
- Minimize the number of parts.
- Design parts that can be used for multiple products.
- Design for ease of manufacture.
- Use materials for multiple products.
- Design for ease of assembly and minimal possibility of errors.
- Minimize the use of tools.
- Design for automated production.
- Design for handling, stocking, and shipping.
- Design for maintenance and repairs.
- Simplify the processes.

We will discuss simplification and standardization further in Chapter 3.

Process Selection

Understanding the processes you manage is fundamental to success as an operations manager. Knowledge of those processes, of their strengths

DFMA RESOURCE
The standard resource for DFMA is *Product Design for Manufacture and Assembly* by **TOOLS** Geoffrey Boothroyd, Winston Knight, and Peter Dewhurst, revised and expanded (Marcel Dekker, 2002). It is strictly for goods, organized according to specific manufacturing processes.

and weaknesses, gives you the ability to find the best applications for your processes. Matching processes to the needs of the enterprise is crucial to meeting strategic objectives. In addition, it's imperative to give process managers the tools needed to succeed.

Process Analysis

Flowchart
Analyze Flowchart - clarify/simplify
includes performance metric to be used.

The best way to understand a process is by analyzing it. This is true whether the process is actually in use or the process is in the planning stage. The best way to begin analyzing a process is by diagramming the basic process elements—typically tasks, inputs and outputs, flows, storage or buffer areas, and decision points.

SIPOC diagram A simple macro map of a process, showing Suppliers, Inputs, **KEY TERM** Process, Outputs, and Customers and defining the start and end of a process.

Starting with a SIPOC Diagram

A SIPOC diagram is a simple macro map of a process, showing Suppliers, Inputs, Process, Outputs, and Customers. It defines the start and end of a process.

Exhibit 2-1. SIPOC diagram. Typically under each part of the diagram you can list the processes and activities involved.

A SIPOC diagram is the first step in mapping a process. In essence, it shows how a process is connected with its context, but shows none of the activities within the process. It ensures that the team members understand the limits of the process, what goes into it, and what comes out of it.

Flowcharting the Process

Diagramming with a *flowchart* shows what is happening in that process, breaking it down and spreading out the steps to make it easier to people understand.

First, define the process boundaries with a start point and an end point. This can be problematic, because what one person might chart as separate processes, another person might chart as multiple stages within a single process. This is not really a problem, however.

GO WITH THE FLOW   SMART

"Until you draw a flow diagram, you do not understand your business."
—W. Edwards Deming   MANAGING
Quality Theorist

What matters is to chart production or service activities in any way that creates a complete and detailed map.

Then map each step in the process in order according to the type of activity—oval for start point and stop point, diamond/ rhombus for decisions, parallelogram for an input or an output, rectangle for processing, inverted triangle for storage (buffer), and half circle (elongated capital D) for delay (time gap between steps or stages of a process). Connect the shapes with arrows to show the flow.

There is no standard way

Flowchart A map of a process, showing the steps as various shapes in sequence, connected by   **KEY TERM** arrows. The primary shapes represent decisions (diamond/rhombus), processing (rectangle), inputs and outputs (parallelogram), storage (inverted triangle), delay (half circle or elongated capital D), and start and stop points (oval).

to create a flowchart and no general agreement on any but the most basic symbols. You should do whatever works for your operations, be consistent, and provide a legend or a key listing your symbols and their meanings.

If a process involves more than one department, it may make more sense to use a *deployment flowchart* (*cross-functional flowchart*). Draw a column for each department and identify it by a heading. Then create a flowchart, placing each step in the column of the department responsible for that step.

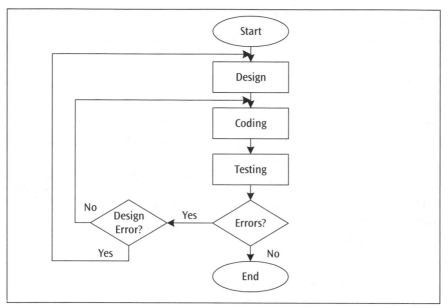

Exhibit 2-2. Simple flowchart for software development

Buffer Temporary storage for work-in-process or finished goods between two successive stages in a process, which allows them to operate independently of each other. Without **KEY TERMS** buffering, the first stage would have to produce outputs at the same rate as the second stage requires inputs. Otherwise, the result would be *blocking* or *starving*.

Blocking Problem that arises when a process or a stage of a process cannot take inputs from the preceding process or stage as quickly as they are produced, causing the faster process or stage to slow or to stop.

Starving Problem that arises when a process or a stage of a process cannot provide outputs for the following process or stage as quickly as they are needed, causing the faster process or stage to slow or to stop.

It's best to have the people who are responsible for the process create the flowchart, since they know what actually happens, not just how the process is designed.

To create an effective flowchart:

1. Define the process boundaries with a start point and an end point.
2. Sketch out the major parts of the process, in order.
3. Break each major part into component steps, in order.

4. Connect the steps with arrows.

5. Label each step.

6. Identify any time delays.

Have other people involved in the process review the flowchart and offer comments. A complete, detailed flowchart should show everything that happens in a process from beginning to end.

> **Deployment flowchart** A map of a process that shows which department or team is responsible for each step in the process. It consists of a standard flowchart superimposed on columns, one labeled for each department or team. Also known as a cross-functional flowchart.
>
> **KEY TERM**

Test the flowchart by trying to follow the map through the process; a simple operations concept is "to staple yourself to the order." In other words, follow the order from start to finish and chart the physical and information flows. If any problems arise, note any discrepancies between reality and the flowchart and then correct the chart. A good test is to give the flowchart to someone unfamiliar with the process; if he or she can follow the map and walk through all of the steps of the process correctly, then the flowchart is probably ready to use.

> **FLOWCHARTING APPLICATIONS**
> Ask 20 operations managers which flowcharting application they'd recommend and you'll probably get at least 50 opinions. Dozens of flowcharting tools exist on the market, with capabilities ranging from very simple drawing functions to advanced mapping and even simulation. Your best bet may be to ask other operations managers in your industry, but you could also check your industry journals for reviews or at least for ads. Make sure that whatever program you use to map your processes allows you to update the charts easily—because you're hoping to make important changes.
>
> **TOOLS**

When you have a complete, detailed, and accurate flowchart, you can analyze the process.

Analyzing the Process

Analysis of a process may be considered in four phases:

- process *clarification*
- process *simplification*

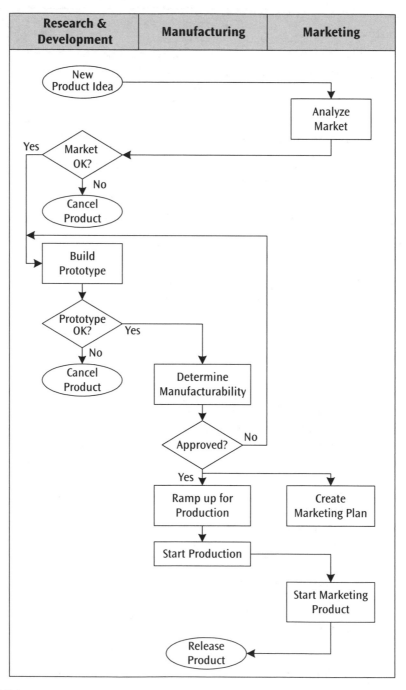

Exhibit 2-3. A simple deployment flowchart for a new product development process

- process *acceleration*
- process *innovation*

At this point we'll focus on clarification, on understanding the process, identifying the key points and areas of actual or potential weaknesses. We'll discuss ways to reduce or eliminate these weaknesses in Chapter 3.

There are several key points in any process, each with aspects that you should examine and measure:

- *Inputs*—quality, availability (supply sources, quantity, and location)
- *Activities or stages*—capacity, labor, efficiency, variations in capacity

DON'T FORGET THE THINKING
Remember to include mental steps, such as decisions. It's easy to forget these steps if you're familiar with the process. However, mental steps are critical to the flow of a process.

USES OF FLOWCHARTS   SMART
You can use your process maps for more than just analyzing processes. They can serve as a MANAGING reference that shows graphically what procedure instructions and manuals express in words. They can also help when training employees who will be staffing the processes or working with the processes. It is easier for most people to learn from a good process map than from descriptions.

- *Layout*—order and flow, timing, pace of an item through the process connections between adjacent activities or stages, difference between capacity and demand, bottlenecks

Inevitably, there will be activities that are not actually part of processing. Some may be necessary and useful, such as buffers, but others may waste time and resources, especially human. These include:

- Decisions
- Transportation
- Inspections and review cycles
- Documentation and other paperwork

Finally, there may be activities that do not add value to the product:

- Delays
- Duplications
- Unnecessary steps

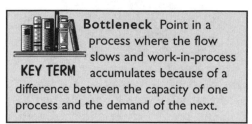

Bottleneck Point in a process where the flow slows and work-in-process **KEY TERM** accumulates because of a difference between the capacity of one process and the demand of the next.

These are activities that likely could be eliminated, and the operations manager should combine this scientific approach to the art of determining which activities should be curtailed.

Characteristics of Processes

Operations management at its basic level is defined by processes. Understanding types of processes, mapping processes, adapting and improving processes, and institutionalizing them are essential responsibilities of an operations manager.

A *process*, as defined earlier, is any part of an organization that transforms inputs into outputs, with the intention that the output will be of greater value than the input. There are many thousands of organizations in the United States, and each contains dozens, hundreds, or thousands of processes. All of those processes can be categorized according to certain basic characteristics, each with advantages and inherent potential problems.

Intermittent or Repetitive. All processes are either more or less intermittent or more or less repetitive. There are two fundamental differences between these two types, which are actually two directions on a continuum:

- The degree to which the processing requirements of the products are different or similar
- The volume of products produced

Intermittent processes produce a variety of products, with different processing requirements, in lower volumes. Good examples of intermittent processes might be a restaurant or an auto body shop.

Since the products that intermittent processes produce have different processing requirements, the processes tend to require more labor and the workers must have more skills, more flexibility, and usually more freedom to make decisions. Intermittent processes usually involve little or no automation.

Repetitive processes produce one or a few products, with the same or similar processing requirements, usually in higher volumes. The best example of a repetitive process might be any segment of a production line or an assembly line or any station in a cafeteria line.

Since the products that repetitive processes produce have the same or similar processing require-ments, the processes tend to be more capital-intensive in the equipment and facilities, to produce large volumes of products more efficiently and with greater consistency. Re-petitive processes are more likely to involve automation.

>
>
> **KEY TERMS**
>
> **Intermittent process** Process that produces a variety of products, with different processing requirements, in lower volumes.
>
> **Repetitive process** Process that pro-duces one or a few products, with the same or similar processing require-ments, usually in higher volumes.

The type of process deter-mines other aspects of operations management, such as equipment, organization around the process, and inventories of materials and fin-ished goods. In terms of organization and inventory of materials, for intermittent processes, resources are grouped by function, which is logi-cal for all the various processes, and products are then moved from resource to resource, according to processing needs. In contrast, for repetitive processes, resources are arranged in order according to need, for easiest access, which is most efficient for the ongoing activities of the process. In terms of inventory of finished goods, intermittent processes *make to order* or *assemble to order*, so there's little or no inventory main-tained, whereas repetitive processes *make to stock*, so there is an inven-tory of finished goods waiting for orders.

These two types of processes, intermittent and repetitive, as men-tioned earlier, are actually two directions on a continuum. Each can be divided into two subtypes according to those two basic criteria:

- The degree to which the processing requirements of the products are different or similar
- The volume of products produced

Intermittent processes can be divided into *project processes* and *batch processes. Repetitive processes* can be divided into *line processes* and *con-tinuous processes.*

KEY TERMS

Make-to-stock A strategy that produces goods or services in anticipation of demand. Customers receive goods or services more quickly, but are not able to customize them.

Assemble-to-order A strategy that produces standard components that can be combined to customer specifications. Also known as *build-to-order*. Customers are able to customize goods or services to some degree and delivery takes more time than in the ordering-from-stock strategy, but less than for goods and services made to order.

Make-to-order A strategy that produces goods or services to customer orders and specifications. Customers receive the goods or services that they want, but it takes longer than if they ordered from stock.

Project processes produce one-of-a-kind products to customer specifications, usually with the customer involved in decisions about the product design.

Batch processes produce products in small groups (batches) according to customer orders or product specifications.

Line processes produce large volumes of standardized products. This is generally called *mass production* and these processes are often called *assembly lines*.

Continuous processes produce very high volumes of standardized products, operating nonstop. The products are often mass quantities (such as liquids, gases, grains, and flour), rather than count quantities (discrete units). These processes usually have a single input and a single output or a limited number of outputs. Because the product is so standardized and the processing is continuous, these processes are generally very capital-intensive and very automated.

Make-to-Order vs. Make-to-Stock (Pull vs. Push). A critical question is deciding whether an operational process will be designed to make to order (pull) or make to stock (push).

Make-to-order processes are activated only in response to an actual order. This "pull" approach minimizes inventory and, in theory, might lengthen response time. However, many firms have been able to use *mass customization*, delaying differentiation of goods or services in order to reduce the tradeoff between personalization and response time, for competitive advantage. Consider, for example, Burger King's "Have It Your

Way" campaign. Service operations are often characterized by a pull approach, as services are frequently delivered for immediate use or consumption and cannot be stocked in inventory. It is very difficult to sell an airplane seat for a flight that departed ten minutes ago.

Typically, a make-to-stock process holds finished goods in inventory and subsequently fills customer orders as they come. Retailers often build up inventory in advance of a promotion, in anticipation of orders.

Some fast-food restaurants, such as McDonald's for one, minimize production time through make-to-stock processes, thus gaining a competitive advantage. A make-to-stock process is controlled by two factors: the anticipated orders and the current inventory. A target level of stock is often set to designate a reorder point.

> **Mass customization** The use of flexible processes and information technology to allow a high degree of cus- **KEY TERM** tomization of products and services while taking advantage of the lower costs of mass production.

Make-to-stock processes are also used to satisfy seasonal demands, such as sunglasses for summer or snow shovels for winter. Running make-to-stock operations constantly can create stockpiles for periods of heavier demand and keep production employees working during times when demand is lower. In fact, balancing operations so that supply meets demand is a key tenet of operations management as a way of maximizing predictability and avoiding the cost and quality issues typically associated with peaks and valleys.

Most firms find success with hybrid processes that mix make-to-stock and make-to-order processes. Frequently, they create a generic product that is subsequently customized to order, in mass customization.

Process Performance Metrics

Once you've analyzed what the flowcharted process is doing, the next step is to determine how well it is doing what it's doing. *Process performance metrics* are measurements of process characteristics that provide a quantitative understanding of a process and a way to assess the effects of any changes to the process.

Many ways exist to measure and trace performance, depending on the specific aspects of the process. Some basic metrics that operations managers commonly use include:

- capacity
- throughput time
- process velocity
- productivity
- utilization
- efficiency

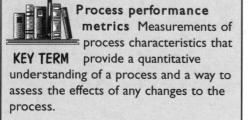

Process performance metrics Measurements of process characteristics that

KEY TERM provide a quantitative understanding of a process and a way to assess the effects of any changes to the process.

Capacity is the output of a process within a specified time, typically expressed in units of output per time period. *Design capacity* is the ideal output rate under normal conditions, the rate for which the process was designed. *Maximum capacity* is the top output rate that the process could achieve; this capacity is possible only for short durations, because of the greater need for labor and energy and the impossibility of performing scheduled preventive maintenance.

Capacity   = Output in units per time period
Capacity utilization = Actual output/Design capacity

Throughput time is the average amount of time it takes a product to move through a system, both processing time (value-added time) and any waiting time. The lower the throughput time, the better the process.

Process velocity is the amount of time wasted in a process. It is calculated by dividing throughput time by value-added time (time spent processing the product):

Process velocity = Throughput time/Value-added time

The closer this ratio is to 1.00, the less time is being wasted in the process.

Productivity is the efficiency of transforming inputs into outputs. It is calculated by dividing output (e.g., total $ value, products, customers served) by input (e.g., total $ value, per employee, per labor hour). Productivity can be calculated for each category of input: *labor productivity* (e.g., hours worked, number of employees, cost of labor), *capital productivity* (e.g., money invested, machine hours), *materials productivity* (e.g., units of materials used, money spent), and *energy productivity* (e.g., units of energy consumed, money spent).

Productivity = Output/Input

Utilization is the time that a resource (e.g., equipment or labor) is actually being used relative to the time that it is available for use.

Utilization = Time in use/Time available

Efficiency is the actual output relative to some standard of output, theoretical capacity, or benchmark.

Efficiency = Actual output (in units)/standard output

There are other process performance metrics that will help you get a more complete picture:

Cycle time is the average time between completions of successive units.

Setup time is the time required to prepare a machine or system to make a particular item or unit.

Throughput rate (also known as *flow rate*) is the average rate at which units pass a specific point in the process. The maximum throughput rate is the process capacity.

Capacity Output of a process within a specified time, typically expressed in units of output per time period.

KEY TERMS

Throughput time Average amount of time it takes a product to move through process or a system: processing time (value-added time) plus any waiting time.

Process velocity Amount of time wasted in a process: throughput time divided by value-added time (time spent processing the product).

Productivity Efficiency of transforming inputs into outputs: output divided by input.

Utilization Time a resource is used relative to the time it is available for use: time in use divided by time available.

Efficiency Output relative to a standard output: actual output divided by standard output.

$$\text{Throughput rate} = 1/\text{cycle time}$$

Takt time is the maximum time allowed to produce a product in order to meet customer demand. Takt time is used to match the pace of work to the average pace of customer demand.

$$\text{Takt time} = \text{Net time available to work (e.g., minutes per day)/}$$
$$\text{Rate of customer demand (e.g., units required per day)}$$

Once you've determined which performance metrics you should be using for a process, you can add a process flow description to your flowchart for that process. The process flow description, in addition to describing the process flow in detail, should capture the process performance measurements. These measurements will provide the criteria by which the effects of changes to the process will be evaluated.

Cycle time Average time between completions of successive units.

KEY TERMS **Setup time** Time required to prepare a machine or system to make a particular item or unit.

Throughput rate Average rate at which units pass a specific point in the process, also known as flow rate.

Takt time Maximum time allowed to produce a product in order to meet customer demand.

Operations Manager's Checklist for Chapter 2

☑ The design of a product—whether goods or services—consists of deciding on the purposes, characteristics, materials, customer benefits, and performance standards of the product.

☑ The design of the process to produce that product consists of deciding on the activities, the flows of those activities, the facilities and equipment, the materials, the labor, the time, and the costs.

☑ Decisions about product design and process design are typically made at the same time, together. They both determine product quality, product cost, and customer satisfaction.

☑ Together, product design and process design represent an important strategic decision for an organization, because they contribute to shaping the competitive position of the organization, defining its identity and image, and helping or hindering its growth.

☑ The operations manager must work with representatives of stakeholder functional areas to make decisions about product design and process design.

☑ Service design consists of both the service and the service concept. Design considerations must include not only the actual service provided, but also aesthetic and psychological benefits–any factor that causes customers to choose one brand of service over another. The service and the concept together constitute the *service package*.

The product design process generally consists of four phases:

- idea development
- screening of ideas
- preliminary design testing
- final design

☑ Diagramming a process with a flowchart shows what is happening in that process by breaking it down and spreading out the steps. Standard formats for flowcharts or flowcharting do not exist.

☑ Process performance metrics measure process characteristics that provide a quantitative understanding of a process and a way to assess the effects of any changes to the process. These measurements should be recorded in a process flow description and will provide the criteria by which the effects of changes to the process will be evaluated.

Improving Production Processes:
The Best Keeps Getting Better

We all want to improve something in our lives—and it seems we're surrounded by suggestions and recommendations, techniques and tools, theories and methodologies for improving anything and everything from A to Z. That's certainly true for business processes. It's easy to feel confused, overwhelmed, and frustrated.

How do you improve production processes? That depends in part on the following:

- *The processes*—simple (one stage) or complex (multiple stages)
- *The scope*—within a single work area or involving two or more areas
- *The type of change you want*—incremental or radical
- *The resources available*

However, it's possible to structure a general process in a way that works for virtually all improvement projects. Depending on your situation, your time, and your familiarity with the processes, it may be necessary or at least advisable to manage all or much of the process improvement effort as a project. (Project management is the subject of Chapter 7.)

Process for Improving Processes

Improving a process generally involves the following steps:

- Document the current process.
- Identify the problem areas. *(ask those involved)*
- Quantify the effects of each problem area.
- Prioritize the problem areas. *pareto chart – 80/20 Rule*
- Determine the causes of the problems. *Five whys: Fishbone Diagram*
- Generate possible solutions for the problems. *benchmarking. brainstorm,*
- Prioritize the possible solutions. *simplify + standardize*
- Decide on the improvement project. *impact/effort; cost benefit, criteria matrix*
- Set baselines. *measurement of current level (10 pc/hr)*
- Set targets. *qualitative + quantitative*
- Develop the new/revised process.
- Plan for making the changes.
- Make the changes as planned. *document everything*
- Evaluate the effects of the changes.

Document the Current Process

The documentation should consist of a flowchart of the process ("as is"), as explained in Chapter 2, and a process flow description, which describes the process flow in detail and records the process performance measurements, which will provide the criteria for evaluating the effects of changes to the process.

Identify the Problem Areas

Several ways exist to identify process problem areas. Start with the people who know the systems and component processes. Survey the employees and suppliers. Review any problems that they currently have with the systems or processes as well as any concerns or suggestions. Not only is this a good way to generate a list of problems, but it also shows that the operations manager cares about people's perspectives and insight as well as processes.

If the processes directly affect your customers, you may want to talk with your marketers, customer service reps, and any other employees in contact with your customers. They are the best situated to know what customers perceive as problems in the processes that affect them directly.

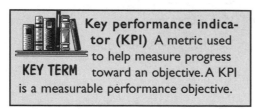

KEY TERM **Key performance indicator (KPI)** A metric used to help measure progress toward an objective. A KPI is a measurable performance objective.

Analyzing process flowcharts and metrics should reveal weaknesses and problem areas.

Look for gaps between actual performance of a system and expected performance according to *key performance indicators* (KPIs). A KPI is a metric that is used as a criterion by which system performance is assessed.

You may already have KPIs. If not, you probably have certain expectations for the system, thoughts about what it should be doing or not doing. The most important performance metrics for the system or component processes should be your KPIs. Each KPI must be clearly defined.

For example, if you decide to use *capacity* as a KPI, you might define it as, for example, "the number of units of acceptable quality produced in an eight-hour shift." If you decide to use *productivity* as a KPI, you might define it as "the quotient of the dollar value of output divided by the number of direct labor hours on the process."

SMART MANAGING **HOW MANY KPIS? HOW FEW?** How many KPIs should you have? That depends on the particular system and situation. However, experts have suggested that it's difficult to focus on more than seven KPIs.

How few KPIs can you have? It can be risky to have only one or even two or three. It is smart to have at least four KPIs.

You can also find problem areas in a system or a process by identifying the *disconnects*. A disconnect makes a process less effective or less efficient. It may be an input, a step, or an output that is missing, unnecessary, or substandard. It may be an activity that occurs at the wrong time, or as performed by the wrong person or work unit, or it may be an activity done wrong, or an activity done manually when it could be automated.

Flowcharts make it easier to identify redundancies, extraneous actions, processes that can be eliminated, bottlenecks, delays that are unnecessary or at least unnecessarily long, and steps that add no value to the product for the customer. Process flow loops or movement back and forth between two operations or workers may indicate unnecessary transfers.

Quantify the Effects of Each Problem Area

How serious are the prob-lems? How much are the

> **Disconnect** *"Anything that impedes the effectiveness or efficiency of the process"* (Geary A. Rummler and **KEY TERM** Alan P. Brache, *Improving Performance: How to Manage the White Space in the Organization Chart* [Jossey-Bass, 1995]).

problems that employees have noted affecting the systems or processes? How big are the gaps between performance and expectations?

Quantifying the effects of problem areas depends on the systems and processes and on the performance metrics you use. You should question people in any work unit affected by the problem areas.

For each problem, you can ask questions like the following:

- Where is the impact? On production capacity? On scheduling? On quality? On sales? On profitability? On deliveries? On customer service? On other areas of the organization? On relationships with suppliers? On relationships with customers?
- How much time is being lost because of this problem?
- Who is involved in dealing with the effects of this problem? How much is their time worth? What is the value of the work they should be doing?
- How is this problem costing the organization? In production downtime? In scrap—cost of materials and labor, cost of disposal? In time spent on products that don't meet specifications—cost of reworking or scrapping? In delays—effect on subsequent systems and processes, effect on delivery to customers? In unscheduled overtime? In lost customers?
- What do you think this problem is costing the organization?
- How has this problem affected employee morale?

The impact of problems is not always easy to quantify in terms of dollars—but that's the best way to compare the effects of problems, and it's the only metric that works in cost-benefit analyses or in convincing marketing of the true cost-to-serve.

Prioritize the Problem Areas

At least three ways exist to prioritize problem areas. The first approach uses the sole criterion of dollars (or euro or yen). The second approach also considers the relationship between the problem area and operations strategies. The third approach allows for soft factors, such as the effects of the problem areas on people in ways that cannot be quantified. Whichever approach you decide to use, the next step is to assess the relative effects of the problem areas. A tool that is commonly used for this purpose is a *Pareto chart* (or *Pareto diagram*). Most people understand the 80-20 rule, which is also known as the Pareto principle—20 percent of the activities yield 80 percent of the results.

Pareto Chart. A *Pareto chart* consists of a simple bar graph used to plot values in descending order, with a line graph that shows the cumulative totals across the bars from left to right; it is a typical graphic representation of the effects of problem areas.

KEY TERMS

Pareto chart A type of bar graph used to illustrate problems or causes by displaying each of them according to its importance relative to the effects of all of them, to distinguish the most important factors, and identify the biggest opportunities for improvement.

Pareto principle A generalization that states that, for many events, roughly 80% of the effects come from 20% of the causes. Also known as the *80-20 rule*.

On the left vertical axis you can mark cost increments, and on the horizontal axis you can name the problem areas, starting with the most costly and going across in order to the least costly. Then you create a bar for each problem area, to show its cost. After you've drawn the bars, you can total the costs of all the problem areas charted, add a right vertical axis to show the total and percentage increments of that total, and plot a line of the cumulative values to show how much each problem area contributes to the total cost. (Exhibit 3-1 shows an example.)

Determine the Causes of the Problems

To determine the causes for your problem areas, begin with your process flowcharts. Work upstream from the problem areas to try to identify

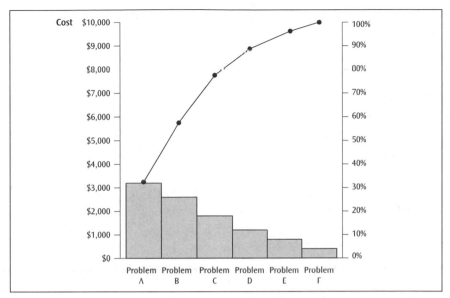

Exhibit 3-1. Pareto chart of process problem areas

SIGNIFICANT FEW VS. TRIVIAL MANY

TRICKS OF THE TRADE

The principle behind the Pareto diagram derives from the work of Vilfredo Pareto, an Italian economist and sociologist who studied wealth and poverty in the early 1900s and found that 80% of the land in Italy was owned by 20% of the people.

Management consultant Joseph M. Juran turned those percentages into the *Pareto principle*, also known as the *80-20* rule. He asserted that the "significant few" things will generally account for 80% of the whole, while the "trivial many" will account for about 20%.

This generalization has become a rule of thumb used in many business situations.

possible factors. A simple yet often effective approach is the *Five Whys*.

Five Whys. The *Five Whys* is a technique for exploring the cause-effect relationships for a problem area by probing with a single question—"Why?" There's nothing magic about the number five; the point is to

Five Whys A technique for exploring the cause-effect relationships for a problem area by probing with a single question—"Why?"—to determine the root cause of the problem.

KEY TERM

dig beneath superficial answers to the question to arrive at the root cause of a problem. The sidebar shows an example of the Five Whys.

WHY DID IT FAIL?

FOR EXAMPLE

A piece of equipment has failed.

Why did the equipment fail? Because a circuit board burned out.

Why did the circuit board burn out? Because it overheated.

Why did the circuit board overheat? Because the ventilation system wasn't working properly.

Why was the ventilation system not working properly? Because the filters had not been changed recently.

Why were the filters not changed recently? Because that was not on the preventive maintenance schedule.

At this point, the operations manager could apply the obvious solution—add changing the filter to the preventive maintenance schedule—and maybe review the schedule to ensure that no other maintenance tasks were missing. The operations manager could also ask "Why?" again, to get to the reason why changing the filter was not on the schedule. It may be wise to revise the procedures for developing preventive maintenance schedules.

The technique of the Five Whys has been criticized for its simplicity and because the "Why?" is often answered only through deduction and speculation. This technique works only to start an investigation into causes. It's important to remember that there could be more than one answer to each "Why?" question; a simple test for each answer is to ask, "If I get rid of this cause, will the problem disappear?" This technique works best if each answer can be verified before asking the next "Why?"

Another tool often used in determining the causes of problems is the *fishbone diagram* or *Ishikawa diagram*

FIVE WHYS

CAUTION

This technique is a straightforward approach to push investigation of a problem area beyond the immediate and most obvious cause. It's important to make sure the "Why?" answers are in the form of "what" and never "who," in order to avoid the blame game and fix the process or system. You should rephrase the answer in your follow-up "Why?" question in order to keep the focus on "what" and away from "who."

(named after Dr. Kaoru Ishikawa, the Japanese quality control statistician credited with inventing it), or *cause-and-effect diagram*.

Fishbone Diagram. Begin by drawing a horizontal line; this is the "spine of the fish." Next, at one end of the line, write the problem; this is the "head of the

> **Fishbone diagram** A tool that provides a systematic and graphic way of identifying possible causes for a **KEY TERM** problem, using categories to focus and structure the thinking, in order to work toward determining root causes. Also known as the *Ishikawa diagram* (after Dr. Kaoru Ishikawa, the Japanese quality control statistician credited with inventing it) and *cause-and-effect diagram*.

fish." Next, draw diagonal lines running up or down from the horizontal line, slanting away from the "head," and label each with a category; these are the "bones of the fish."

The following categories are typically used, if only because it's easy to remember them:

- *Methods, Machines, Materials, Maintenance, Manpower, Measurement, Mother Nature (Environment)*—the 7 M's
- *Place, Procedure, People, Policies*—the 4 P's
- *Surroundings, Suppliers, Systems, Skills*—the 4 S's

Use whatever categories help you organize the diagram. A good, basic set of categories is unfortunately less easily remembered:

- Equipment
- Process
- People
- Materials
- Environment
- Management

You can add categories if possible causes arise that don't fit the categories you've charted. Use idea-generating techniques to identify factors within each category that may be contributing to the problem. Write each of these on a short horizontal line from the diagonal for the appropriate category. (See Exhibit 3-2.)

Repeat this procedure for each factor in each category to generate factors within each factor. Probe until the team members feel that you've

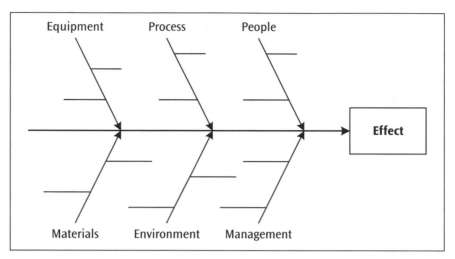

Exhibit 3-2. Fishbone diagram

exhausted the possibilities of factors and factors within factors and factors within factors within factors…. You want to achieve a point at which the final factors are variables that are specific, measurable, and controllable.

Analyze the results. Are there any factors that appear in more than one category? If so, these are the most probable root causes of the problem. Prioritize these factors in terms of probability. Then state each root cause clearly and specifically. These root cause statements are your problem statements.

Generate Possible Solutions for the Problems

Sometimes a solution is obvious, a matter of applying common sense and/or experience.

For example, if your analysis of the flowcharts reveals activities that are not adding value to the product or service, such as redundancies and unnecessary steps, try to eliminate them. There may be activities that are not actually part of processing—decisions, transport of work-in-process, inspections and review cycles, and documentation and other paperwork. You may be able to reduce the time spent on these activities if you are unable to eliminate them.

If delays occur, determine whether they are necessary; if not, eliminate or at least reduce them. If a delay is necessary because two connected processes work at the same average speeds but the speeds vary, consider inserting a buffer between them so that there are no delays when the first process is going slower than the second and no downtime if the first process is going faster than the second.

Sometimes the solution to a problem may seem obvious, but you lack the specifics for taking action. For example, if the problem is that a process is producing too much waste or productivity is inconsistent, you may believe that the solution is in reducing variations, but not know how. In that case, the best step might be to consider using statistical methods, such as the methodology and tools of Six Sigma.

Benchmarking. In many situations, it may be possible to find solutions by examining similar processes within your organization or in other organizations. Through *process benchmarking,* you identify and examine how others are doing what you want to do. This is also known as *best practices benchmarking,* although it may be more realistic to aim at finding *better* practices.

Specifically, if you are searching for possible solutions, this is *problem-based benchmarking.* It is essential to distinguish between *benchmarks* and *benchmarking;* benchmarks are the "whats" but more importantly, benchmarks uncover the "hows" and

> **Benchmarking** The process in which an organization identifies other organizations (within its **KEY TERM** industry or not) with better products, services, or processes and then adapts that information to change or improve its own products, services, or processes. This term is often used to at least imply that the comparison is with the best in the field or with *best practices.*

> **ON BENCHMARKING** **SMART**
> "Paul Allaire [then chair of Xerox] says the primary objective of benchmarking is understanding exemplary business **MANAGING** practices. Four things count in benchmarking: the process on which you focus, the organizations you visit, the best practices you find and the changes you institute. Target-setting is secondary."
> —Robert C. Camp, "A Bible for Benchmarking, by Xerox," *Financial Executive,* July 1, 1993

"whys." For example, Michael Phelps's world record of 4:03.84 in the 400-meter individual medley set in Beijing established a true benchmark, but

THINK "PROCESSES"

When you think of a production system as a series of processes, you can learn more from other organizations, even if they are not in your industry or selling products or services like yours.

Suppose you want to create a system for producing a schnurxo and you want to find the best way to construct the system. You won't find it out there, since no organization is producing anything like a schnurxo.

But if you break down production of the schnurxo into processes (P1, P2, P3, ...), you may find several organizations using P1 processes, and a few organizations using P2 processes, and so forth. Learn about those processes and apply that knowledge to create better processes and structure them into a system to produce schnurxos.

it is his total dedication to the sport, the thousands of hours he spent in the pool, Bob Bowman's coaching, and his family's unwavering support that is most relevant to those pursuing his benchmark. That's what benchmarking uncovers.

Brainstorming. It may be necessary to use idea-generating (*ideation*) techniques such as brainstorming. We all know about brainstorming. It's a technique commonly used to enable a group of people to creatively and efficiently generate a lot of ideas on any topic in an environment that is free of judgment.

However, the word "brainstorming" is often used for *unstructured* brainstorming, which is usually a group session without any rules in which the participants offer ideas at any time and someone tries to record all the ideas.

It may be more efficient and more effective to use *structured brainstorming*. The process is relatively simple:

1. State the problem and write it on a board or flip chart to keep it on display.
2. Announce, and then enforce, this basic rule—"No idea is judged by anybody in any way."
3. Have each member of the group, in turn, give an idea.
4. Write each idea as it is offered, in large letters on a board or flip chart.
5. Keep going around the group, allowing members to pass if they have no ideas to offer, until all members have passed.

6. Review the list of ideas to make sure that all members understand them.

7. Combine similar ideas and discard any duplicates.

PAPER IS SAFER

TRICKS OF THE TRADE

If the members of the group might not feel comfortable with the freedom of the activity, you can ease into it slowly and safely. Give each member a small pad of paper and ask them all to jot down their ideas and suggestions, one to a slip. Allow them a few minutes. Then collect the slips. Read them aloud and have someone record each on the board or flip chart. This approach gets contributions out anonymously and makes it easier for group members to risk sharing their thoughts in the traditional brainstorming method.

Perhaps the most important point to keep in mind when trying to generate possible solutions for a problem is not to focus so much on the problem that you become fixated. Focus instead on what you're trying to do that you cannot do well because of the problem. This means asking three basic questions:

- What are we trying to do?
- What other ways can we find to do that?
- Which other ways would work here?

Simplification and Standardization. Sometimes the best way to solve a problem is to apply the simplification and standardization that are much of the essence of Design for Manufacture and Assembly, as mentioned in Chapter 2, and that can be applied to providing services as well as to manufacturing and assembling.

- *Simplify the design and reduce the number of parts.* Each part represents an opportunity for defects and assembly errors or, in providing services, for mistakes and wasting time. (Also, the more parts or steps, the more it costs to produce the goods or provide the services.)
- *Standardize similar designs and processes as much as possible.* This makes activities easier to understand and mistakes less likely.
- *Use common parts and materials.* This reduces the amounts and types of inventory necessary and reduces time spent finding and transporting parts and materials.
- *Mistake-proof processes however possible.* To err may be human, but

you can reduce the chances of error without making anyone less human.

■ *Automate processes.* This saves time and labor and reduces the need for thinking and, of course, the possibility of making mistakes.

Some basic principles apply to processes of all types and reduce problems.

Prioritize the Possible Solutions

You probably won't be able to try to solve all of the problems at one time. To decide which problems to solve and how to prioritize them, you can use a simple tool, the *impact-effort matrix* (also known as *effort-impact matrix*).

Impact-Effort Matrix. The members of the group rate each solution option according to impact (what the option would achieve) and effort (what the option would require), using a scale from one to five (for example). Then, a vertical axis and a horizontal axis are drawn and marked with increments from zero to five. The vertical is marked "Impact" and the horizontal is marked "Effort." The options are then plotted on the chart according to their rating values.

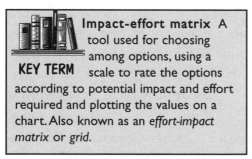

KEY TERM — **Impact-effort matrix** A tool used for choosing among options, using a scale to rate the options according to potential impact and effort required and plotting the values on a chart. Also known as an *effort-impact matrix* or *grid*.

The chart is then divided into four quadrants of equal size and marked: the upper left is "1," the lower left is "2," the upper right is "3," and the lower right is "4." Options in quadrant 1 (higher impact, lower effort) are best, particularly the closer they are to the upper left corner. Options in quadrants 2 (lower impact, lower effort) and 3 (higher impact, higher effort) are next best, depending on the resources available. Again, the closer the options are to the upper left corners of their quadrants, the better. The options in quadrant 4 (lower impact, higher effort) would be the lowest priority.

(The use of quadrants is unnecessary if there are sufficient options clustered in the upper left of the chart. If not, the quadrants make it

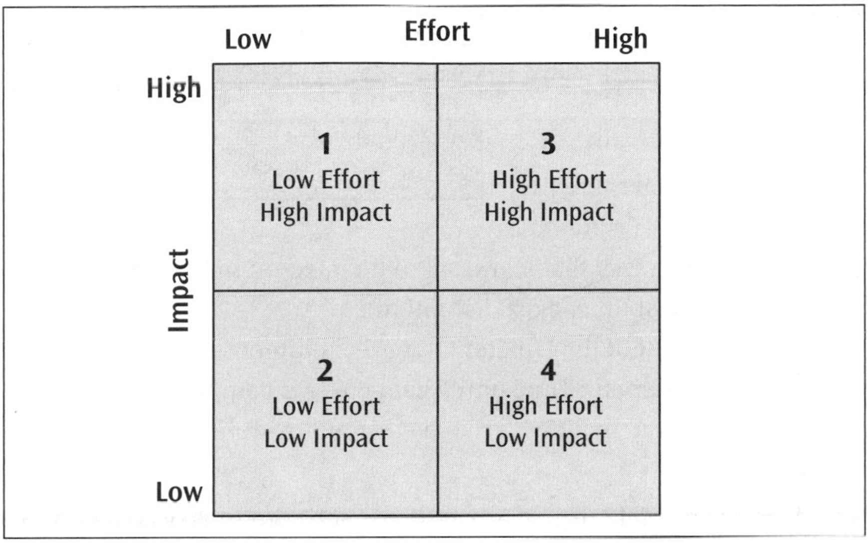

Exhibit 3-3. Impact-effort matrix

easier to compare lower-impact, lower-effort options and higher-impact, higher-effort options.)

Criteria Matrix. A *criteria matrix* is a systematic approach to choosing among options, by weighting each criterion and then rating each option for each criterion. It is particularly useful when there are more than 10 options for a solution and when there are more than a half-dozen crite-

> **AGREE ON DECISION CRITERIA** 
> **CAUTION**
> Whenever a group is making decisions about improvement ideas, it's smart to identify in advance the criteria to be used. If group members decide on decision criteria early in the process, they can use the same standards and minimize misunderstandings and conflicts.

ria. This technique allows for quantifying qualitative criteria.

Step 1. Create an objective statement; this problem statement will be the basis for choosing and weighting the criteria to be used.

Sample problem statement: *To increase productivity of widget assembly line.*

Step 2. Develop a list of criteria for judging the options. What factors are essential considerations for a solution to this problem?

Criteria:

- Cost
- Time to Implement
- Disruption of Activities

> **Criteria matrix** A systematic approach to choosing among options, by weighting each criterion and then rating each option for each criterion.
>
> **KEY TERM**

Step 3. Specify what each criterion means. Make sure that each is stated in a way that allows all to be rated on the same scale (e.g., 1 = most cost, most time, most disruption).

- Cost: Total cost of time, materials, and equipment
- Time to Implement: Time until changeover is completed
- Disruption of Activities: Negative effect on operations during implementation

Step 4. Assign a weight (e.g., 1-5 or 1-10) to each criterion based on importance.

- Cost   7
- Time to Implement   8
- Disruption of Activities   6

Step 5. Create a table, listing each option as a column head and each criterion to the left of a row. (See Exhibit 3-4.) (Depending on the number of options, the number of criteria, and the dimensions of the paper or board, it may work better to put the criteria across the top and the options on the left.)

Step 6: Rate each option 1-10 according to each criterion. Mark the rating in the left half of the appropriate cell.

Step 7. Multiply each rating by the weight assigned to that criterion. Mark the score in the right half of the appropriate cell.

Step 8. Total the scores for each solution option. (See Exhibit 3-5.)

Cost-Benefit Analysis. A traditional technique used in deciding among potential solutions is to do a cost-benefit analysis for each of them. This technique is relatively simple for anyone with experience doing budgets and estimates. You calculate the benefits expected from applying a solution and subtract the costs you expect to incur.

The costs may be one-time or ongoing; many solutions are likely to involve both. The benefits are most often going to come over time. You

Evaluation Criteria	Wt.	Options			
		A	B	C	D
Cost					
Time to Implement					
Disruption of Activities					
Total Weighted Scores					

Exhibit 3-4. Criterion matrix, showing options and criteria

Evaluation Criteria	Wt.	Options			
		A	B	C	D
Cost	7	6 / 42	7 / 49	4 / 28	5 / 35
Time to Implement	8	4 / 32	5 / 40	8 / 64	6 / 48
Disruption of Activities	6	5 / 30	4 / 24	6 / 36	6 / 36
Total Weighted Scores	21	104	113	128	119

Exhibit 3-5. Criterion matrix, showing ratings, scores, and totals

should calculate a *payback period*, the time it takes for the benefits of a change to outweigh the costs. (The payback period is often known as the time to the break-even point, as discussed in Chapter 2.) You can calculate the costs and benefits at time intervals, such as six months, a year, 18 months, two years, and so on.

SMART MANAGING

IT'S MONEY THAT MATTERS, BUT TIMING IS EVERYTHING
The payback period or break-even point may be a crucial consideration. This is especially true if the improvement project involves big capital expenditures or borrowing, or if the investment in improvement entails a significant cost of lost opportunity. Time to break-even may be the decisive factor in choosing the problem for your improvement effort.

The costs side could include extra time, training, equipment, the value of productivity lost during the implementation, lost sales, and so on.

The benefits side could include the value of the resulting increase in productivity, time saved, and so forth. You'll want to work with someone from finance when you do your cost-benefit analysis.

It's generally better to account only for financial costs and financial benefits. However, you should consider as well the intangible costs and benefits—e.g., the boost in morale, the increased stress on the process manager and workers, and the positive effects on the organization's image. It's tricky to estimate the value of intangibles, but it seems naive to ignore those costs and benefits. You should at least note the intangibles you expect to result, both bad and good.

Decide on the Improvement Project

By now you should have enough information to decide on the problem and solution. If not, you may need to continue discussing the options, maybe include other people in the decision making, and revisit the criteria matrix and/or the cost-benefit analyses.

Set Baselines

Set your baseline, the measurements for the process performance metrics that you'll be using as the basis of comparison for evaluating the effects of the changes you'll be making. The baseline should include measurements of the process outputs. You should pay particular attention to your KPIs, the key performance indicators.

Set Targets

You should have qualitative goals—what you expect to do—and quantitative improvement targets—how well you expect to do it. Setting targets helps you focus better on what you want to improve. You should set targets for the overall process, not simply the problem area. Make sure you have a baseline measurement for every metric for which you set a target. This is especially important for your KPIs.

> **Baseline** A set of measurements used to establish the current level of performance for a system or a **KEY TERM** process, usually before starting improvement activities.

How much do you expect to be able to improve on your baseline measurements? What performance levels will you consider acceptable?

Develop the New/Revised Process

Start by challenging basic assumptions and beliefs about the current process. Often people can't remember or never knew why the current process was structured as it is or if it simply evolved.

Using the Five Whys may be useful here, to dig into assumptions and beliefs. Ask questions like the following—and probe the answers with "Why?"

- Why does this process exist? What is its purpose?
- Why are the activities sequenced as they are?
- Why is activity A part of the process? Why is it necessary?

Once you've questioned assumptions and beliefs and dissociated the group members from the familiarity of the current process, you can start working toward something new.

First, establish the purpose of the process. What output(s) are necessary? What input(s) does the process need to produce the output(s)?

Then, try to open up the discussion to design a new process, from zero. This may or may not work, depending on the process and the people in the group.

If the discussion stalls here, ask questions about the activities in the process. For example:

- What if we changed the sequence of the activities?
- What if we dropped activity A, activity B, activity C...?
- What if we split activity A, activity B...?
- What could we do to reduce or eliminate errors in activity B?
- What could we do to speed up activity C?

At some point, you should be able to start designing a new process from zero, with questions like the following:

- What should we do first to transform the input into the output? What needs to happen?
- What should we do next?
- Can we get from input to output any faster, any more efficiently, any more simply?
- Follow up answers with "Why?" This helps keep the discussion logical and the design simple. When the group has agreed on each step in the new process design, mark it on the board or flip chart.

Keep going until your new process can produce the necessary output(s). Then review the process step by step. Is each step necessary? Is the sequence of activities logical? Can the process be simplified in any way?

Create a flowchart for the process as it should be, following the same guidelines as used to create the flowchart for the current process (Chapter 2).

Plan for Making the Changes

The best way to plan for implementing an improvement project is by using the methods and tools of project management, which are presented in Chapter 7. Be sure to specify the basics:

- *What* is to be done?
- *Who* is responsible for doing it?
- *How* is it to be done?
- By *when* is it to be done?

Also, note any potential problems that you anticipate and the means by which you should be able to detect them as soon as they develop.

Make the Changes as Planned

Check to make sure each person involved in the change knows what he or she is responsible for doing, is able to do it, and does it according to the schedule, as planned. Monitor the changes—and the effects. Check for problems. Document everything.

SMART

MANAGING

PLAN THE WORK AND WORK THE PLAN

We cannot always plan our work as well as necessary. But we should always try to work our plan as well as possible.

"A poor strategy executed well is always better than a great strategy executed poorly."

—Michael Porter, Institute for Strategy and Competitiveness, Harvard Business School

On the other hand ...

"Taking the few extra minutes to outline your strategy often means the difference between achieving your objectives and losing everything. Remember, a great strategy poorly executed will always achieve better returns than a poor strategy executed well."

—David Goldsmith, MetaMatrix Consulting Group, LLC

Evaluate the Effects of the Changes

Get measurements for the process performance metrics that you used for your baseline and compare the "before" and "after." Pay particular attention to the KPIs—the "vital signs" of the process.

Check for any problems that may have resulted from the solution. If you are removing or reducing a bottleneck, for example, you should expect another to develop. Whenever there are multiple activities operating at different speeds, you may need to add a buffer.

Theory of Constraints   *PRoduction planning*

A discussion of improving production processes would not be complete without the Theory of Constraints (TOC). This is an approach to management and improvement developed by Eliyahu M. Goldratt and introduced in his book *The Goal* (North River Press, 1984).

TOC pursues the goal (global objective) of a system through an understanding of the underlying cause-and-effect dependencies and variations in the system. TOC applies cause-and-effect thinking processes to understand and improve systems, including organizations. The TOC thinking processes have been used to create solutions in various business functions, including production, distribution, and supplier relations. TOC has been labeled "a process for creating processes of improvement" (John Tripp, *TOC Executive Challenge: A Goal Game*, North River Press, 2007).

The core principle in TOC is that every system is limited by a constraint—something that keeps the system from achieving its goal more efficiently or more completely. There may be a few constraints, but not many.

Theory of Constraints
KEY TERM An approach to management and improvement that emphasizes an understanding of the underlying cause-and-effect dependencies and variations in systems and an application of cause-and-effect thinking processes to understand and improve systems in business functions. TOC was developed by Eliyahu M. Goldratt. It has been labeled "a process for creating processes of improvement."

Constraints can be within the system or outside it. To improve a system to any significant degree, we must identify the constraint and manage the system accordingly.

In other words, a chain is only as strong as its weakest link, and we need to understand the entire chain, not only focus on individual links.

Whether an organization is producing goods or providing services or both, the performance of any system is determined by its constraint. There are two main types of constraints: physical (resources, e.g., people, facilities, machines, equipment, materials, time) and policy (almost everything else that is intangible).

TOC uses three fundamental operational measures—*throughput, inventory,* and *operating expense*—rather than traditional cost accounting measures. These three measures should be used to guide and improve decision making. These measures are based on the premise that all operations are basically "money-making machines."

- *Throughput* (T) is the rate at which the system produces money. It is calculated by subtracting direct costs (usually costs of materials) from the sales price.
- *Inventory* (I) is all the money invested in things the organization intends to sell (not just materials).
- *Operating Expense* (OE) is all the money poured in continuously to convert inventory into throughput.

For the system or any operations within the system, the following formulas are used:

DON'T MAINTAIN POLICY CONSTRAINTS

Your most limiting constraints may be *policies*, according to Goldratt:

CAUTION

"Our systems today are limited mainly by policy constraints. We very rarely find a company with a real market constraint, but rather, with devastating marketing policy constraints. We very rarely find a true bottleneck on the shop floor, we usually find production policy constraints. We almost never find a vendor constraint, but we do find purchasing policy constraints. And in all cases the policies were very logical at the time they were instituted. Their original reasons have since long gone, but the old policies still remain with us."

—Eliyahu M. Goldratt, *What Is This Thing Called Theory of Constraints and How Should It Be Implemented?* (North River Press, 1990)

Profit	= Throughput − Operating Expense
Return on Investment	= (Throughput − Operating Expense)/Inventory
Cash Flow	= (Throughput − Operating Expense) + Inventory

TOC is a process of ongoing improvement. There are five "focusing steps" for maximizing the performance of a system by ensuring that improvement efforts focus on constraints:

1. Identify the *system constraint*—the part that prevents the system from achieving its goal more fully.
2. Decide how to exploit the system constraint, how to use its capacity to the fullest.
3. Subordinate and synchronize all other processes to support the above decision, what you do with the constraint.
4. Elevate the system constraint until it is "broken" or solved. Increase the capacity of the constraint permanently, if possible.
5. Don't let inertia become the system constraint! If you solve the constraint problem, another part of the system then becomes the new constraint. And if you stop working on constraints, then inertia becomes the constraint.

In TOC, the improvement process is structured around three questions:

- *What to change?* What is the problem?
- *What to change to?* What is the solution?

- *How to cause the change?* How can we implement the solution?

The three questions provide the framework for the *TOC Thinking Processes.* To solve the problem of a constraint, we must:

- Understand the process interdependencies that contribute to delivering a product or a service.
- Understand the effects of those interdependencies and variations in the processes on the performance of the system.
- Buffer to allow for those interdependencies and variations so that performance can be consistently high.

Drum-Buffer-Rope

Drum-Buffer-Rope (DBR) is the method for achieving optimal material flow in *synchronized production* (aka *synchronous manufacturing*), the Theory of Constraints approach to production planning introduced by

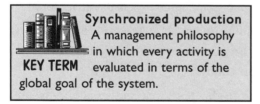 **Synchronized production** A management philosophy in which every activity is **KEY TERM** evaluated in terms of the global goal of the system.

Eliyahu M. Goldratt and Robert E. Fox in their book, *The Race* (North River Press, 1986).

This method for optimizing flow through a system in consideration of a constraint pulls materials through the system, rather than pushing them into it. It is named for its three components.

The *drum* is the physical constraint in the system that limits the capacity of the system. (Why "drum"? Because the production rate of the constraint is like a drumbeat the rest of the system must follow.) It's essential to make sure that this capacity-constraining resource always has a flow of work and that anything it has processed is used, not wasted. This makes the most of its limiting capacity.

The *buffer* is a way of ensuring that the drum always has work flowing to it. The unit of measure for buffers in DBR is *time*, rather than quantity of material. The system operates according to the time at which work-in-process is expected to be at the constraint. Traditional DBR usually calls for buffers at several points in the system—not only the constraint, but also material release points, synchronization points (divergences and convergences), and shipping.

The *rope* is a connection from the constraint back to the gating mechanism that releases work into the system. The rope functions as the work release mechanism: it ensures that work cannot be put into the system too soon

> **Drum-Buffer-Rope (DBR)** The method for achieving optimal material flow in synchronized production, the Theory of Constraints approach to production planning. DBR was introduced by Eliyahu M. Goldratt and Robert E. Fox in 1986.
>
> **KEY TERM**

or in excessive quantities. The "rope length" is equal to the buffer duration; the gating rate is equal to the drum rate. Putting work into the system earlier than a buffer time means a high amount of work-in-process and slows down the entire system.

DBR is a method, a way to operate a system. It works only with proper buffer management to monitor and control the system.

Operations Manager's Checklist for Chapter 3

☑ The process of improving a process generally consists of the following steps:
- Document the current process.
- Identify the problem areas.
- Quantify the effects of each problem area.
- Prioritize the problem areas.
- Determine the causes of the problems.
- Generate possible solutions for the problems.
- Prioritize the possible solutions.
- Decide on the improvement project.
- Set baselines.
- Set targets.
- Develop the new/revised process.
- Plan for making the changes.
- Make the changes as planned.
- Evaluate the effects of the changes.

☑ Theory of Constraints (TOC) is an approach to management and improvement that emphasizes an understanding of the underlying cause-and-effect dependencies and variations in systems and an application of cause-and-effect thinking processes to understand and improve systems in business functions. TOC has been labeled "a process for creating processes of improvement."

☑ Drum-Buffer-Rope is the method for achieving optimal material flow in synchronized production, the Theory of Constraints approach to production planning introduced by Eliyahu M. Goldratt and Robert E. Fox in 1986.

Quality and Operations Management:
The Journey Without End

W hether you produce goods or deliver services, whether your company is a small LLC serving a local area or a huge multinational corporation, quality matters to your customers. However they perceive it and however you define it, quality should be important to you.

What Is Quality?

What does quality mean to your customers? How do you know what it means?

Don't read any further unless you can answer both questions. Gurus such as W. Edwards Deming, Joseph M. Juran, and Philip B. Crosby have defined and discussed quality—but they're not buying your goods or services.

Know what your customers expect from your goods or services. Make sure that your processes can provide it consistently. That's "Quality" with a capital "Q."

Quality has been defined as excellence, conformance to specifications, fitness for use, and value for the price. It's all that—and more. Quality in products means reliability, durability, serviceability, and more. Quality in services means reliability or consistency, caring about your customers, and more. That "more" is whatever people want and expect

SMART

MANAGING

QUALITY IN PERSPECTIVE
"Fitness for use" (with "fitness" defined by the customer).
—Joseph M. Juran

"Conformance to requirements."
—Philip B. Crosby

"Degree to which a set of inherent characteristics fulfills requirements" (i.e., "needs" or "expectations").

—*International Organization for Standardization,* ISO 9000:2005—Quality management systems—Fundamentals and vocabulary

"A subjective term for which each person or sector has its own definition. In technical usage, quality can have two meanings: 1. the characteristics of a product or service that bear on its ability to satisfy stated or implied needs; 2. a product or service free of deficiencies."
—American Society for Quality

"Quality in a product or service ... is what the customer gets out and is willing to pay for."

—Peter F. Drucker, *Innovation and Entrepreneurship: Practice and Principles*

from your goods and services. But be careful, because the Kano Model suggests that "today's delights are tomorrow's expectations."

Exhibit 4-1. The Kano Model

> **Kano Model** A theory of product development and customer satisfaction developed in the 1980s by Noriaki Kano that classifies customer preferences into five categories:
> - attractive
> - one-dimensional
> - must-be
> - indifferent
> - reverse
>
> **KEY TERM**
>
> Other people have given these categories various names (delighters/exciters, satisfiers, dissatisfiers, etc.) and modified the model. An essential point is that customers may be surprised and delighted by some characteristic when it's new to them, but they will soon come to expect it.

How Do You Ensure Quality?

Make Quality a Strategic Issue

Planning for quality must be part of the organization's comprehensive business planning. Ask this basic question: Why, specifically, are we focusing on quality? What do we want to achieve? The answers should determine how you plan for quality.

Any focus on quality must be championed by effective leaders who understand at least the basics of quality, who believe in it as a strategic necessity, and who engage in training and improvement activities personally, not just sign memos about them and give speeches in support. The leaders must lead by example.

Promote Teamwork and Provide Training

Quality is not the responsibility of a quality assurance department or quality control units. It's the responsibility of every employee in every area of the organization; it has to be built into any product or service that you deliver. For you, this means that any employee involved in any production process should understand at least the basics of quality thinking, techniques, and tools and should take personal responsibility for providing the best goods and services possible—and for suggesting ways to improve those goods and services and the processes that produce them.

You need to provide training in the basics of quality so that it becomes a way of life—the methodology and the essential tools. You will also need to form teams to improve production or service delivery processes. The employees who execute the processes are the experts in how those processes work—not just as they were designed to work, but also how they work in real life. They own those processes, and they should have authority and responsibility for improving them.

Meet or Exceed Your Customers' Expectations

Focus on satisfying the customers. Those are the people who buy the goods and services. Those are the people who define "quality" through their needs and wants. And their requirements extend throughout the supply chain—the sequence of connected activities that results in providing the goods and services, from design through delivery, from raw materials to satisfaction.

The strategy to meet or exceed customer expectations must be linked vertically to the customer and horizontally to other parts of the enterprise. The main objective of a *category strategy,* as explained in Chapter 1, is to translate the critical attributes of the target market segments into the requisite competitive dimensions that can be operationalized.

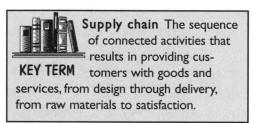

Supply chain The sequence of connected activities that results in providing customers with goods and services, from design through delivery, from raw materials to satisfaction.

Each link in the supply chain is responsible for satisfying the customers. Every person working in the chain is a member of a team that exists to produce goods or services that meet or exceed the customers' expectations.

Improve Key Processes Continuously

When can you stop improving your designs and processes? Never. Quality is a journey without end. Even if your designs and processes are perfect now—which is highly improbable—and even if you are currently delighting your customers, don't expect that perfection and that delight to last.

We're all only too human: something that knocks our socks off today may not impress us as much tomorrow. We tend to want something better, something more, something that costs less. Continuous improvement means always working to provide what customers want, even before they realize they want it. Uncovering latent demand is the key to engendering lifetime customer relationships.

Work with Information: Get It, Analyze It, Apply It

A central tenet in any approach to quality is that you must base what you do on facts, not assumptions, guesses, hopes, or fears. To manage operations, you need the following information:

- Information about what potential and current customers want and expect you to offer in your goods and services
- Information about your markets and your industry, particularly your competitors, both *direct* and *indirect*
- Information about your current processes, similar processes used by other organizations, and possibilities for improving your processes through technology and zero-based thinking
- Information about the organization's financials
- Information about critical business issues—issues identified during strategic planning or operational goal setting as objectives for ensuring the growth or survival of the organization

Direct competitor Any organization offering the same goods or services in the same markets.

Indirect competitor Any organization offering the same or similar goods or services, but in other markets, or any organization offering similar goods or services in the same markets—both are potentially direct competitors.

KEY TERMS

These terms depend on how your organization positions itself and how it understands its goods and services. If you rent DVDs, for example, are you competing with other DVD rental companies, with movie theaters and cable TV as well, or with any company that is providing any type of entertainment—live theaters, music concerts, bowling alleys, professional sports, etc.?

In the following sections of this chapter, we will focus on this last essential point for ensuring quality—getting, analyzing, and applying information.

Design for Quality

Chapter 2 covered designing goods and services and the processes that produce or deliver them. Here we can only reiterate two things:

- Design products and services according to information about what potential and current customers want and expect.

■ Design processes according to information about
your current processes,
similar processes used by
other organizations, and
possibilities for improving
your processes through
technology and zero-
based thinking.

KEEP CURRENT AND KEEP IMPROVING
CAUTION

"When the rate of change inside an institution becomes slower than the rate of change outside, the end is in sight."
—Jack Welch, former Chairman and CEO, General Electric

Later, we'll briefly outline a methodology for designing products, services, and processes.

Six Sigma for Quality Improvement

A basic approach to improving products, services, and processes can be found in the Six Sigma methodology for quality management. It focuses on customer requirements and reducing variation in processes.

Six Sigma uses a specific approach and tools to improve processes and products by using data to reduce process variation. The technical goal of Six Sigma is to reduce unacceptable output to no more than 3.4 defects per million opportunities (DPMO).

KEY TERMS

Six Sigma A business management strategy for improving the quality of process outputs by identifying and removing the causes of defects and variation in the processes.

Sigma A Greek letter (σ) that is used to represent standard deviation, a measure of variation in a statistical population.

The term is used in Six Sigma methodology process to represent 99.9997% consistency—six standard deviations between the process mean and the nearer of two specification limits.

Defects per million opportunities (DPMO) A standard measurement in Six Sigma methodology, used to facilitate measurement and comparison of processes.

Defect Any undesired result or any variation in a required characteristic that does not conform to requirements.

Opportunity Any area within a product, a service, or a process in which a defect could occur.

Tools

Six Sigma uses dozens of techniques and tools, depending on the specific improvement project. Some tools are often used during more than one phase, for different purposes; others may not be used at all.

Here we can only discuss a few of the most commonly used. However, according to Kaoru Ishikawa, a quality pioneer, the seven basic tools—flow charts, cause-and-effect diagrams, Pareto charts, histograms, scatter diagrams, run charts, and control charts—are sufficient for removing 95 percent of all defects, variations, and inconsistencies from any process.

Variation

The objective of the Six Sigma approach to quality is to reduce variation in processes in order to produce outputs that better satisfy customer requirements as consistently as possible and to minimize waste. So, what is *variation*?

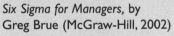

SIX SIGMA BASICS

Here are two references that should be useful for learning more about Six Sigma:

Six Sigma for Managers, by Greg Brue (McGraw-Hill, 2002)

Rath & Strong Six Sigma Pocket Guide, revised (Rath & Strong, 2006)

TOOLS

It's the spread of data around the average value, quantified in terms of standard deviation, as mentioned above.

Variation occurs in every process. If it's natural to the process (that is, due to inherent causes, called *common causes*), the variation is predictable and the process is considered to be *in control* and *stable*. If the variation cannot be attributed to common causes, but rather to *special*

Common cause A cause of variation that is inherent in the process.

KEY TERMS   **Special cause** A cause of variation that is extrinsic to the process.

Stable/in control State of a process in which any variation is due to common causes only.

Unstable/out of control State of a process in which there is variation due to special causes.

causes, the variation is uncontrolled and the process is considered *unstable* and *out of control.* As you might expect, for an operations manager, it is always better to control the variation.

Six Sigma Methodology

The Six Sigma structure for improvement projects generally consists of these five phases, often described as DMAIC:

1. Define
2. Measure
3. Analyze
4. Improve
5. Control

Within each phase, the activities can vary widely, depending on the specifics of the situation and the person leading the initiative. Here we outline most of the usual activities and describe the tools used most often.

Define

Form an improvement project team.

Create a project charter. The charter should contain the following:

- Business case for the project—quantify the results expected, especially the effect on the bottom line
- The problem statement
- The scope of the project
- The goals and objectives of the project
- Plan and milestones for the project

- The members of the team (including champion, sponsor, and process owner) and their roles and responsibilities

Determine the customers' needs and requirements. Get input from marketing, customer service, and any other units in direct contact with customers. Use a *critical to quality* (CTQ) tree to break down the product or service into factors that customers consider critical to quality.

The procedure for growing a CTQ tree is similar to the procedure used to develop the cause-and-effect diagram (fishbone diagram or Ishikawa diagram, explained in Chapter 3), but the result is structured more like the traditional hierarchical organizational chart.

For more complex scenarios, the team may also use a *cause-and-effect matrix* or *quality function deployment* (QFD). Both tools are used to evaluate the interrelationships among characteristics and contributing factors identified with the CTQ tree and to prioritize those factors in order of their importance.

(For a brief explanation of the cause-and-effect matrix, also known as a *prioritization matrix,* see *Rath & Strong Six Sigma Pocket Guide,* revised [Rath & Strong, 2006]. For a good explanation of QFD, see *www.qfd-world.com/what_is_QFD.htm.*)

QFD is one approach to gaining cross-functional buy-in across the enterprise. The QFD process begins with studying and listening to customers (e.g., usage and attitude results, marketing, etc.) to determine the characteristics of a superior product. With the usage and attitude results as a starting point, you can define the customer requirements. Work with marketers to weight those characteristics based on their relative importance to customers and to determine the characteristics that are most important to customers. It is also possible to evaluate how those characteristics compare with current products and competitors' products. The end result is a better understanding and a focus on characteristics that require improvement.

> **Quality function deployment** "Method to transform user demands into design quality, to deploy the functions forming quality, and to deploy methods for achieving the design quality into subsystems and component parts, and ultimately to specific elements of the manufacturing process."
> —Yoji Akao, "Development History of Quality Function Deployment"
>
> **KEY TERM**

Customer requirement information also forms the basis for a matrix called the *house of quality.* With a house of quality matrix, you can use customer feedback to translate customer requirements into concrete category goals and to make downstream decisions. This process encourages people from various functions of the extended enterprise to work more closely together and to better understand each other's goals and issues as they collaborate to identify and detail the important product characteristics for developing a product that satisfies customers. (For instructions on building a house of quality, consult "House of Quality: Steps in Building a House of Quality," by Jennifer Tapke, Allyson Muller, Greg Johnson, and Josh Sieck, *www.public.iastate.edu/~vardeman/IE361/f01mini/johnson.pdf*).

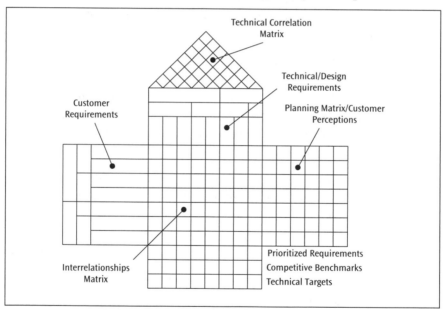

Exhibit 4-2. House of quality

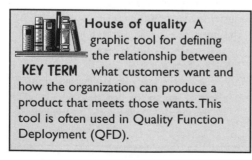

House of quality A graphic tool for defining the relationship between **KEY TERM** what customers want and how the organization can produce a product that meets those wants. This tool is often used in Quality Function Deployment (QFD).

Create a high-level map of the process. This consists of a SIPOC diagram with essential information: this map names the process, establishes the start point and the stop point, lists outputs and customers, lists inputs and suppliers, and shows the process as five to seven basic steps.

Measure

Refine the Y or Y's that will be the project focus. The team should determine exactly what it will measure and how.

Define essential concepts. The team should define at least what will be meant by *defect*, *opportunity*, and *unit* (smallest measurement of output).

The team will be measuring overall performance of the process in terms of *sigma level*. This is calculated in terms of *defects per million opportunities* (DPMO), so those three concepts must be understood well enough to measure them.

A TOOL, NOT A DEFINITION

In most QFD studies, the house of quality is not the starting point. In fact, the team may not even create a house of quality. Although the house of quality is commonly associated with QFD, Yoji Akao, the co-founder of QFD, has said many times, "The house of quality is not QFD."

Sigma level A standard measurement in Six Sigma methodology, used to facilitate measurement and comparison of processes, based on defects per million opportunities (DPMO).

These are the equivalents of six sigma levels in terms of DPMO:

1 sigma = 691,462 DPMO
2 sigma = 308,537 DPMO
3 sigma = 67,000 DPMO
4 sigma = 6,200 DPMO
5 sigma = 233 DPMO
6 sigma = 3.4 DPMO

Develop a more detailed process map. This should break down the basic steps of the high-level process map and enable the project team to identify key metrics for inputs, outputs, and the process.

Create a data collection plan. A *data collection plan* is a chart consisting of columns containing the following information:

- *Characteristics to measure*—the requirements determined in the Define phase
- *Metrics* (generally one to three) for measuring each of the following—
  - How well your suppliers are meeting your requirements for the inputs you need
  - How well you are meeting your customers' requirements with your outputs

- How efficiently your process is working (e.g., cycle time, cost of materials, cost of labor, value added)

■ *Type of data*

DISCRETE AND CONTINUOUS

Two basic types of data exist—*discrete* and *continuous*.

Data is *discrete* if the number of possible values is finite, that is, if you can count the values or if you can record them as either/or (e.g., off/on, good/bad, red/white/blue). Discrete data is also known as *attribute(s)* data.

Data is *continuous* if the values exist on a continuum, that is, if each value could be divided *ad infinitum* (e.g., measures of height, length, width, weight, minutes, days). Continuous data is also known as *variables* data.

Discrete data is usually easier to collect and interpret. Continuous data allows us to measure with greater precision, to measure extent or magnitude, which gives us an advantage over measuring with discrete data.

■ *Operational definitions and procedures*—specifics on how the data will be collected and recorded, so that all parties involved will understand means of measuring, sampling methods, and so on

■ *Targets* (the ideal levels for the customers) and/or specifications (the lowest acceptable levels for the customers)

KEY TERMS

Continuous data Data for which the values exist on a continuum, that is, if each value could be divided *ad infinitum* (e.g., measures of height, length, width, weight, minutes, days). Also known as *variables data*.

Discrete data Data for which the number of possible values is finite, that is, if you can count the values or if you can record them as either/or (e.g., off/on, good/bad, red/white/blue). Also known as *attribute(s) data*.

■ *Data collection forms*

If collecting discrete data, the team should create a check sheet. It should define what constitutes a defect (as determined at the start of the Measure phase), create a grid for recording the data, specify the types of defects, and set the time frame for collecting the data.

If collecting continuous data, the team should create a frequency distribution data sheet or frequency plot check sheet. As the data is recorded, it develops a plot of the distribution of the values, like a histogram (bar graph).

■ *Sampling method(s)*— means of ensuring that the sample(s) used for collecting data be representative of the total available and taken at random

> **Sampling** The practice of using data from only part of the total available. For the results of data analysis **KEY TERM** to be valid, any sample must be representative of the whole and it must be taken at random. *Random sampling* means that any part of the whole has an equal probability of being sampled as any other.

Implement the data collection plan.

Calculate the current sigma level of the process (baseline). Here's the easiest way:

■ Count the number of units processed.

■ Count the number of units with defects.

■ Calculate the defect rate (defective units divided by units processed).

■ Count the opportunities for defects in each unit.

■ Calculate the defects per opportunity (defect rate divided by opportunities).

■ Calculate the defects per million opportunities (defects per opportunity multiplied by 1,000,000).

■ Convert DPMO into sigma value, using a DPMO-sigma table or a sigma calculator. (Note: Sigma tables are calculated in two ways— with or without the effect of a shift, generally calculated at 1.5 σ. It's assumed that the process mean can shift by that amount over time.)

Set performance targets. The team should specify the results it hopes to achieve, in line with the business case made in the project charter.

Analyze

Analyze the data collected in the Measure phase. The methods and tools used for data analysis depend on whether the data is discrete or continuous.

For *discrete data*, the statistical tools most commonly used are the Pareto chart (explained in Chapter 3) and the pie chart. Either tool enables the team to use the data from the distribution check sheet to determine which factors are most important and should be the focus.

DON'T SKIP AND DON'T SKIMP

CAUTION

The Analyze phase of Six Sigma methodology is essential. Unfortunately, project teams often have ideas about improving processes. As soon as the Measure phase quantifies the need for improvement, they feel ready to start the Improve phase, foregoing analysis. A project can be botched when the team jumps to conclusions.

For *continuous data*, if the data is collected using a frequency distribution check sheet, it's already in a form allowing analysis. The shape of the distribution reveals whether any one of the variables is exerting more influence on the process than any other variable—*special cause variation*—or no one variable is exerting any special influence on the process—*common cause variation*.

If the distribution is shaped like a bell, that's an indication of common cause variation. However, if the distribution is *skewed* (if one of its tails is longer than the other), that's a sign of special cause variation.

If the distribution shows two peaks, indicating two central tendencies, it's *bimodal*. (A *mode* is the most frequent value in a set of data.) This indicates that the process is not homogeneous: there are two or more factors influencing the process.

If the continuous data was collected on a run chart, it's already in a form allowing analysis. A *run chart* tracks some value over time, so we can see if there are any shifts or trends in the data.

Run chart A graph that plots performance of a process over time, usually showing the data as a line, with the Y axis showing what is being measured and the X axis showing time measurements.

KEY TERM

If a run chart shows a trend—defined as seven points or more in a row, in increasing or decreasing order—it's evidence of special cause variation.

Analyze the process in greater detail. If the project goals are more focused on improving efficiency, process analysis is critical. The team creates a more detailed map of the process and analyzes that map in search of inefficiencies, examining the activities within the process steps.

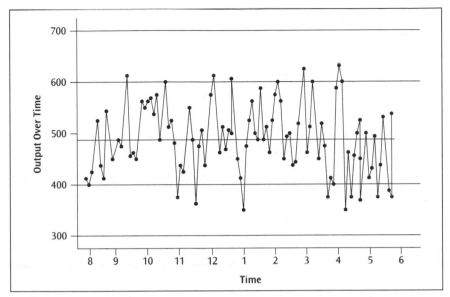

Exhibit 4-3. An example of a run chart

Create one or more small problem statements. Whether the team is analyzing data or analyzing the process, it concludes the analysis by posing "Why?" questions—e.g., "Why is _____ happening?

A project team generally creates one small problem statement for the data and one for the process. That's enough. If more questions arise, it's likely to mean the team has not analyzed the data or the process adequately.

Analyze the root causes of the effects. Six Sigma uses a simple, basic equation—Y = f (x)—where Y represents the small problem statement, x is a process variable, and f is the function (the way x causes Y).

First, the team generates as many x's as possible—process variables that could cause the Y in the small problem statement. The method commonly used is brainstorming, as explained in Chapter 3.

Next, the team narrows down the possible causes. One way to do this is through *multivoting*. (This method works better than conventional voting because there may be more general support for an item that may not be any member's top choice than for any of the top choices.)

List the potential causes on a flip chart or board and number each one.

Allow each team member to cast five to 10 votes, depending on the number of items.

Give each member that number of slips of paper (five in this example). Each is to choose the five potential causes that seem most likely, write each on a slip of paper, and then add a ranking for each—five for the top choice, four for the second choice, and so on.

> **KEY TERM**
> **Multivoting** A technique used by teams to select the highest-priority projects or most significant factors from a list, generated through ideation activities, most often brainstorming.

Collect the papers. Record the ranking score of each vote on the flip chart or board next to the potential cause receiving that vote. Total the ranking scores for each potential cause of the small problem.

Finally, the team tests the prioritized possible causes in order to validate at least one. There are three ways to test the potential root causes and validate x's in the $Y = f(x)$ equation:

- data collection
- scatter analysis
- Design of Experiments

The team usually starts with basic data collection methods. The team then creates a scatter diagram, plotting an x that can be measured with continuous data and Y. The point is to determine whether there's a correlation between x and Y and, if so, how much.

Correlation. An upward trend—if the data points form a linear cluster going up to the right, a *positive slope*—indicates a positive association between the two variables: as x increases, Y increases.

> **KEY TERM**
> **Correlation** An indication of the strength and direction of a linear relationship between two random variables, often measured as a *correlation coefficient*. In statistics, this term is not applied to any type of relationship, as in colloquial use, but only to those that are linear.

A downward trend—if the data points form a linear cluster going down to the right, a *negative slope*—indicates a negative association between the variables: as x increases, Y decreases.

The more the data points are scattered, the less correlation exists between the two variables.

It's very important to understand and keep in mind that *correlation* is *not* necessarily *causation*. In general, it's very difficult to establish a cause-and-effect relationship between two correlated vari-

CORRELATION DOES NOT IMPLY CAUSATION   CAUTION

Two variables can be correlated without any cause-and-effect relationship existing between them. We must test to determine whether or not a correlation is *statistically significant.*

ables. However, we have statistical tools that enable us to determine whether or not a correlation is *statistically significant.*

LINEAR REGRESSION

To study the correlation between the variables, we can draw a *line of best fit.* This is a straight line that best represents the data plotted on a *scatter diagram*, minimizing the distances between the data points and the line. By using *linear regression,* we can calculate the *correlation coefficient* for the line of best fit. That number—between 0 **TOOLS** and 1—expresses the correlation. The higher the coefficient, the greater the correlation. If the coefficient is 0 or very low, no correlation exists between the two variables.

Statistics Simplified

For more on statistics and Six Sigma, you might find this book useful: *Statistics for Six Sigma Made Easy!* Warren Brussee (McGraw-Hill, 2004).

Design of Experiments. If two or more *x*'s could be affecting *Y*, the project team can use a structured methodology for systematically testing variables, *Design of Experiments (DOE).*

DOE (also called Designed Experiments) enables us to test the effects of variables more efficiently than through the traditional method, in which only one variable is changed and tested in each experiment. DOE tests the effects of a combination of several variables in a single experiment, in order to determine the effects of each variable with fewer runs. DOE also has the important advantage of capturing interaction effects among the variables. (A good explanation of DOE can be found in *Rath & Strong's Pocket Guide to Advanced Six Sigma Tools* [Rath & Strong, 2004], Chapter 8.)

KEY TERMS

Design of Experiments (DOE) A systematic method for testing variables in combination, rather than separately, enabling determination of the effects of each variable with fewer runs and capture of interaction effects among the variables.

Failure mode(s) and effect(s) analysis (FMEA) A methodology for analyzing potential problems early in the development or improvement process, by identifying relationships between process and product requirements and anticipating the potential for unacceptable outputs and their effects, enabling teams to take action to reduce risk and increase reliability.

List root causes and propose solutions. The team concludes the Analyze phase by listing the root causes it has validated and, and proposing a solution for each of them.

Sometimes, the analytical results are such that it is necessary to revise the problem statement and start the process again.

If the process is complicated or new, the team members may also decide to do a *failure mode(s) and effect(s) analysis (FMEA)*. They list each process step or input, identify anything that could go wrong, list the possible causes and effects of each possible failure mode, specify the controls currently in place, recommend actions, identify the person responsible for taking action, and list any actions taken. They then prioritize each potential failure mode according to three criteria—severity, probability of occurrence, and probability of detection. (For a good explanation of FMEA, see "Performing Failure Mode and Effect Analysis" by Erik Fadlovich, *www.embeddedtechmag.com/content/view/181/121/*.)

Improve

Implement the solutions the project team has proposed for the root causes. The team should prioritize its proposed solutions and implement them one at a time or in groups. After each solution is implemented, the team should calculate the process performance sigma.

It may be wise to test the proposed solutions on a small scale first. The team can then tweak and optimize the solutions before implementing them fully.

Verify the results of the process changes with independent data. The team calculates the process performance sigma. If the calculation shows that the team has achieved its improvement goals and objectives, it can then begin the Control phase.

Determine process capability. This key metric is calculated historically in terms of process capability (C_p) and process capability index (C_{pk}), with formulas using the upper and lower specification limits, process mean, and standard deviation. (Most calculators can do these metrics, including some online, such as *www.sqconline.com/cpk.html.* It helps to enlist the aid of someone with knowledge of statistics.)

Control

Determine a method of technical control. The team members must make sure that the newly improved process continues to perform at the sigma performance level that the changes have enabled it to achieve. They verify the long-term capability of the process. They standardize the process to ensure consistency. They develop any standard operating procedures (SOPs) the process owner will need. They recommend training for the employees working the process, if necessary. They also validate the measurement systems that will be used to monitor process performance (measurement system analysis) and write out procedures for the employees who will be taking measurements. (This may involve some training to ensure that they follow the procedures and measure in the same way.)

A common method of technical control is a *statistical control chart.* This is a tool used to determine whether a process is in a state of statistical control or not (as explained in the discussion of variation).

A control chart consists of a line graph with a central line that represents an estimate of the process mean (average) and an *upper control limit* and a *lower control limit*, which form the control area. If the plotted data points are within

> **Control chart** A graph used to determine whether a process is in a state of statistical control or not. It **KEY TERM** consists of a line graph with a central line that represents an estimate of the process mean (average) and an *upper control limit* and a *lower control limit*, which form the control area. If the plotted data points are within the control area, the process can be considered *stable, in control.* A data point outside the control area indicates that the process is *unstable, out of control.*

the control area, the process can be considered *stable, in control:* any variations are due to *common causes.* A data point outside the control area indicates that the process is *unstable, out of control,* because the variation is due
to *special causes.* These special causes of variation must be eliminated.

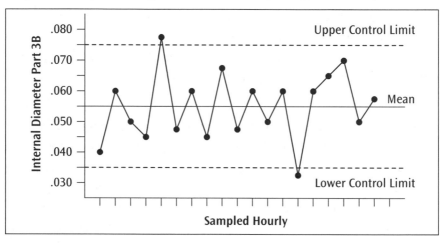

Exhibit 4-4. Control chart

Create a response plan. Things change. It's inevitable. So you plan for it.
The project team creates a plan to hand off to the process owner as the
improvement project ends.

The *response plan* resembles the data collection plan. It includes a
high-level map of the improved process (the "should be" map), the most
important metrics for the process, the specifications or targets for those
metrics, the forms to be used to collect data on the process, the control
method chosen by the team (e.g., control charts), and—the bottom line
for the project—the most important process improvements (the results
in terms of the project goals and objectives).

Using the response plan, the employees working the process collect
data and monitor performance with the specified control method. If data
shows that the process is not working consistently up to its capability, the
employees in the process try to figure out a cause.

Close the project. The team transfers control of the process to the process
owner. The members conduct a review of the project and then archive all
records of the project. Finally, it's time to celebrate!

Design for Six Sigma

Another version of Six Sigma, similar to the DMAIC approach, is structured for developing designs of products, services. and processes. The most common version is known as DMADV, from the five phases that structure the methodology:

1. *Define* the goals for the design and the deliverables for the customers.
2. *Measure* the customer requirements and specifications.
3. *Analyze* the process options for meeting the customer requirements and specifications.
4. *Design* (detailed) the process to meet the customer requirements and specifications.
5. *Verify* the design performance and ability to meet customer requirements and specifications.

> **DESIGN FOR SIX SIGMA BASICS**
>
> Here are two books for learning more about design for Six Sigma: *Design for Six Sigma,* by Greg Brue and Robert G. Launsby (McGraw-Hill, 2003)
>
> *The Design for Six Sigma Memory Jogger,* by Dana Ginn, Barbara Streibel, and Evelyn Varner (GOAL/QPC, 2004)
>
> **TOOLS**

Continuous Improvement

If quality is to be truly a strategic issue for an organization, the people in that organization must commit to continuous improvement. That means constantly adapting to changes and always seeking opportunities to make processes more efficient and to make products and services meet the customers' needs and wants more effectively.

Operations Manager's Checklist for Chapter 4

☑ Quality has two definitions: one is technical—the extent to which a product or service is able to satisfy stated or implied needs—and one is subjective, depending on the individual and the specific situation.

☑ Quality must be a strategic issue, part of the organization's comprehensive business strategy, and championed by effective leaders who are actively involved in quality initiatives.

☑ A central tenet in any approach to quality is that you must base what you do on information, not assumptions, guesses, hopes, or fears.

☑ The Six Sigma methodology for quality management provides a structured approach to improving products, services, and processes and a structured approach to designing products, services, and processes.

☑ If quality is to be truly a strategic issue, the organization must commit to continuous improvement.

Chapter
5

Lean Thinking
(and Doing)

The concept of lean has developed into so many adaptations and variations and applications, almost all of them generating dozens of books and hundreds of articles, that it's absurd to even consider giving it only a short chapter in this book. But we'll keep it lean by focusing on the thinking, the principles, and the spirit.

Lean Production, Lean Thinking, Lean Principles

The term "lean production" was coined by John Krafcik, who used it in an article he published in 1988, "Triumph of the Lean Production System." James P. Womack, Daniel T. Jones, and Daniel Roos used it in their influential book, *The Machine That Changed the World* (Rawson Associates, 1990). In their next book, *Lean Thinking* (Simon & Schuster, 1996, 2003), Womack and Jones stated five principles of "lean thinking."

1. **Value.** Determine exactly what *value* means for the customer for a specific product (good, service, or combination).
2. **Value stream.** Identify for each product or, in some cases, for each product family the entire *value stream*—the series of specific actions required to bring a specific product to the customer.
3. **Flow.** Make the remaining, value-creating steps *flow*.
4. **Pull.** Customers should *pull* products and services through their orders; the organization should not push its products and services.

5. **Perfection.** Pursue *perfection* by reducing effort, time, space, cost, and mistakes while offering products of ever greater value to customers.

> **KEY TERM** **Lean thinking** Philosophy based on defining value from the customers' perspective, reducing all forms of waste (time, materials, energy, money), and running the enterprise by pull rather than by push. More concisely, the point of lean thinking is to provide more value with less work.

Principle 1—Value

"Value can only be defined by the ultimate customer. And it's only meaningful when expressed in terms of a specific product (a good or a service, and often both at once) which meets the customer's needs at a specific price at a specific time." And how does this happen? "Lean thinking must...start with a conscious attempt to precisely define value in terms of specific products with specific capabilities offered at specific prices through a dialogue with specific customers."

This action requires paying closer attention to what customers are saying and what they're buying—and why. And, something difficult for many operations managers, "The way to do this is to ignore existing assets and technologies and to rethink firms on a product-line basis with strong, dedicated product teams. This approach also requires redefining the role for a firm's technical experts...and rethinking just where in the world to create value."

Principle 2—Value Stream

Womack and Jones describe the *value stream* as "the set of all the specific actions required to bring a specific product (whether a good, a service, or, increasingly, a combination of the two) through the three critical management tasks of any business: the *problem-solving task* running from concept through detailed design and engineering to production launch, the *information management task* running from order-taking through detailed scheduling to delivery, and the *physical transformation task* proceeding from raw materials to finished product in the hands of the customer."

Analyzing value streams will "almost always" reveal three types of activities—steps that "unambiguously" create value, steps that create no value but are "unavoidable with current technologies and production assets," and steps that create no value and are "immediately avoidable."

Womack and Jones identify these last steps as a type of "*muda.*" This is the term for waste used by Taiichi Ohno, a Toyota executive who fought to remove all types of waste from Toyota production systems. He identified seven types, to which Womack and Jones have added an eighth:

- defects (in products)
- overproduction
- inventories (in process or finished goods)
- unnecessary processing
- unnecessary movement of people
- unnecessary transport of goods
- waiting
- "design of goods and services which do not meet users' needs"

Principle 3—Flow

"The next step in lean thinking—a truly breathtaking one: Make the remaining, value-creating steps *flow.*" This comes after specifying what value means to the customer, after mapping the value stream for a specific product, and after eliminating steps that are "obviously wasted." Going for the flow is tough; Womack and Jones warn that "this step requires a complete rearrangement of your mental furniture."

Why? Because flow thinking seems counterintuitive. Because we inherit "a commonsense conviction" that

LOST IN TRANSLATION, 1
There's nothing special about specifying seven types of waste, at least not for technical reasons. In Japanese culture, the number seven has a great power, a special significance. So, when Taiichi Ohno listed seven *muda*, that number had more impact than if he'd listed six or eight. The significance of seven may be lost in translation into English, but less when the *muda* are labeled "The Seven Deadly Wastes."

The Japanese have a saying, "Ask 'Why?' seven times," which just means to keep searching until the root answer is found. That expression was appropriated by Japanese TQM gurus. It's the same approach as the Five Whys technique discussed in Chapter 3, but the number seven gives it a special significance.

work activities should be "grouped by type so they can be performed more efficiently and managed more easily" and that we should perform similar activities in groups or batches. "We all need to fight departmentalized batch thinking," they assert, because we can "almost always" do tasks more efficiently and more accurately when we work on a product "continuously from raw material to finished good."

instead of Batches

Principle 4—Pull

"*Pull* in simplest terms means that no one upstream should produce a good or service until the customer downstream asks for it," say Womack and Jones, "but actually following this rule in practice is a bit more complicated." It involves questioning and challenging economic beliefs and taking a leap of faith. More importantly it requires that credible information, collected at the source and shared throughout the value chain, drives the process.

When an organization transforms from batches and departments to flow and product teams, according to Womack and Jones, the time it takes to go from concept to launch, from raw material to customer, drops significantly. In fact, they claim, "if you can't quickly take throughput times down by half in product development, 75 percent in order processing, and 90 percent in physical production, you are doing something wrong."

Principle 5—Perfection

"As organizations begin to accurately specify *value*, identify the entire *value stream*, make the value-creating steps for specific products *flow* continuously, and let customers *pull* value from the enterprise...suddenly *perfection*, the fifth and final principle of lean thinking, doesn't seem like a crazy idea. Why should this be? Because the four initial principles interact with each other in a virtuous circle." They expose the *muda* in the value stream. "There is no end to the process of reducing effort, time, space, cost, and mistakes while offering a product which is ever more nearly what the customer actually wants."

Beyond the Five Principles

Lean thinking is not limited, of course, to the five principles that

Womack and Jones stated in *Lean Thinking*. Under the "lean tent" you will find a variety of strategies and systems. Here are a few that are most closely related to lean thinking.

Mura and *Muri*

These two terms are traditionally associated with <u>muda</u>—a general term for any <u>activity that's wasteful</u>, that <u>doesn't add value</u>, that's

> **LOST IN TRANSLATION, 2**
> Three words *muda, mura,* and *muri*—are often used together in Japanese, known as the three *mu*'s. *Muda* means waste, *mura* means irregularity or unevenness, and *muri* means strain or overburden. These terms may not translate very well into English because they were chosen for sound as well as for meaning, but it doesn't take a rocket scientist to know that for an operations manager they all spell **mu**ch heartache.

unproductive. <u>*Mura* means irregularity, unevenness, or inconsistency</u>. <u>*Muri* means strain, overburden, unreasonableness, or absurdity</u>.

Taiichi Ohno and Shigeo Shingo linked the three as problems to eliminate in the Toyota production process; the repetition of the *mu-* made the three words a powerful slogan. In practice, more attention has been focused on *muda* than on *mura* and *muri*.

> ### DON'T FOLLOW ALPHABETICAL ORDER
> CAUTION
> "It's striking to me how much effort we've expended on eliminating *muda* and how little attention we have given to *mura* and *muri*…. In most companies we still see the *mura* of trying to make the numbers at the end of reporting periods (… completely arbitrary batches of time). This causes sales to write too many orders toward the end of the period…. This wave of orders—causing equipment and employees to work too hard…—creates the overburden of *muri*. This in turn leads to downtime, mistakes, and backflows—the *muda* of waiting, correction, and conveyance. *The inevitable result is that* mura *creates* muri *that undercuts previous efforts to eliminate* muda."
> —James P. Womack, "Mura, Muri, Muda?" *www.leanorg.com*
> He suggests that a more logical sequence would be "*mura, muri, muda*."

5S

5S is a methodology for organizing the workplace to improve efficiency, safety, and morale. It's structured around five Japanese words that, when transliterated, begin with the letter S. The five guidelines were translated into English using words that also begin with S. As usual with Japanese, something is lost in translation. These terms may seem simple, even silly, but understood as guidelines they make sense:

- **Seiri** (tidiness)/Sort or Sift. Go through all materials in the workplace and keep only essential items. Store or dispose of everything else.
- **Seiton** (orderliness)/Straighten or Set in Order. Arrange all materials in the workplace to promote flow.
- **Seiso** (cleanliness)/Sweep or Shine. Clean the workplace regularly and systematically.
- **Seiketsu** (standardization)/Standardize or Systematize. Make sure that practices, procedures, and policies are consistent.
- **Shitsuke** (discipline)/Sustain the discipline. Maintain standards and review them periodically

---

SMART MANAGING

KNOW WHY YOU'RE DOING WHAT YOU'RE DOING

"What's the purpose of 5S? If you said, to keep things clean and neat, then you have a good example of how a tool can be misused without the right thought process. If 5S is implemented...without understanding that the principle behind it is to spot problems instantly, it becomes nothing more than a housekeeping exercise and will fail as a sustainable tool. To truly understand 5S, you must internalize the ability to immediately identify problems to enable quick responses."

—Jamie Flinchbaugh, "The Lean Toolbox," *Quality Digest*, October 2003

TOOLS

LEAN BASICS AND BEYOND

Lean Lexicon: A Graphical Glossary for Lean Thinkers, 4th edition (Lean Enterprise Institute, 2003), www.lean.org

The Lean Toolbox, 4th edition, John Bicheno and Matthias Holweg (PICSIE Books, 2008)

Further Connections

In *Cause and Effect Lean* (PICSIE Books, 2000), John Bicheno called "lean operations" one of "three principal priorities for operations in the new millennium," with Six Sigma quality and supply chain management. "These interlink," he said, and they must be "embedded in a background of three related forms of thinking"—lean thinking, systems thinking, and statistical thinking.

It should be noted that a hybrid has developed from lean thinking and Six Sigma, the approach to quality discussed in Chapter 4. Lean Six Sigma is a synergistic methodology. As Michael L. George succinctly explains in *Lean Six Sigma: Combining Six Sigma Quality with Lean Speed* (McGraw-Hill, 2002), "The fusion of Lean and Six Sigma is required because . . . Lean cannot bring a process under statistical control [. . . and] Six Sigma alone cannot dramatically improve process speed or reduce invested capital."

Operations Manager's Checklist for Chapter 5

☑ Improve your organization through the five principles of lean thinking.

☑ Eliminate all types of waste—*muda, mura, muri*—seven, eight, or however many you find.

☑ Apply the five guidelines of 5S.

☑ Interlink lean operations with Six Sigma quality and supply chain management within three related forms of thinking—lean thinking, systems thinking, and statistical thinking.

Operations Management as a System: Supply Chain—The Tie That Binds and Creates Value

As described in Chapter 1, the *supply chain* is the series of processes by which inputs are transformed into outputs and delivered to downstream customers. In addition to the processes within the organization, the chain necessarily includes suppliers, sub-tier suppliers, distributors, and downstream distributors. The processes are linked by logistics and, more importantly, information.

Supply Chain

The supply chain is simply that network of operations across all the companies that provide the goods or services to the end consumer. Take, for example, that kid's meal that you bought last weekend. The supply chain consists of all the companies that worked together to produce that meal—the farmers who raised the chickens and cows and grew the wheat, the manufacturers that produced the paper cup and packaging material, the trucking companies that transported the meat and milk and cheese and paper cup, the company in China that made the toy (which is why your kid wanted you to buy the meal), the quick-service restaurant that cooked and served the food, and the other companies along the way.

Someone once described a supply chain as the entire series of activities from "cradle to grave," "womb to tomb," or "lust to dust" that provide something that the customer values. A good analogy is the Boeing commercial airliner, which can be described as "hundreds of thousands of parts flying very closely in formation." That's what the supply chain does; by using information and inventory, it coordinates the activities of suppliers and distributors from around the world, so that these parts can be brought together and United Airlines can get you from Baltimore to Los Angeles.

Exhibit 6-1 depicts this interlocking supply chain (or *extended enterprise*, which will be described later). The flow of products starts with raw materials and passes through processors, manufacturers, distributors, and retail stores to the customers, with each link connected to the next by modes of transportation. There's also a flow of information that moves upstream from the customers and points-of-purchase, with information loops in both directions, linking each member of the chain to other members upstream and downstream. There's a third flow, much simpler and yet, in a very basic way, the most important—money. It flows from the demand upstream through the chain to the very beginning of supply.

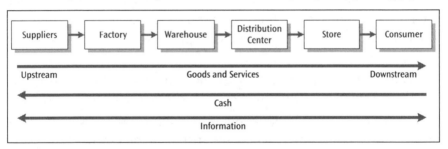

Exhibit 6-1. The supply chain (or extended enterprise)

A chain is only as strong as its weakest link, and nowhere is this truth more relevant than in the supply chain. The operations are inextricably connected together through information and shared interests. Supply chains that work to address customer needs, thrive on complexity, act efficiently, deliver quickly, and continuously add value for the customers, drive competitive advantage, and enhance revenues.

Supply—or Demand?

Some people have argued that what's traditionally called the *supply chain* should more accurately be called the *demand chain*. After all, the supply chain exists to meet the demand; without the demand there's no need for the supply. This logic makes even more sense because of the growing interest in lean thinking and the emphasis on *pull* rather than *push*, as discussed in Chapter 5.

Actually, the most logical term for the chain we're discussing here is *supply-and-demand chain* or, in order not to put the cart before the horse, *demand-and-supply chain*. Demand provides the impetus— the beginning of the flow of information that moves upstream to trigger the effect—supply, which then moves downstream to the customers, the source of the demand.

Vertical and Horizontal

Although the supply chain is usually depicted horizontally, with a company handling a single activity or group of activities as one link in the chain, it can also be vertical, with a company performing a long series of activities in the chain. Both orientations have advantages, of course.

The more activities a company performs, the more control it has over costs and quality. But a vertically integrated company generally spreads out in its investments and its organization, so it may be less focused and efficient in any of the activities and less agile to respond to changes in its markets.

The more a company specializes, the more efficiently it can execute its core activities and focus on adding specialized value to the products and services passing through its supply chains. However, it's inherently affected by all of the other companies upstream and downstream. Every action in the supply chain has a corresponding equal and, hopefully, positive reaction, upstream or down. It's like pulling on a rope. When someone tugs on the end, once the slack in the system is taken up, the other end of the rope feels the pull. Fortunately, the recent emphasis on quality standards and the development of technologies have enabled companies to take greater competitive advantage of both orientations, horizontal and vertical. Also, a company may be vertical in its supply chains for certain products or services and certain markets and horizontal in its supply chains for other products or services and markets.

Supply Chain Strategy

Supply chain strategy forms the plan for operating the supply chain in line with the organization's business strategy and as an extension of operations within the organization. The *business strategy* provides the general direction and guidelines for the organization. The supply chain strategy, in effect, operationalizes or implements the

Supply chain strategy
Plan to operate the supply chain in line with the organization's business strategy and as an extension of operations within the organization.   **KEY TERM**

business strategy by orchestrating the operations of the organization and, by extension, the supply chain in order to achieve specific objectives across the extended enterprise.

A supply chain strategy should do the following:

- Guide operations to maximize efficiencies and reduce costs.
- Prescribe how managers are to work with other members of the supply chain—suppliers, distributors, and customers.

THE COMMUNITY

SMART

MANAGING

The term *extended enterprise* (alternatively called the *supply* or *value chain*) describes the entire community of players that combine their activities to provide products and/or services to the market. Firms in the extended enterprise may operate independently, for example, through market mechanisms, cooperatively through agreements and contracts, or, more importantly, through a combination of formal and informal information-sharing mechanisms that support one another. According to Professors Ed Davis and Robert Spekman of the Darden Graduate School of Business, to execute the extended enterprise effectively, the operations manager should:

- Start with the marketplace: segment customers based on product/service needs.
- Listen to the market: demand forecasting is important throughout the supply chain (not just supply).
- Reduce cost of ownership system-wide.
- Leverage, leverage, leverage.
- Share Technology system-wide; information must be owned by the supply chain partners.
- Use performance measures that span the system; one cannot do well at the other's expense.
- Pursue connectivity, community, and collaboration.

Developing a Supply Chain Strategy

Start by understanding the business strategy. That may seem obvious, but it's fundamental. The supply chain strategy extends the business strategy to the exterior. It must be totally in alignment with that strategy and support it fully.

You may want to start out with a mission statement and/or a vision statement for your operations and extended supply chain. Then, you can develop it in terms of the realities of your situation.

Form a team to assess the capabilities within your organization and through the supply chain. Make it detailed and be realistic. How well do your organization's assets support the business strategy? How competent are your core competencies? If you have not recently and systematically benchmarked your operations, the time is now.

After you've assessed your capabilities, have your team generate recommendations for developing the mission statement and/or vision statement into a strategy. Here are some general questions to consider:

- How will your supply chain strategy support your business strategy?
- How will your strategy enable you to improve operations?
- How will your strategy help you build your competitive advantage?
- How will your strategy help position your company for the future?
- How will your strategy promote your core competencies and address the realities of your current operations?

Forming a Plan to Work the Strategy

The step is to form a plan for acting on your supply chain strategy. Your team should discuss in greater depth its assessment of your organization's capabilities—the realities of your current operations.

It may be appropriate to do a *SWOT analysis.*

- What are the current and potential *strengths* of your operations and the entire organization in terms of your supply chain?
- What are the current and potential *weaknesses* of your operations and the entire organization in terms of your supply chain?
- What *opportunities* exist in developing your supply chain?
- What *threats* could cause risks in developing your supply chain?

At this point, the procedure for planning to implement your supply chain strategy is much like the procedure for any other strategy. You and your team establish priorities, outline actions, define requirements, analyze the risks you anticipate, and develop a plan that includes activities and tasks, roles and

> **S WOT analysis** A strategic planning method for evaluating the *Strengths, Weaknesses, Opportunities,* **KEY TERM** and *Threats* involved in undertaking a business venture. It involves specifying the objective and identifying factors should be considered in planning.

responsibilities, a timeline with milestones, and metrics by which to assess your supply chain.

The first phase in your plan should definitely be to further develop your internal processes, both business and operational. There are two sound reasons for this recommendation. First, only if you have the appropriate business processes in place and working effectively can you be sure that you're providing the right and accurate information to your chain partners. Second, if you cannot make sure your operational processes are working effectively and efficiently, what hope do you have of developing a supply chain that works effectively and efficiently?

Evaluating the Results

As with any other plan, you should periodically—at least annually— evaluate the results of your supply chain strategy.

- Assess your progress toward the goals of the business strategy.
- Evaluate your relationship with each member of the chain.
- Examine the situation of each member of the chain. Have there been any changes that are affecting any of the relationships and for which you should make adjustments or consider seeking other suppliers?
- Identify any changes in your markets or your industry. Should you modify your supply chain?

It might also be wise to do another SWOT analysis.

Supply Chain Management Basics

Just as the success of your supply chain strategy depends on how well you implement it, the success of your supply chain design depends on how well you manage your chain.

KEY TERM

Supply chain management Processes and activities involved in the *identification, procurement, logistics,* and *management* of goods and services within an organization and with its suppliers and its customers.

"In essence, Supply Chain Management integrates supply and demand management within and across companies."
—Council of Supply Chain Management Professionals (*www.cscmp.org*)

Supply chain management (SCM) consists of the processes and activities involved in the *identification, procurement, logistics,* and *management* of goods and services within an organization and with its suppliers and its customers. A company can and should have a supply chain for each product and service it offers and for each market it serves. Differentiation between supply chains encourages focus on building the supply chain that is most appropriate for specific customer needs. For a company to manage its supply chains successfully, it must have cross-functional integration within the organization and throughout each network of companies that form its supply chains.

Cost vs. Differentiation

It's been noted that companies tend to focus their supply chain strategies on either cost or differentiation. Companies focused on *cost* want to derive benefits that will enable them to reduce their costs. They want immediate, short-term, bottom-line benefits. Companies focused on *differentiation* typically have a more ambitious, long-term perspective. Their competitive advantage is usually in their core competencies and capabilities and they consider their supply network as another means of achieving their strategic objectives. Differentiation strategies require more complex, collaborative relationships, and necessarily greater information sharing.

Integration

It's generally agreed and established that the more integrated the supply chain, the better. However, there's no general agreement on any precise definition of "integration."

One good, simple definition has been proposed by Mark Pagell, an operations management professor, in his study, "Understanding the Factors that Enable and Inhibit the Integration of Operations, Purchasing and Logistics." He defines integration as "a process of interaction and collaboration in which manufacturing, purchasing and logistics work together in a cooperative manner to arrive at mutually acceptable outcomes for their organization." It's been further suggested that the goal of an integrated supply chain is to remove all boundaries to ease the flow of material, cash, resources, and information.

> **Supply chain integration** **KEY TERM**
> "Process of interaction and collaboration in which manufacturing, purchasing and logistics work together in a cooperative manner to arrive at mutually acceptable outcomes for their organization," with the goal of an integrated supply chain being to remove all boundaries to ease the flow of material, cash, resources, and information.

Supply chain management treats the supply chain as a single entity, an integration of processes and functions and entities, not as a series of autonomous units with transactional connections. It requires strategic decision-making.

Organizations that have succeeded in building integrated supply programs have gained many benefits, including the following:

- improved supplier relations
- ability to increase supply of materials quickly
- reductions in inventory
- more efficient use of space
- increased employee productivity
- greater efficiencies in purchasing administration
- benefits in the receiving function
- more efficient payment processes
- knowledge of costs
- shorter time to market

Principles for Optimal Supply Chain Management

It's been noted that top managers want supply chains that are integrated, interactive, collaborative, adaptive, and—of course!—virtual. But we can't build the chains we want unless we think differently about how to manage three huge factors—complexity, relationships, and change.

The following basic principles can help your company optimize its use of its supply chains and improve its profits.

Build and maintain your internal system of business processes—purchasing, shipping, inventory, accounts receivable, accounts payable, and so forth. Simplify those processes, improve the flow, and make them faster through technology.

Maximize the linkages in your supply chain, the logistics that connect all the members. Again, it's most important to take full advantage of information technology. However, technologies are only tools. You should also maintain relationships with your chain partners. Build and manage those relationships as *strategic alliances*.

KEY TERM **Strategic alliance** A relationship between seller and buyer with a common goal of improving product performance, sharing risks, and maintaining trust at a level that enables extensive cooperation in strategic business areas and product development without fear of possible negative effects of sharing information, such as espionage. Strategic alliances are intended to be long-term relationships.

Plan more comprehensively. This means forecasting with greater accuracy, of course, and being aware of market trends and other external events that influence demand and supply. But it also means anticipating internal events, such as promotions and entries into new markets, and preparing for them by communicating with your chain partners.

Emphasize performance of your supply chains. Just as you expect the units within your organization to meet or surpass certain standards and expectations, you should expect the same of your supply chain partners. This means measuring performance across your chains, setting standards, communicating your expectations, and enforcing your standards. An important part of emphasizing per- formance is maintaining relationships with your chain

SMART MANAGING **GO FOR THE GOAL** "The primary goal of any supply chain management system should be to get the right product to the right place, at the right time, at the right price, and at the right cost."
—Syed M. Kamal, President and CEO, Gillani, Inc.

partners—and being prepared to end relationships that are not working well enough and to create new relationships.

Managing Relationships

As we develop chains and networks in a business world that's more and more complex and competitive, it's critical for companies to strengthen their relationships, build new relationships, and work together better.

Competitive pressures are mounting across all fronts of business in the form of market price erosion and the need to reduce product time to market and delivery lead time. In response, companies are increasingly relying on the collective capabilities of their extended enterprises. But, as mentioned earlier, the supply chain is only as strong as its weakest link, so establishing and managing effective and differentiated relationships at every link in the chain is becoming vital to success. Consequently, opera-

---

THE HUMAN SIDE

SMART

MANAGING

Two terms are commonly used in business circles—*supplier relationship management* (SRM) and *customer relationship management* (CRM). Generally, these two terms are applied to information technologies. However, we must not neglect the human side of SRM and CRM.

Managing relationships with supply chain partners is a core competency that should be valued and developed. It's challenging, largely because no two relationships are the same. Every partner relationship is the result of many factors, including the following:

- the nature of the good or service
- market characteristics and conditions
- the power differential between partners
- the supply chain policies and practices of each partner
- the type of relationship
- the personalities of the individuals involved in the relationship

Although we've been generally using the terms "partner" and "partnership," the partnership is only the most common supply chain relationship. Companies develop supply chain relationships that can be traditional and adversarial, opportunistic, or open and based on trust.

Supply chain relationships are an area of growing interest, unfortunately beyond the scope of this chapter and this book. Perhaps the most important thing to understand and remember is that chain relationships are not all business—not just dollars and cents and bottom lines.

tions managers recognize that, at least for the foreseeable future, it will be *supply chains* that compete, not *companies*.

Dependency and Certainty

It's been argued that the primary dynamic is not economic power, which is only one factor. The primary dynamic is actually a trade-off between the level of *dependency* that a company is prepared to accept and the level of *certainty* that it considers realistic.

The main proponent of this theory is Paul D. Cousins, a professor of operations management, director of the Supply Chain Management Research Group, and co-author of *Strategic Supply Management: Principles, Theories, and Practice* (Prentice Hall, 2008).

He says that companies face a dichotomy when they attempt to develop collaborative or partnership relationships with their major suppliers or customers. This dichotomy exists because they are attempting to collaborate "within the framework of competition (opportunism)." The concept of these "collaboratively competitive relationships" has been labeled "co-opetition."

If these relationships are "managed properly and with full awareness of the possible pitfalls," Cousins notes, they can be very successful. But if they're managed incorrectly, they can be "disastrous" to the buyer, the supplier, or both.

Managers must understand relationships with other companies not as entities, as states of being, according to Cousins, but rather as processes or courses of action. Their role then is to deliver some business outcome—a price reduction, an exchange of cost information, or whatever. They must focus relationships on delivering something. That's the measure of success. So "relationship processes" must be focused "at the level of the product or service (and not the firm)" and the type of business outcome must determine the level of relationship process and the course of action required.

As mentioned above, the primary dynamic of supply relationships is a trade-off between the level of *dependency* that a company is prepared to accept and the level of *certainty* that it considers realistic.

Dependency is defined as "a mechanism that creates a reliance" on the buyer, the supplier, or both. The reasons for a dependency may be

economic (cost of switching to another supplier), historic (previous interactions), technological (competencies and capabilities), and/or political
(policies and internal politics).

Certainty is defined in terms of risks. Four levels or types of certainty
have been defined: contractual (certainty that the other company will
perform as agreed), competence (certainty that the other company is
capable of performing as agreed), goodwill (certainty that the other will
be willing to go beyond contractual obligations if needed), and political
(political risk or gain in dealing with the other, from either an internal or
an external perspective).

OK, so what does all that mean in practical terms?

Four Basic Relationship Management Strategies

It means that the balancing of dependencies and certainties results in
four basic relationship management strategies that exist on a continuum:

1. With little or no dependency or certainty, a relationship will likely be
   traditional, "adversarial," or open-market negotiating. Unless those
   two factors change, don't expect more than an arm's-length contractual relationship, i.e., confined to a well-defined activity (typically
   price-based) with little or no spillover into other business areas.
2. If dependency increases but not certainty, expect a relationship of
   opportunism or simple cooperation—if either party can dominate, it
   will be able to take advantage of the situation.
3. If certainty increases but not dependency, the relationship will tend
   to be a *tactical* degree of *collaboration,* or, more accurately *coordination*—not a partnership, but an arrangement involving a significant
   level of coordinated activity, and information or work flow
   exchanges.
4. If dependency and certainty are both high, the relationship can be a
   strategic collaboration, with potential for both parties to work the
   relationship for mutual gain, to share risks and rewards, and to
   undertake joint ventures—requiring a great degree of investment
   and offering great returns for both parties. This level of relationship
   is typically characterized by supply chain integration, technology
   sharing, and joint planning.

Two final points.

■ As mentioned earlier, a _relationship process_ must be focused "at the level of the product or service" and the type of business outcome must determine the level of relationship process and the course of action required. In other words, it's not a relationship between two companies: it's a process about a product or a service. Two companies may have a number of relationships, each different in terms of the importance of the product or service, the amount of risk involved, and the balance of power/dependency relative to the product or service.

■ Know what you want to get out of supply chain relationship and be aware of the dynamics influencing the situation. Don't expect too much and don't settle for too little.

Traditional, Adversarial—Open-Market Negotiation. This is a simple transactional relationship. It can be labelled as discrete or market-based or buy-the-market. The contract is short-term and very specific. Little or no face-to-face contact occurs; there is relatively little, if any, sharing of information beyond the necessary minimum, and no trust exists between parties.

Opportunism—Cooperation. As mentioned above, in this type of relationship, with at least a certain level of dependency but not certainty, if either party can dominate, it will be able to take advantage of the situation. If your company can dominate in this type of relationship, you should keep in mind that you can take advantage of the relationship only until the other party decides that enough is enough. What's the risk of losing an advantageous position?

Tactical Collaboration—Coordination. This relationship is based on a higher level of certainty but not dependency. You can try to develop tactical collaborations by increasing the dependency of the other party, maybe by using time and good deals or offering technological competencies and capabilities that the other party lacks and needs.

Strategic Collaboration—Partnership. As explained above, this type of relationship can be the most advantageous, providing the greatest long-term benefits. Seek opportunities for ensuring that the relationship benefits both parties equitably; one truly can attain a "win-win" scenario.

Even when a partnership relationship is appropriate, it may be poorly set up as a cozy and friendly arrangement. The focus should always be about business benefits. A partnership should be a performance-based, market-driven, symbiotic relationship, subject to dissolution if either party becomes dissatisfied with the relationship. The best collaborations have built-in self-correcting mechanisms based on market conditions.

The success of a supply chain partnership depends on the following factors:

- Partners should both bring special competences and capabilities to the table. If the strategies of both are based on differentiation, as explained above, they will each contribute something of special value to the relationship.
- Partners should be committing to a long-term relationship that permits them to share strategic objectives, even a vision. Their contracts should be expected to renew automatically, as long as both parties are performing as agreed and agree to continue to perform together.
- Partners should build trust. How? By being trustworthy and by trusting—with care. It may be difficult to trust, especially at first. Be cautious but confident.

> **SMART MANAGING**
>
> **TRUST, BUT VERIFY**
> That was the approach of former President Ronald Reagan in working with the Soviet Union after four decades of the Cold War. He noted that it was a translation of a Russian proverb. That wisdom is universal and eternal.

- Partners should share information that enables their partnership to provide greater value to each party. This could include information about costs, as in open-book costing, specifications for new product designs, or plans for the future, for example.

> **KEY TERM**
>
> **Open-book costing** A partnership in which a supplier and a retailer examine together a breakdown of all the costs involved in any given area to help them find ways to reduce them through initiatives such as group purchasing and joint logistical planning and share the savings equitably. Also known as *open-book transparency*.

OPEN WITH CARE

Open-book costing is potentially risky, of course. It requires a degree of trust and should be considered only under certain conditions. Generally, this type of arrangement is to provide a basis for cost reduction and continuous improvement by enabling both partners to engage in methods to better manage the cost drivers with a shared sense of urgency defined by market conditions. It can be a smart tactic—if you're smart enough not to hurry into it.

Changing Relationship Strategies

As mentioned above, relationships are not entities or states of being, but rather processes, courses of action. You may decide to change a relationship, maybe to increase the dependency and certainty, maybe to decrease either or both factors, or maybe to terminate a relationship.

Before you make a relationship change, make a business case for your decision. That may seem obvious, but not all managers and companies do it. What are the benefits you expect? What are the potential costs? Weigh the advantages and disadvantages, just as you should for any important decision.

Supply Base Rationalization or Reduction. We will address the fundamental concepts of sourcing and procurement in Chapter 9, but several of the basic constructs are also important when you look across the supply chain or extended enterprise. *Rationalizing* or, most often, *reducing* the number of suppliers that your company uses for a product or service means terminating a relationship or, if the decision is to drop a supplier for one product or service but not for others, adjusting a relationship. In rare situations such as commodity-like products or where assurance of supply is an issue, the operations manager may actually want or need to increase the number of potential suppliers. Supply base reduction may make sense in theory, on paper, but it's not a simple decision in terms of relationships, unless they're only transactional.

Supply base reduction can offer substantial advantages, including the following:

- better relationships with remaining suppliers
- greater leverage with suppliers
- lower unit cost or price
- better quality

- more dependability, less risk or uncertainty
- greater flexibility and responsiveness
- better delivery performance
- decrease in inventories
- better service
- increased involvement with suppliers builds goodwill and trust
- better communication and information sharing
- more opportunity to integrate suppliers in product development

Disadvantages also exist in implementing supply base reduction activities:

- risk of decreasing competition among suppliers
- necessity of developing formal system for evaluating suppliers

Of course, the advantages and disadvantages would depend greatly on how it's decided which suppliers to keep and how those relationships are managed.

If you're increasing purchasing from any supplier, you should probably try to improve the relationship process, in areas such as standardizing and rationalizing specifications, improving quality and service, shortening lead times for introducing products, and improving product functionality. Only within close relationships with suppliers can phrases such as "value alignment," "harmonization of interest," "competence compatibility," and "technology integration" really begin to mean something.

Reciprocity. *Reciprocity* is the practice of selecting as suppliers companies that are customers of the organization. It's simply "I'll buy from you if you buy from me."

Reciprocity The practice of selecting as suppliers companies that are customers of the organization. **KEY TERM**

There's a legal line to consider here. Reciprocity is legal if you buy from your customers at fair market prices and if there are no economic threats or any intent to restrict competition. However, if the arrangement restricts competition and trade, reciprocity can be illegal.

Legal issues aside, there are good business reasons not to develop reciprocal relationships. Reciprocity may cause buyers or sellers to lower their standards or expectations. For example, a buyer may accept paying slightly higher prices or receiving slightly inferior service because of the reciprocal relationship and a seller may accept that payments arrive a little late. Suppliers can become complacent in the security of reciprocity and reduced competition. Customers may be less diligent about checking other suppliers regularly.

Contract Management — s/be win/win

Contract management is the process that ensures that the parties to the contract understand fully the obligations of each and, in so doing, maximizes the probability that the parties will fulfill their obligations.

Contract management involves the following responsibilities:

- Identify and manage the risks.
- Manage the expectations of the other party or parties.
- Manage the relationship between or among the parties.

In other words, it's not about negotiating the best contracts (although that's essential), or using the best contract management software (although that makes the process easier), or having the best attorneys ready in case of breach of contract (although that may be necessary). Contract management is basically another aspect of relationship management. You do what you can to make this part of the relationship—whether it's transactional or a strategic collaboration—work out for the best for both or all parties.

A basic principle of optimal supply chain management listed earlier is to emphasize performance of your supply chains. That entails the following responsibilities:

- Measure performance across your chains.
- Set performance standards.
- Communicate your expectations.
- Enforce your standards.
- Be prepared to end relationships that are not working well enough and create new relationships.

Contract management remains a major challenge. Even with increased emphasis on supplier relationship management and strategic sourcing, companies continue to leave money on the table by not effectively managing their portfolios of contracts.

Power of Information

Information is power. This truth is becoming more and more significant as organizations are making greater use of information to power supply chains as information technology develops. Operations managers are more effective if they collect this information once and close to the source and then share it when and where it makes sense. In other words, become a broker of the information you acquire.

Technology

Information technology is essential to the success of any supply chain, ensuring communication among chain partners and supporting collaboration, as well as making the processes within each partner organization perform better and more efficiently.

Our focus here is on technologies for capturing and communicating data, not on technologies for storing, retrieving, manipulating, or reporting data. (Technologies will be discussed more fully in a later chapter.)

For years, "data exchange" meant Electronic Data Interchange (EDI), a technology developed for transmitting electronic documents for common types of transactions. Many companies around the world still use EDI systems, even as new data communication technologies, such as XML, have developed. XML (eXtensible Markup Language) is a technology for transmitting data in formats that are more flexible than EDI and extensible (allowing for future growth). One advantage of that flexibility is that XML systems can work with EDI systems.

Data communication has improved incredibly with the development of the Internet and with broadband technologies. Companies are able to connect and exchange data more quickly, more easily, less expensively, more flexibly, and more widely—across town and around the world. Data—purchase orders, acknowledgments of receipt, invoices, electronic payments, forecasts, and more—can move from partner to partner. A company can communicate with other chain partners—whether dozens or hundreds—almost instantaneously.

Technology can do wondrous things—if we use it properly, and if we use it with the right partners. We cannot overstate the importance of choosing good supply chain partners, building and maintaining strong relationships with them, and helping them become better. In the final analysis, information technology is often easier in most organizations than information sharing. Understanding what constitutes the right information and knowing how and when to apply it are often the greatest challenges for the operations manager.

Metrics

The emphasis of supply chain management on performance requires measuring performance across your chains. The basic premise is that "what gets measured gets rewarded, and what get's rewarded gets done." And nowhere is this principle more important to the operations manager than in executing across the supply chain. After all, the supply chain is an extension of your company operations, so it makes sense to extend your measurements. Unfortunately, that logic is where the simplicity ends.

METRICS ARE ESSENTIAL, BUT . . .

"It is generally believed that a well-crafted system of supply chain metrics can increase the chances for success by aligning processes across multiple firms, targeting the most profitable market segments, and obtaining a competitive advantage through differentiated services and lower costs.

"The lack of proper metrics for a supply chain will result in failure to meet consumer/end-user expectations, suboptimization of departmental or company performance, missed opportunities to outperform the competition, and conflict within the supply chain.

"However, there is no evidence that meaningful performance measures that span the entire supply chain actually exist."

—Douglas M. Lambert and Terrance L. Pohlen, *Supply Chain Management: Processes, Partnerships, Performance*, 3rd edition (Supply Chain Management Institute, 2008)

Your company has been in business for a while, maybe a long while, and people there have been measuring performance in various ways at least long enough for you to know that no set of metrics is perfect, at least not in practice. Certainly the TQM and Six Sigma experts have taught us all that there are so many things to measure in our processes and inputs and outputs that we could all go crazy striving for perfection in metrics and measurements.

Chain Performance Measured as Shareholder Value

Douglas M. Lambert and Terrance L. Pohlen, in *Supply Chain Management: Processes, Partnerships, Performance*, 3rd edition (Supply Chain Management Institute, 2008), explain at length the difficulties of measuring the overall performance of a supply chain. They then propose a framework for developing metrics that translate supply chain performance into shareholder value. Their seven-step framework aligns performance at each supplier-customer link in the chain, beginning with the linkages at the focal company and moving outward link by link:

- Map the supply chain from beginning to end to identify "key linkages."
- Analyze each customer-supplier link to determine where value can be added.
- Develop P&L statements for both customer and supplier to assess for each the effect of that relationship on profitability and shareholder value.
- "Realign supply chain management processes and activities to achieve performance objectives."
- Decide on non-financial measures that "align individual behavior with supply chain management process objectives and financial goals."
- Compare shareholder value and market capitalization with supply chain objectives and revise performance measures as necessary.
- Repeat the first six steps for each link in the chain.

This measurement system works, they conclude, because the P&Ls "capture cost trade-offs and revenue implications" and any action taken by one company affects both P&Ls. As a result, combining the analyses of all the P&Ls throughout the chain provides the foundation needed for improving the chain's performance.

Supply Chain Operations Reference Model

The Supply Chain Council offers its members the Supply Chain Operations Reference (SCOR) model (*www.supply-chain.org/resources/scor*). This is "a process reference model that has been developed and endorsed by the Supply Chain Council as the cross-industry standard

KNOW THE SCOR

Supply Chain Excellence: A Handbook for Dramatic Improvement Using the SCOR

TOOLS *Model,* by Peter Bolstorf and Robert Rosenbaum, 2nd edition (AMACOM/American Management Association, 2007)

99 SUPPLY CHAIN MEASURES

Larry Lapide offers a list of 99 possible supply chain meas-

TOOLS ures in nine categories in an excellent white paper from the ASCET Project, *What About Measuring Supply Chain Performance?*, reprinted in *The Supply Chain Yearbook, 2001 Edition,* John A. Woods and Edward J. Marien, editors (McGraw-Hill, 2001).

diagnostic tool for supply chain management." With the SCOR model, users can "address, improve and communicate supply-chain management practices within and between all interested parties."

The SCOR model describes supply chains in terms of "process building blocks" and with "a common set of definitions." As a result, according to the Supply Chain Council, the model can be used to describe chains that are "very simple or very complex," for "global projects as well as site-specific projects."

Operations Manager's Checklist for Chapter 6

☑ Think of the supply chain as the *supply-and-demand chain* or, more logically, as the *demand-and-supply chain.* Demand is the cause, the beginning of the flow of information that moves upstream to trigger the effect, supply, which then moves downstream to the customers, the source of the demand.

☑ Work to get your company to position the supply chain as a strategic partner. Otherwise, you risk losing a competitive advantage.

☑ Make your supply chain strategy the plan for operating the supply chain in line with the organization's business strategy and as an extension of operations within the organization.

☑ Evaluate the results of your supply chain strategy periodically—at least annually.

☑ Focus on the goal of an integrated supply chain: to remove all boundaries to ease the flow of material, cash, resources, and information.

☑ Manage relationships with supply chain partners as a core competency. No two relationships are the same. Every partner relationship is the result of many factors.

☑ Remember that a *relationship process* must be focused "at the level of the product or service." It's not a relationship between two companies; it's a process about a product or a service.

☑ Know what you want to get out of a supply chain relationship and be aware of the dynamics influencing the situation. Don't expect too much and don't settle for too little.

☑ Work at contract management. Companies continue to leave money on the table by not effectively managing their portfolios of contracts.

☑ Broker information as if your life depended on it; your supply chain certainly does.

Managing Projects
Creating the Light at the End of the Tunnel

As an operations manager, you're almost certainly going to be responsible for projects. Managing projects effectively means delivering the desired results on time and within budget and leaving the stakeholders feeling satisfied and the team members feeling proud—or at least relieved. So, you need good project management skills.

Creating "Unique Products or Services"

In *A Guide to the Project Management Body of Knowledge* (affectionately known as the *PMBOK® Guide*), the Project Management Institute (PMI) defines a *project* as "a temporary endeavor undertaken to create a unique product or service." It can be defined less simply as a series of tasks with a starting point, a deadline or a target date, a specific goal or goals, and a budget of resources (financial, material, temporal, and human). Most importantly, projects have a clearly defined end (that may or may not be in sight) but allow for a celebration of victory when the end occurs.

A project is temporary or finite, and its purpose makes it unique or at least a one-off

> **KEY TERM** **Project** "Temporary endeavor undertaken to create a unique product or service"; a series of tasks with a starting point, a deadline or a target date, a specific goal or goals, and a budget of resources (financial, material, temporal, and human).

gig. In contrast, processes or operations—the normal work of an operations manager— are permanent or at least of lasting or indefinite duration, and their purpose is to produce products or services with consistency.

PMBOK® GUIDE

A Guide to the Project Management Body of Knowledge (PMBOK® Guide), produced by the Project Management Institute, is recognized internationally as the standard resource on the fundamentals of project management.

TOOLS

Because of these inherent differences, projects require management skills that differ from those used to manage processes and operations. That's why this chapter is here—and why you should be reading it.

In fact, the *PMBOK® Guide* identifies nine management skill areas ("knowledge areas") for project managers:

- integration management
- time management
- cost management
- scope management
- procurement management, aka contract management
- human resource management
- communication management
- risk management
- quality management

Using a Systematic Approach

Since a project is an endeavor undertaken "to create a unique product or service," it should not surprise you that there's no one project management approach that works for all projects. You need an approach that ensures that you cover the basics, but you should be aware of any particular conditions for which you should adapt and adjust your approach.

What we present here is a standard, traditional structure that consists of five phases:

Project manager The person identified and authorized to be responsible for achieving the project objectives on time, within budget, and according to quality requirements.

KEY TERM

1. Initiate
2. Plan
3. Execute

KNOW WHAT YOUR CULTURE EXPECTS

This chapter presents a generic approach to project management. That's all you'll find in any book—generic approaches with different flavors. Before you start following any of them, find out how projects are presented and planned in your organization. There may be formal instructions; there may be only informal expectations. To give your projects the best chance of succeeding, play by the rules.

✳ THINK AHEAD ✳

SMART

Four basic criteria exist to measure project success:

- Achieve the project goals.
- Finish the project on time.
- Finish the project within the budget of resources (money, material, and human).
- End with the team members satisfied and interrelationships intact.

MANAGING

The first three are critical for the current project. The fourth is critical for projects in the future.

4. Control
5. Close

That seems simple enough. Well, it's not quite so linear, since phases two, three, and four are linked into a cycle. So the structure is somewhat like a traffic circle or rotary: "Initiate" is the road that you take into the circle, where you go around and around through "Plan," "Execute," and "Control" again and again . . . until finally you leave the traffic circle by way of "Close."

Project Phase 1—Initiating

During this phase, a problem or opportunity is identified, a project sponsor is selected, and the project manager is authorized to plan for the project.

Understand the Project. A *project* starts when someone recognizes a need. *Project management* starts when you understand that need and you determine what the project must accomplish. You define the overall project goal and objectives and define the general scope of the project.

Assess the Feasibility of the Project. The second step is to think about what could keep the project from accomplishing what you've just decided it must accomplish. Think in terms of types of limitations or constraints—finances, technical aspects, time, resources, legalities, politics, workplace culture, traditions, schedule conflicts, knowledge and skills, technology, geography, and so on. List every potential limitation as specifically as possible, as a problem statement.

Do a Preliminary Cost-Benefit Analysis. First, do the cost side of the equation. What types of costs would this project involve? What would it take to overcome the limitations you've listed? Break down the types of costs and estimate a dollar amount for each cost.

In Reality ...

The process outlined in this chapter is logical. However, in reality, projects can start in various ways. In many companies, the structure and culture determine a less than ideal SOP for projects. It may be that managers on high decide that something must be done about something and that it should be done within a certain length of time and with a certain amount of resources—and then they select a project manager.

Constraint Anything that limits a project—such as finances, technical aspects, time, resources, legalities, politics, workplace culture, traditions, schedule conflicts, knowledge and skills, technology, and geography.

KEY TERM

Next, do the benefit side of the equation. What benefits would result from this project? Consider all the people who would be affected—the stakeholders. Think of each person or group and how he, she, or they would be better off after the project is completed. Include both tangible and intangible benefits. Quantify each benefit, if possible, in terms of money. That's not the only thing that matters, of course, but it's hard to compare costs and benefits if you've got apples and oranges.

Make a Case for the Project. What you do next depends on the power structure and formality of your organization. Write a recommendation for the project. It should consist of a project statement (i.e., a description of the need and how the project would meet that need), the results of your feasibility assessment, and the cost-benefit analysis. It should also fit the project into the context of the organization's strategic plans, goals, and initiatives.

KEY TERMS

Project sponsor Person with ultimate authority over the project and responsibility for its success, who provides funding, authorizes major changes, resolves issues, exerts the necessary power to overcome obstacles, approves major deliverables, and champions the project within the organization.

Project charter Document that formally authorizes a project. It should contain a statement of the project and define the authority of the project manager. It may also provide preliminary information about the scope, the objectives, the stakeholders, and the members of the project team and their roles and responsibilities.

Identify the Project Sponsor. The *project sponsor* approves funding and is ultimately responsible for the project. You want someone with enough authority, of course, but your sponsor should also be interested in the project and be willing and able to be a strong champion.

Obtain Authorization to Plan the Project. Depending on your organization and the project, authorization could be informal or formal. It may take the form of a *project charter.*

A project charter should contain a statement of the project, identify the project manager, and define his or her responsibilities and authority. It may also provide preliminary information about the scope, the objectives, the stakeholders, and the members of the project team and their roles and responsibilities.

Project Phase 2—Planning

In this phase, the project is planned in detail. This involves creating a project plan, a schedule, a change control plan, a quality control plan, a risk management plan, a communications plan, a procurement plan, and possibly a completion plan.

Start Creating the Project Plan

This plan should contain the basics: goal, objectives, scope, deliverables, constraints, and approach. The project plan can run from just a few pages long for shorter, simpler projects to 50 pages for longer, more complicated projects. Start with your goal and objectives; after that, the planning steps can come in whatever order makes the most sense to you, as long as you take all the steps by the end of this planning phase.

goal: why doing project
objective: what expect to achieve

Define the Project Goal and Objectives. You defined the goal and objectives in the first phase. The goal statement documents your purpose and serves as the basis for the rest of the plan: it states why you're doing this project. The objectives specify what you want the project to achieve: they will serve as criteria by which you assess any changes proposed during the project.

> ### PLAN PROJECTS PROPERLY
> **SMART**
>
>
>
> **MANAGING**
>
> "The planning processes are perhaps the most important...because proper planning can significantly reduce the time spent in the execution processes...[s]urveys conducted over the past 20 years indicate that for every hour spent in planning, 20 to 100 hours can be saved in execution."
> —Nancy Mingus, *Alpha Teach Yourself Project Management in 24 Hours* (Alpha Books, 2002)

Determine the Project Scope. You also defined the scope in the first phase. In your scope statement here, you outline in a few sentences the significant work activities of the project. As you're summarizing what you and your project team will do, you should also summarize what you will not do—the exclusions to the scope.

scope: Include what will not do

When you assessed the feasibility of the project in the first phase, you identified potential problems. If you do not intend to address them, restate them here. Again, the essence of strategy is not what you will do but rather what you will not do. The scope, together with the project objectives, will guide you through the rest of the planning process and then through the project if any suggestions for changes arise.

> ### SCOPE—FIRST AND FOREMOST
> A project manager must simultaneously manage the four basic parameters or constraints—*time, resources, money,* and *scope.* Many articles and books on project management stress the need to balance the first three, but it's actually scope that's the most important. It's the *what* of the project; the other three are the *how*.
>
> Any project scope change must be matched by a change in time, resources, and/or money. If not, the project manager should not allow the scope to change.
>
> The problem is often with the "little" changes—otherwise known as *scope creep.* Each change may seem insignificant, but small changes can add up to a big headache for the project manager.

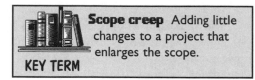

Scope creep Adding little changes to a project that enlarges the scope.

KEY TERM

Specify Project Deliverables. These are the results of your work, what the project sponsor, the stakeholders, and others are expecting of you, either during the project or after it's been completed. At the end of the planning phase, you will need to identify and deliver some key thoughts and ideas to the sponsor. As the project ends, you will be delivering whatever you specified in your project objectives.

Evaluate the Project Constraints. You considered constraints when you were assessing the feasibility of the project in the first phase. Now you itemize them in the project plan, describing each in a sentence or two. You list the constraints for two reasons: to help you in further planning and to inform project stakeholders about the limitations and potential problem areas.

Describe the Project Approach. How are you going to achieve the project objectives? You don't have to have it all figured out at this point, just by the end of the planning phase. Write down your ideas, whether you've got one approach in mind or several possibilities. The approach or approaches you're considering will help you determine the resources you'll need and identify the people who will be affected by your project.

Determine the Resources. Return once again to your assessment of the feasibility of the project and the constraints you identified. What resources will you need to overcome those constraints? These resources will include money, of course, and materials, but you should also think about the human resources—the skills and knowledge required and maybe even personality traits such as tact, creativity, intelligence, and so on. If specific individuals come to mind as you make your list, jot down their names. Again, you don't need to finalize your list until the end of the planning phase.

Identify the Project Stakeholders. Who's going to be affected by your project, in addition to members of the project team? You thought about stakeholders while you were doing the preliminary cost-benefit analysis in the first phase. Now that you know more about what you're doing, you can list all the stakeholders, starting with the project sponsor and any clients (either external or internal, such as managers and process owners). List their names, their titles, and how they will be affected. You'll be using this list in making your communications plan, so think about anybody who should know about your project at any point and why.

Itemize the Project Assumptions. We all make assumptions when we think about things, do things, or say things. Unfortunately, we're usually not aware of what we're assuming.

> **START WITH THE IMPROBABLE**
> **TRICKS OF THE TRADE**
>
> If you have trouble itemizing your assumptions, open up your mind by considering the most improbable possibilities. For example, what if a meteorite falls on your office or every employee but you retires? Well, obviously you're assuming those things won't happen. But your mental wandering should soon be bringing up possibilities that are not improbable, things that could happen—and you realize you're assuming they won't.

Think about all the things that are in your mind but not yet on paper as you think about this project. What are you taking for granted, as givens of your situation? List only the major assumptions. (If you're signing a contractual agreement, you should list all your assumptions, for maximum protection.)

Specify the Criteria. This is basically a listing of criteria by which to assess the results of your project. How would you describe "success" in terms of time, resources, quality, and—of course—your objectives? Write one succinct sentence for each criterion.

List Work Activities

When you determined the project scope, you outlined the significant work activities of the project. Now you want to expand those few sentences into a list of activities. How many activities? In what detail? As usual, it depends on the complexity of the project. The purpose is to make sure that when you start scheduling the activities and component tasks, you don't neglect anything necessary.

Create a Work Breakdown Structure

Now you start breaking the project into bite-sized chunks, using the → *work breakdown structure* (WBS). The purpose of the WBS is to define a project team's work activities and organize the component tasks so you

Work breakdown structure (WBS) A tool for defining a project team's **KEY TERM** work activities and organizing the component tasks in order to better manage the project.

can better manage the project. Traditionally, the WBS structured three levels of work activities, but with project management software there's no limit—and no standardi-

zation of terms or formats.

Basically, you can approach and structure project work activities in any of three ways:

PROJECT MANAGEMENT SOFTWARE

TOOLS There are so many project management programs that it's overwhelming for novices. Three of the top-rated programs overall and in terms of ease of use are Project (Microsoft), MindView (Matchware), and Project KickStart (Experience in Software).

- *By stage or phase*—with work broken down into tasks sequentially within each stage or phase (the best way in terms of the resulting Gantt chart).

- *By deliverable or output*—with work broken down into tasks required to produce each deliverable or output.

- *By skill involved or role*—with work broken down into tasks by person with those skills or assigned to that role.

You can structure your WBS in various ways. Two common ways are as a diagram like an organization chart (Exhibit 7-1) and as an outline (Exhibit 7-2). Both figures show a breakdown consisting of three levels with a logical three-part numbering system.

You need to decide how much detail to include in your WBS. Also, you need to decide at what level you want to track progress and what metrics you'll use. The more closely you track your progress, the sooner you can detect any problems or potential problems. Also, depending on your metrics, the information you collect will enable you to plan projects in the future, if you can track use of time and material resources by task. On the other hand, tracking a project so closely takes more effort and is more likely to annoy team members sensitive to what they could perceive as "micromanaging." If you track the project by deliverables, you'll know when things are going well, but not how much time and material

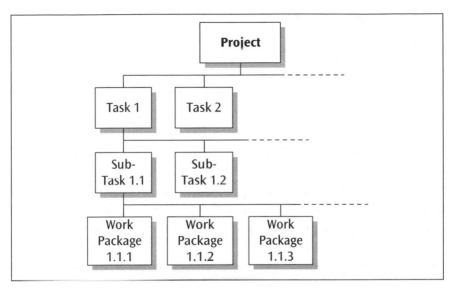

Exhibit 7-1. WBS diagram

Level 1	Level 2	Level 3
Task 1		
	Subtask 1.1	
		Work Package 1.1.1
		Work Package 1.1.2
		Work Package 1.1.3
	Subtask 1.2	
		Work Package 1.2.1
		Work Package 1.2.2
		Work Package 1.2.3
Task 2		
	Subtask 2.1	
		Work Package 2.1.1
		Work Package 2.1.2
		Work Package 2.1.3

Exhibit 7-2. WBS outline

resources it took to produce each deliverable—and not how things are going until the deadline for the deliverable.

Form a Project Team

At several points in these first two phases, you've thought about human resources—the skills, knowledge, and maybe even personality traits your project requires. Maybe you've noted the names of some individuals who have some of the necessary ingredients. Now you consider this "sourcing" more closely, deciding what skills and knowledge and other intangibles you need and which people have at least adequate levels of what you need. List each skill, area of knowledge, and other intangibles and the level needed for the project. Then match up the people who could meet any of those needs. Indicate the availability of each person, in number of hours per week, for example.

The next step is to consider "fit." You may not be taking this step if there's only one person for each skill or knowledge area. In most situations, however, the project manager must make at least one choice. On the best teams, the members work well together. That doesn't mean they all agree or they all think the same way. In fact, quite the opposite. It's a matter of mixing personality types and thinking styles. You want a good fit, a balance. Many people describe projects as evolving through a group of phases that Bruce Tuckman articulated in 1965: *"Forming, Storming, Norming, and Performing."* Getting the right people together at the start will help the operations manager navigate through the storming phase when different ideas compete for attention and to the subsequent phases of working together to attain high performance levels. In the final analysis, high-performance teams set ambitious goals, but, more importantly, they are committed to one another on all levels.

Structure the Project Team. Now you need to assign types of work activities and responsibilities to your team members and decide how they will work together and with you. Who will be doing what, when, and with whom?

The *when* question may be the most difficult, at least for team members with more rigid work schedules or who work less than full-time and/or irregular schedules. You may have to go with your second choice to fill a position on the team if your first choice is too difficult to schedule.

The next question may, in some situations, be better asked earlier: Can we get the people we want for the team? It should be easy to get the employees who report to you; it's "just" a matter of shifting their normal work responsibilities to allow for project team responsibilities. If you want to borrow employees who report to other managers, you may need to negotiate with those managers or you may ask the project sponsor to negotiate, depending on how your company handles projects, on the importance of your project and the stakeholders, and maybe on your relationships with those other managers.

Estimate Time, Resources, and Costs

In your preliminary cost-benefit analysis in the first phase, you made some cost estimates. They may have been rough, just enough to make the business case for this project, or they may have been as accurate as you could get. Now you need to estimate task durations based on your WBS and estimate the costs of employee time and material resources.

Check your WBS carefully. Make sure you haven't forgotten any tasks and you've organized the tasks effectively and assigned the right people to those tasks.

Estimate the duration for each task. You can use your own experience, and you can consult with the employees who will be responsible for the project work activities and managers with knowledge and experience in estimating time and costs.

An *estimate* is basically a guess—but it should be an educated guess.

You may want to try using the PERT weighted-averages formula or ask others to make

> **PERT Program Evaluation and Review Technique**, a project management model designed to represent and analyze the tasks involved in a project. **KEY TERM**

estimates and then use your best judgment to decide on the best estimate.

You may want to calculate a fudge factor into your estimates. This percentage should account for meetings, project-unrelated interruptions, phone calls, conversations with coworkers, bathroom and water cooler breaks, and so on. Your experience should guide you to the appropriate percentage—maybe 10 percent, maybe 20 pecent. If employees on your project team will be switching back and forth between their normal jobs

TOOLS

PERT Weighted Average Formula

The formula often used in PERT calculates a weighted average for the duration of an activity from three estimates:

$$(O + 4M + P)/6$$

O is the optimistic (best-case scenario) estimate, M is the most likely estimate, and P is the pessimistic (worst-case scenario) estimate.

SMART

MANAGING

Close Enough

Estimates of task time within 10% of the actual times are usually considered very good. Just don't stick with the estimates you made in your preliminary cost-benefit analysis. Preliminary estimates tend to be 50% to 70% under the actual time and costs. Of course, this fact does not mean that you should increase your preliminary estimates 50% to 70%. Also, remember that these percentages are themselves only estimates.

and project tasks, that percentage could be adjusted upward.

For each task, multiply the duration estimate by the cost per hour for the employee assigned to that task. That cost should be not only the hourly wage but also the cost of employment taxes and benefits (health insurance, workers' compensation, and additional benefits).

Finally, estimate the costs to be incurred for material resources and any other costs. The calculations should be relatively simple.

Create a Network Diagram

Now you begin what many people consider the heart of planning, moving activities and tasks from a list into a schedule. The next step is to create a *network diagram* (aka *logic diagram*), which is a schematic display of the logical interrelationships among project activities and tasks, ordered from left to right to show chronology of activities.

In some projects, the activities or tasks would be sequenced one after the other, running in series, to use an electronics term; in other projects, the activities or tasks would be sequenced in parallel, all running simultaneously. In most projects, however, the activities and tasks are chronologically interrelated in ways that require more complex arrangements.

These chronological relationships, known as *dependencies*, consist of four types (in order of frequency):

- *Finish to start*—A FS B = B starts only after A has finished

- *Finish to finish*—A FF B = B finishes only after A has finished
- *Start to start*—A SS B = B starts only after A starts
- *Start to finish*—A SF B = B finishes only after A starts

Network diagram
Schematic display of the logical interrelationships among project activities and tasks, ordered from left to right to show chronology of activities. Also known as a *logic diagram*.

KEY TERM

Using project management language, in these examples A would be the *predecessor task* and B would be the *successor task*. Sometimes a predecessor task and a successor task can overlap or require a gap between them. Then we apply terms such as lead time and lag time. *Lead time* (aka *overlap time* or *negative lag time*) is the amount of time that a predecessor task runs before a successor task starts. *Lag time* (aka *gap*) is the amount of time that passes between the finish of a predecessor task and the start of a successor task. Both lead time and lag time can be expressed in terms of percentage of the duration of the predecessor task or in time units; lead time is usually expressed as a percentage and lag time is usually expressed as time.

Sometimes activities in sequence can be further time-constrained. An activity can be labeled "as soon as possible" (ASAP) (i.e., minimum lag time) or "as late as possible" (ALAP) (i.e., maximum lag time).

Lead time Amount of time that a predecessor task runs before a successor task starts. Also known as *overlap time* or *negative lag time*.

KEY TERMS

Lag time Amount of time that passes between the finish of a predecessor task and the start of a successor task. Also known as *gap*.

Once you've established the interrelationships among the activities and tasks in your project, you can chart them. Basically, it's a lot like drawing a flowchart for a process, as discussed in Chapter 2. If you numbered activities and tasks in your WBS, you might want to use the same numbers in your network diagram.

This diagram is just to help you schedule, so you can do whatever works best or at least most easily for you. The point is to show all the activities and tasks as a network—e.g., squares or rectangles connected by arrows or whatever your PM software uses. (And it's probably easiest

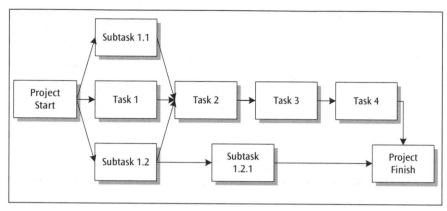

Exhibit 7-3. Network diagram

with software, unless you enjoy drawing and erasing and drawing and erasing until you get it right.)

As you diagram your activities and tasks, mark the durations for each that you estimated earlier in this phase.

PERT vs. CPM. Two major variations exist of the network diagram—PERT and Critical Path Method (CPM).

PERT (Program Evaluation and Review Technique) was developed in the late 1950s by the U.S. Navy to simplify the planning and scheduling of the Polaris project, which was very large and complex. PERT made it possible to schedule a project without knowing the exact durations and details of all the activities.

CPM was developed by the DuPont Corporation in 1957 to work out a process for shutting down chemical plants for maintenance and then restarting them. CPM enables project managers to calculate the time required to complete a project and to determine which activities are critical to the duration of a project and which are not.

So, what's the difference?

Both methods lead to the same end: a *critical path* (explained below). The main difference between these methods is how they treat activity time. PERT treats activity time as a variable: as noted earlier, it allows for calculating task durations by means of weighted averages. CPM treats activity time as fixed: it allows for only a single time for any task.

PERT is more applicable for projects for which estimates of duration

[handwritten margin notes: use variable time / focuses on time / use fixed time / includes analysis between cost & time]

are uncertain. CPM is best suited for projects for which time and costs can be calculated more accurately. Another difference is that PERT is focused exclusively on time, while CPM includes analysis of the tradeoff between time and cost.

Critical Path. If your project is urgent, you may want to calculate the *critical path* (CP). This is the string of tasks that represents the longest distance through a project. Any delay of an activity on the critical path results in delaying the planned project completion date. (In other words, there's no *float* or *slack* on the critical path.) Any change in the duration of tasks along the critical path will change the duration of the project.

Once you've identified the critical path, you can determine whether you can increase resources for any of the tasks and thus shorten the critical path and the project duration. Maybe you can run more tasks in parallel rather than sequentially, if there's no dependency to prevent that arrangement. You can also know which tasks to monitor most closely and which ones should not worry you as much. You can even take away resources from the tasks that are not critical, if you need them elsewhere at the same time or you want to reduce costs. Unfortunately, that approach works only for certain tasks, like assembling widgets by hand. Other tasks will take X amount of time no matter how many people you assign to them, such as assembling widgets with the only assembly machine.

KEY TERMS

Critical path (CP) String of tasks that represents the longest distance through a project. Any change in the duration of tasks along the critical path will change the duration of the project.

Float/Slack Amount of time that a task in a project network can be delayed without resulting in a delay in subsequent tasks or the project completion date.

Create the Schedule

You've got your project team and their work schedules, your estimates of task durations, and your network diagram. Now it's time to create your schedule.

Are there any date constraints—for example, you must finish by a certain date or begin after a certain date, or you must deliver some output before a specific date, or a necessary input will be available only after a specific date?

Are there any potential schedule conflicts that will affect your scheduling? A team member may be unavailable due to a prior commitment, for example, or there may be a holiday coming up.

As you start scheduling, you will need to mark the duration for each task on your network diagram. Next, it's time for—football! Well, actually it's time to calculate the critical path, through a process that consists of what the project management people call a forward pass and a backward pass.

The *forward pass* consists of working forward through the network, from the first task to the last. In the upper left corner of any tasks that can begin the first day, mark a 1. That's the early start date. Then, for each of those tasks, add the early start date and the task duration and subtract 1. The result is the early finish date, which you write in the upper right corner. As you move toward the right, each task will have an early start date that's calculated as the early finish date of the preceding activity plus 1.

Continue calculating and marking early start and finish dates for all the activities. When you've completed the forward pass, the latest early finish date for any of the final tasks will be the early finish date for the project. OK?

Whew! One pass down and one to go.

The *backward pass* consists of working backward through the network, from the last task to the first. In the lower right corner of each of the final tasks, mark the latest finish date. Then, for each of those tasks, subtract from that latest finish date the duration of the task and add 1. Mark that latest start date in the lower left corner of the task. As you move toward the left, each task will have a late finish date that's calculated as the late start date of the succeeding activity minus 1.

Doing the two passes is actually easier than understanding this description.

If you're working on a network diagram manually, Exhibit 7-4 shows an example. The format doesn't matter, as long as you can read the numbers and know what each of them means.

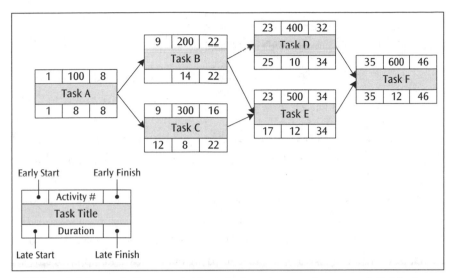

Exhibit 7-4. Network diagram with task durations and start and finish dates

The backward pass reveals that task D shows a difference of 2 between its early and late dates (start and finish) and task C shows a difference of 6 between its early and late dates (start and finish). This time, the float, allows for flexibility in those two activities.

Any task for which the two start dates are the same and the two finish dates are the same is on the *critical path*. In other words, there's no flexibility, no float. In the example (Exhibit 7-4), the critical path would be A-B-E-F.

Create a Gantt Chart

Once you've done a forward pass and a backward pass, you're ready to create a *Gantt chart*. This is a type of bar chart that illustrates a project schedule, showing the start and finish dates of the tasks (sometimes with the dependencies among tasks) and a line to show the current status of the project.

Across the top of the page extends the timeline. The scale you use should generally be in proportion to the length of the project and/or (more important) the durations of the tasks. You can shade any days off, when project work is suspended.

Down the left side of the page are listed the tasks. This works best if you structured the project work activities on your WBS by stage or phase,

 **Gantt chart** A type of bar
chart that illustrates a proj-
ect schedule, showing the

KEY TERM   start and finish dates of the
tasks (sometimes with the dependencies
among tasks) and a line to show the
current status of the project.

with the component tasks
ordered sequentially within
each stage or phase.

For each task, a horizontal
line extends from left to right,
beginning below the timeline
point marking the start date of
the task and ending below the timeline point marking the end date of the
task.

Exhibit 7-5 shows a simple example of a Gantt chart that lists start
date, finish date, and duration for each task.

The final touch for your Gantt chart is to decide on the symbols, patterns, and/or letters you want to use to indicate, for example, progress,
actual dates, reasons for delays, and so on. If you're doing the chart manually, the only limits are your creativity and perhaps your artistic skill. If

	Name		January 1	January 8	January 15
	Project	Days			
1	Begin Project	0 days	◆		
2	Select Architect	1 day	▪		
3	Draw Up Plans	1 week	▬▬▬▬		
4	Corporate Signoff	1 day		▪	
5	Begin Construction	0 days		◆	
6	Lay Floor	1 day		▪	
7	Rough in Walls	2 days		▪▪	
7.1	Hang Drywall	2 days		▮▮	
7.2	Paint Walls	1 day			▮
7.3	Paint Trim	1/2 day			▮
8	Lay Carpet	1 day		▪	
8.1	Install Doors	1/2 day			
9	Install Workstations	2 days			▪▪
10	Hook Up Phones	1 day			▪
11	Project Finished	0 days			◆

▪ = Critical Process   ▮ = Secondary Process   ◆ = Milestone

Exhibit 7-5. Gantt chart (example)

you're using software, you're stuck with whatever codes the program allows, but you save yourself a lot of work.

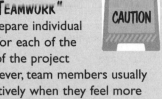

KEEP THE "TEAM" IN "TEAMWORK"
You can prepare individual schedules for each of the members of the project team. However, team members usually work effectively when they feel more like a part of a greater effort.

The main advantage of a Gantt chart is that it clearly shows what's happening. That makes it easy for you to anticipate potential problems and to catch any errors in the scheduling. It also makes it easy for you to share the project schedule with team members and other stakeholders and for all to know at a glance how the project is progressing.

Of course, that works only if you update your chart periodically. A Gantt chart is not just a way to schedule a project; it's also a way to monitor the activity and, as necessary, to motivate the team members.

Develop Control Plans

Now that you've decided what your project will do, how (more or less), and for whom, it's time to make plans to help ensure that you'll deliver. Just as you need a plan for executing the project, you need a plan or a series of plans for controlling it.

Develop Change Control Plan. Since scope is the most important of the four basic project parameters or constraints to control, you need to develop a plan. It should specify how a proposed change is to be evaluated, accepted or rejected, approved if accepted, and reported to stakeholders.

use of change order

First, define "change." Is it any variation in tasks or in deliverables? Or any variation in only one of those two?

Second, use a change form. Your organization may have a standard form or you may need to create a form. It should allow for the following information: name of project and project manager; name of person requesting change and date of request; description of change and reason(s) for requesting change; impact on scope, deliverables, quality, time, and resources; and decision (accepted or rejected) and signatures of project manager and/or sponsor and dates signed.

Third, determine criteria for evaluating proposed changes. This should be in terms of the impact on scope or work activities, deliverables, quality, time, and/or resources.

Fourth, specify which changes the project manager can approve and which changes require the approval of the project sponsor.

WHAT IS "QUALITY"?
You've got to define quality if you expect to monitor and ensure it. Maybe your company has specific standards. If so, then you can state that your project will use those standards. If not, maybe your industry associations have definitions of quality. You should review Chapter 4 as well.

A Supreme Court justice is quoted as having stated, "I can't define pornography, but I know it when I see it." You may feel that way about quality, but it's part of your responsibilities as project manager to define it.

IF YOU CAN ANTICIPATE IT
"If you can dream it, you can do it."
—Walt Disney
"If you can anticipate it, you can plan for it."
—Anonymous program manager

Develop a Quality Control Plan. This plan is for addressing issues of quality, both for the process and for the deliverables. How will you be measuring quality? How will you be monitoring and ensuring quality?

Develop a Risk Management Plan. You've identified problem areas. How do you intend to deal with them? You've identified your major assumptions. What possibilities could upset those assumptions and how would you deal with them? You should make contingency plans.

A risk management plan should contain an analysis of possible risks. For each risk you identify, consider three aspects:

- How would the problem affect the project and/or the stakeholders?
- How likely is the problem to occur?
- How serious would the impact be?

For each risk, your plan should have a strategy. There are four approaches, depending on the type of risk you identify and your answers to those three questions:

■ *Avoid the risk*—Modify your plans to prevent the problem or at least lessen the possibility.

■ *Mitigate the risk*—Take steps to reduce the impact of the problem. This may mean preparing your communications plan to be ready to react immediately, just in case.

■ *Transfer the risk*—Have someone else ready, willing, and able to manage the problem if it occurs.

■ *Accept the risk*—Take your chances, as we all take chances in our lives.

Whatever risk management plan you develop, make sure to review it periodically.

Develop a Communications Plan. Don't skip this one. It's often easy when planning a project to take communications for granted, but it's very important.

Communication for a project is about two things: providing information and managing expectations. You can think about it as sharing, developing, and maintaining a sense of community; things that you want to do; and you can think about it as a good way to manage risks. The better you keep stakeholders informed about progress and potential problems, the less any problems will surprise them. The more you keep stakeholders feeling involved in your project, the less negatively they're likely to react to problems and the more likely they are to help out.

Earlier in your planning, you identified and listed stakeholders, including anybody who should know about your project at any point and why. Now you figure out for each individual or group three things:

■ What to communicate.
■ When to communicate.
■ How to communicate.

For the last point, you've got oral forms of communication (presentations, one-on-one meetings, phone calls, videoconferences, etc.) and written forms of communication (reports, memos, e-mails, newsletters, etc.). Each has its advantages and disadvantages, of course.

Your choices may depend largely on your organizational culture. In many workplaces, certain things are generally communicated in certain ways.

Consider the time and effort involved, both for you and for the stakeholders. You want to provide enough information to satisfy their needs and interests—and convey the importance of your project—but not so much as to bore them. (Most people don't like long meetings or long reports. Also, the longer you talk, the less people are likely to remember—or care—and the more you write, the less they're likely to read—or care.)

Generally, it's best to provide information both ways: orally, if only because it involves greater social contact; and in written form, if only because it provides documentation.

However you decide to communicate with stakeholders about your project, schedule it. When you're working on a project, it's easy to forget to communicate and easy to postpone communicating because other tasks seem more important. Prioritize it now and schedule it so it remains a priority.

Develop a Procurement Plan. This should be easy for you. After all, procurement planning is probably in your job description and you probably do it well enough to keep your operations running.

Develop a Completion Plan. You may not need this plan. To do or not to do it is mostly a matter of organizational culture and particularly how projects are closed.

A completion plan provides answers to two simple questions:

- How will we know when we've completed this project?
- What should we do when we've completed this project?

You should prepare a checklist for the project deliverables and any specifics about handling them. You should find out what reports or other documents are required for the project. These may seem like details now, as you feel overwhelmed by all the tasks and plans and schedules, but you should be preparing for the end before it comes.

Get Approval

Share your project plan with the project sponsor. Get his or her approval and official authority to start executing your plan.

Create Work Packages

A *work package* is basically a project task and related information. You can start developing work packages when you're developing the work breakdown structure (WBS) or you can wait until you've finalized the project schedule.

Now that you've got your schedule completed and approved, and you're ready to meet with your team members, you should prepare work packages for each of them. The format can be simple, maybe only a list of the essentials:

- task name and/or number
- person responsible
- estimated duration
- scheduled start date
- scheduled finish date
- input(s)
- output(s) or (deliverable[s])
- specifications, guidelines, and standards

You'll be handing out these work packages when you meet with the team, along with copies of the project schedule.

> **Work package** Project task and related information, usually task name and/or number, person responsible for the task, estimated duration, scheduled start date, scheduled finish date, input(s), output(s), or deliverable(s), and specifications/guidelines/standards.
>
> **KEY TERM**

Save Documents

Finally, save copies of your project plan, your schedule, and other documents you've generated in the planning phase. These are "for the record": you won't be modifying these copies as the project progresses.

Project Phases 3 and 4—Executing and Controlling

The Executing phase consists of following the project schedule, of doing "the real work."

As mentioned a little earlier, the Controlling phase runs concurrently. As team members do their assigned tasks, you're monitoring those work activities, taking corrective actions as necessary, and managing team members and other stakeholders. You're also following your control plans. In addition, you're evaluating project progress and comparing the results against your plans, particularly in terms of the schedule, the quality of the work, and—of course—time and cost.

Prepare the Project Team

Assemble the members of the project team. Present the project:

- Overall project goal and objectives
- Scope
- Main stages or phases of work
- Deliverables

Ask the team members to introduce themselves briefly: name, title, and department. Then, briefly state what each member will be contributing to the project, in general terms: roles and responsibilities. Explain that you'll be distributing a schedule with the specifics of their responsibilities. Answer any questions about the project in general.

Pass around index cards or sheets of paper and ask them to write down their full name, phone numbers, e-mail addresses, and other contact information you may need. You'll keep this information at hand and make a copy to keep with your communications plan.

Finally, distribute copies of the project schedule and the work packages. Ask them to read the materials carefully and encourage them to come to you with any questions,

Hold Kickoff Meetings

It's a good idea to hold at least one kickoff meeting, especially if that's how projects are launched in your organization. You want to officially announce your project to stakeholders, in one or more meetings, and provide the first of many reports on your project. How you do the kickoff depends on the policy or practices and culture of your organization. It should include providing the same general information as you gave to your team and introducing the team members.

Monitor Work Activities

At this point in the project, two phases actually run concurrently, execution and control. *Monitoring* provides the connection between them.

Deal with Situations. As you monitor project activities, you may notice things for which you haven't specifically planned. You may need to resolve conflicts (involving team members, schedules, or stakeholders). You may need to deal with issues and fight fires. You may need to help team members, by providing information, training, and/or encouragement.

Follow Control Plans. Also, as you monitor project activities, you'll be following your control plans—change control plan, quality control plan, risk management plan, communications plan, and procurement plan.

Track Progress. Throughout this phase of the project, you should be tracking progress. This means, at the very least, making sure that team members start and finish their tasks as scheduled. Record task completions on your Gantt chart. Compare actual task durations against your estimates. This information will help you adjust your schedule, and you should make note of it for the project review and for future projects.

Adjust the schedule for any delays or other changes. Notify the team members responsible for any tasks that you shift as well as any milestones that you move.

You might want to collect information from team members as they complete their tasks. How many hours did they spend on the task? Were there any particular challenges? If so, how did they overcome them? This information will help you improve your ability to estimate effort and duration for future projects and will better prepare you to prepare team members, in this project and future projects, for challenges they might encounter in doing their tasks.

Update the Project Plan

As you monitor project activities and as you adjust your schedule, you may find it necessary to update your project plan. So, you should review the project requirements, the deliverables, and your WBS. Have any requirements changed? Have any deliverables been changed, dropped, or added? How do any changes in requirements or deliverables affect your WBS? And how do any changes in your WBS affect your schedule?

Track Costs

Just as you're tracking the progress you're making, you should be monitoring closely the costs you're incurring. The way you track costs depends on your accounting system and the capabilities of your software. You've estimated the project costs; now you're tracking the actual costs and determining any variances.

Adjust Time, Scope, and/or Cost

As unexpected problems arise during the project, you take corrective action by adjusting the schedule. At some point you may realize that you can't adjust the schedule any more.

You're also reacting to cost variances by adjusting and recalculating expenses. At some point you may realize that whatever you do won't be enough to keep the costs from exceeding your budget.

If worse comes to worst, the only thing you can do to resolve schedule problems is to try to get more time and/or reduce the scope of the project. The only thing you can do to resolve problems with costs is to try to get more money. Prepare an explanation of the causes of the variances and the actions you've taken to adjust the schedule and/or the expenses. Then take your case to the project sponsor.

Report on Progress

This is only a reminder—if you're following your communications plan. You should be reporting to stakeholders at least at every milestone date,

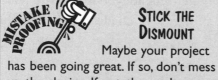

STICK THE DISMOUNT
Maybe your project has been going great. If so, don't mess up the closing. If not, then at least you can end it right. As gymnasts say, "No matter how badly a routine goes, do your best to stick the dismount."

whether you're on schedule or not. This is part of managing expectations, keeping perspectives realistic, and avoiding big bad surprises.

Prepare to End

Review your completion plan or at least draw up a checklist of things that must be done as your project ends. It's important to close a project properly.

Project Phase 5—Closing

This phase consists of finishing the project, reporting to stakeholders, reviewing the project, and following your completion plan.

Finish the Project

Ensure the Quality of Deliverables. Make sure that you and your team have finished the job. Sometimes a team can feel pressured, relieved, or both toward the end of a project and get a little messy. Deliverables leave a legacy, and they matter.

Close the Contracts and Pay the Bills. If there are any contracts, make sure they get closed according to the contract terms. Take care of any remaining financial obligations.

Finalize the Records

After you've ensured that the deliverables have been delivered, closed the contracts, and paid the bills, you can record the final cost and time figures for the project. You'll use these in evaluating your project and making the final report.

Obtain Signoff

This is the official end of the project. The project sponsor formally accepts the project results.

Celebrate

Now's the time to acknowledge the results you and your team have achieved.

This means gathering your team members for a party. It can be casual or formal, according to your organizational culture and how the team members feel. Start with a few words about the project

> **STAND ASIDE**   SMART
>
> "It is better to lead from behind and to put others in front, especially when you celebrate victory when nice things occur."   MANAGING
>
> —Nelson Mandela

and the people who made it happen. But keep it short—it's a party, not a meeting!

Celebrating also means sharing with stakeholders and maybe the entire organization what your team members have achieved and how you feel. This is your penultimate project communication. Be brief about the facts and show your appreciation for your team members.

Evaluate the Project

After celebrating the project and the people who made it happen, it's time to evaluate it, to derive value from it for future projects. Document the results! The purpose is to understand how the project worked—what went well and why, what went badly and why, and how it could have gone better.

Survey your team members. Impress upon them that this is their final obligation of the project, to help those who will be doing projects in the future. You want candor and honesty. It may also be worthwhile to survey other stakeholders as well. Although their perceptions of the project are largely from the outside, they may have insights that are of value.

You may want to conduct a follow-up meeting to allow team members and maybe other stakeholders to discuss the project. Depending on the situation, the personalities of the members, and the team dynamics, this may produce results that you couldn't get through a survey.

Whether you use surveys or a meeting or both, make sure you capture lessons learned. Record them so they'll make sense to others who will be managing projects, so they can benefit from your experience.

Write the Final Report

While all of the details, results, and impressions are fresh, write your final report. It may be required in your organization and there may be an established format. It may not be required. Either way, it's a good idea. You want to provide a succinct overview of the project and analysis of what happened and why. Keep it short enough that people will actually read it. You'll probably need at least three pages—and others will probably not need more than five or six.

Archive

Finally! You've generated a lot of documents before, during, and after your project. Now it's time to store it all in your project file for future reference and use.

Congratulations!

Operations Manager's Checklist for Chapter 7

☑ Managing projects effectively means delivering the desired results on time and within budget and leaving the stakeholders feeling satisfied and the team members feeling proud—or at least relieved. That requires good project management skills.

☑ Projects require management skills different from those used to manage processes and operations. The Project Management Institute has identified nine skill areas needed in managing projects, and four basic criteria exist to measure project success:

- Achieve the project goals.
- Finish the project on time.
- Finish the project within the budget of resources (money, material, and human).
- End with the team members satisfied and interrelationships intact.
- The first three are critical for the current project. The fourth is critical for projects in the future.

Forecasting, Planning, and Scheduling:

Taking the Guesswork Out of Guesswork

S atisfying demand is the essential essence of operations. It's what we do. Jessica, in her role as mother, prepares meals for her three children, as described in Chapter 1.

Every week, she has to know how many kids she'll be feeding (sometimes they invite friends to stay for dinner, and sometimes they eat with friends) and what they'll want to eat (forecasting demand), determine what she'll need in order to prepare those meals (planning), and decide how and when she'll prepare those meals (scheduling). This chapter is all about how operations managers forecast demand, plan to meet that demand, and schedule operations to do so.

Demand

The operations manager needs to understand the demands for each of the company's products or services and to manage those demands and satisfy them. That's *demand management*.

Demand for products and services is either dependent or independent. *Dependent demand* for a product or service is caused by the demand for other products or services. *Independent demand* is, as you might guess,

146

not caused directly by another demand. For example, if a company is assembling 1,000 automobiles, then it will need 1,000 radiators, 4,000 or 6,000 or 8,000 spark plugs, and so forth. This type of demand requires tabulation, not a forecast. On the other hand, who knows how many cars it will need to assemble—particularly if the economy is weak and unstable? There's not a lot to do about dependent demand except basic math, but the operations manager should try to influence independent demand through incentives, campaigns, or price changes, especially to stimulate demand between periods of seasonal demand.

Forecasting

Forecasting is the scientific process of *estimating* without having all the necessary information. It often refers to estimating information over time (time series, cross-sectional,

"A highly iterative process that involves driving to a revenue and profit target through prioritization of customers, channels, products, geographies and the demand stimulation programs available to the enterprise."
—Aberdeen Group, "Demand Management: Driving Business Value Beyond Forecasting: A Demand Management Benchmark Study" (2004)

SMART MANAGING

KEY TERMS

Demand management The science and art of understanding, coordinating, and controlling all sources of demand so that operations can efficiently deliver products or services on time to satisfy demands.

Dependent demand Demand for a product or service that is based on the demand for another product or service. It can be calculated.

Independent demand Demand for a product or service that is not based on the demand for another product or service. It must be forecast.

Seasonal demand Interest in purchasing particular products or services primarily during specific periods of the year. For example, snow ski equipment, ice cream cones, tax preparation, and costumes are subject to seasonal demand.

or longitudinal data). For the operations manager, forecasting provides the basis for making decisions with regard to independent demand planning and scheduling and for mitigating risk and uncertainty.

Forecasts are critical to every business and contribute to nearly every significant management decision. Forecasting provides the basis for

Forecasting Scientific process of estimating without having all the necessary information, often referring to estimating information over time (time series, cross-sectional, or longitudinal data).

long-term corporate planning and for near-term actions. In finance and accounting, forecasts form the basis for budgetary planning and cost control. Marketing relies on sales forecasting to plan and introduce new products, compensate sales personnel, and make other key decisions. Operations uses forecasts to make periodic decisions regarding process selection, capacity planning, and facility layout as well as for continual decisions about production planning, scheduling, and inventory. But as Benjamin Disraeli said, "there are three types of lies: lies, damned lies, and statistics." The operations manager has to ensure that none of these lies or statistics influences the decisions he or she must make.

Demand forecasting, sometimes known as *supply chain forecasting*, is

Demand forecasting Practice of estimating how much of a product or service consumers will purchase, using calculations based on sales data or test marketing and making educated guesses. Also known as *supply chain forecasting,*

the practice of estimating how much of a product or service consumers will purchase, using calculations based on sales data or test marketing and making educated guesses. Demand forecasting may be used to make pricing decisions, to estimate capacity, to schedule operations and activities, or to determine market strategies. It necessarily entails both statistical forecasting and a consensus process.

Forecasting 101—What You Need to Know About Forecasting

First, only two things matter about forecasts: they are wrong or they are damned wrong. And only one major premise exists for the entire body of forecasting: the closer you can get to the situation in question, the more reliable and accurate the forecast will be. In other words, if a meteorologist is predicting the weather for six months from now, it may be a crapshoot. If the forecast is for five minutes from now, he or she can look out the window and have a much better chance of getting it right. Science (or *The Farmer's Almanac*) can help make long-term forecasts more accurate, but basing our activities on this prediction will necessarily be chancier than if we wait until we're much closer to what we're predicting.

However objective and scientific we can be in forecasting demand, we will always be human. So, marketers will forecast optimistically and operations managers will plan and schedule accordingly, preferring to purchase and produce in excess rather than be caught short. And these effects of human nature will be typically repeated and amplified by marketers and operations managers throughout the supply chain in a bullwhip effect (discussed below). That will happen naturally unless the supply chain partners establish truly collaborative information-sharing mechanisms and become more efficient at satisfying downstream demand.

Forecasts are critical for every significant operations management decision. Accurate forecasting will help operations meet consumer demand effectively and efficiently and maintain more appropriate levels of inventory, which means increasing profit margins.

Rather than striving for perfect forecasts, though, it's more important to instill a process and culture of continually reviewing forecasts and learning to live with inaccurate forecasts. A good strategy is to use multiple methods of forecasting and evaluating the results with common sense. No demand forecasting method is 100 percent accurate. Combined forecasts improve accuracy and reduce the likelihood of large errors.

Bullwhip Effect. The *bullwhip effect* (or *whiplash effect*) is a phenomenon observed in forecast-driven distribution channels. Since customer demand varies, companies maintain extra inventory, *safety stock,* to be prepared to meet greater demand. When customer demand is expected to increase, orders increase as the demand moves upstream through the supply chain, with each company reacting to the increase by ordering to meet the demand and add to its safety stock.

On the other hand, when customer demand is expected to decrease, orders decrease as the demand moves upstream through the supply chain, with each company naturally wanting to order less in order to reduce its inventory. The effect is that variations in demand amplify through the supply chain, so that a small change in demand by customers results in ever bigger changes in demand upstream, like a small movement of the handle of a bullwhip results in a great movement of the tip.

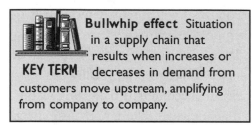

Bullwhip effect Situation in a supply chain that results when increases or decreases in demand from customers move upstream, amplifying from company to company.

There are various causes of the bullwhip effect—e.g., upstream partners not knowing the forecast demands, companies needing long lead times, companies wanting economies of scale in ordering and transporting—and many consequences. There are also several types of countermeasures. However, the one sure way of reducing the bullwhip effect is to order enough materials to meet the demand exactly—no more, no less.

This requires sharing information about demand throughout the supply chain, forecasting more accurately, and not overreacting to changes in demand. The ideal for a supply chain would be better sharing and use of information, with electronic links connecting demand and supply and with information being captured only once and as close to the source as possible, so demand signals transmitted through the supply chain would be more reliable. Smarter use of information within each company means linking production, logistics, and procurement.

It's best if you can determine the demand forecast using a multifunctional approach. It should consider inputs from sales and marketing, finance, and operations, with the final demand forecast being the consensus of all participating managers. You may also want to develop a sales and operations planning group composed of representatives from the departments that would be tasked to prepare the demand forecast.

Sales and Operations Planning

Effective *sales and operations planning* (S&OP) is a process that links supply and demand, leading to more accurate forecasting, more efficient operations, and better bottom-line performance through an aligned planning-and-execution process. S&OP is a company-wide demand-and-supply plan that is integrated and linked to financial plans and targets and focused on planning weekly, monthly, or seasonally. Companies across industries are significantly improving performance through better S&OP by minimizing the typical issues that make operations planning less effective (Exhibit 8-1).

Issue	Description
Subjective forecast inflation	There is subjective inflation of the financial forecast, post-forecasting process, which causes plan variance and gives the supply side an incentive to have their own forecasting process.
Inconsistent forecasting process	Limited consistency in the forecasting process and its outputs within/across the organization/ business units.
Too many forecasting functions	There are at least two (and often more) totally separate forecasting functions being performed, which never reconcile.
Metric inconsistencies	Metrics lack accuracy or consistency (e.g., fill rate is not accurate because orders are not taken if there is no stock).
Limited customer facing input into forecasting process	All required functional groups are not actively involved in forecasting process (e.g., sales, customer development, etc.).
Ineffective communication	There is limited *effective* communication between major functional areas.
Misaligned planning cycles	Demand planning cycle is not aligned with supply planning.
No closed-loop corrective processes	Few instances of accountability for closed-loop corrective action follow-up.

Exhibit 8-1. Operations planning issues

Qualitative and Quantitative Forecasting Methods

Demand is often (perhaps too frequently) modeled based on expert (or inexpert) opinions. *Qualitative forecasts* (i.e., subjective or judgmental), involving intuition and experience and based on estimates and opinions, are used when the situation is less defined and little data exists, such with new products and technologies. Qualitative methods include unaided judgment, predictions, Delphi technique, sales force composites, game theory, judgmental bootstrapping, simulated interaction, consumer market surveys, intentions and expectations surveys (e.g., usage and attitude), and conjoint analyses.

Quantitative approaches are typically characterized as being either time series techniques or causal models. These approaches can be used when the situation is more understood and historical data exist, such as with current products or services and current technology.

Time series forecasts use historical data as the basis for estimating future outcomes based on a set of evenly spaced numerical data that is obtained by observing responses at regular time periods. In the *time series model*, the forecast is based only on past values and assumes that factors that have influenced past and present sales of your products or services will continue in the future.

Causal model forecasts use time series data but with *regression analysis*, a statistical technique that relates a dependent variable (for example, demand) to an independent variable (for example, price, advertisement, etc.) in the form of a linear equation. Forecasting methods that rely on quantitative data include discrete event simulation, extrapolation, quantitative analogies, rule-based forecasting, neural networks, data mining, causal models, and segmentation. A *rolling forecast* is a projection into the future based on past performances, routinely updated with data on a regular schedule.

KEY TERMS **Time series forecast** Forecast using an approach that consists of a various techniques based on the assumption that past and present demand patterns can be used to project demand in the future.

Causal model forecast Forecast using mathematical techniques based on using regression analysis to establishing a functional, causal relationship between or among two or more variables. The reliability of the results depends on correctly identifying significant variables.

Make demand forecasts by following these steps:

- Determine the use of the forecast.
- Select the products or services to be forecast.
- Determine the time horizon of the forecast.
- Select the forecasting model(s).
- Gather the data.
- Make the forecast.
- Validate the results.

TIME SERIES FORECASTS

Several methods exist for making time series forecasts. The *naïve approach* to time series forecasts assumes that demand in the next period will be the same as in the current period (e.g., fall sales will be the same as summer sales). A *moving average* fore- **TOOLS** cast provides an overall impression of data over time and uses a series of arithmetic means; it can be used if little or no trend is present in the data for a fixed sequence of periods and is good for stable demand with no pronounced behavioral patterns.

A *weighted moving average* adjusts the moving average method to reflect fluctuations more closely by assigning weights by intuition to the most recent data, meaning that older data is usually less important. *Exponential smoothing* is an averaging method that gives greater weight to more recent information and less weight to older information; this method is useful if recent changes in data are the results of actual change (e.g., seasonal pattern) rather than random fluctuation. *Time series decomposition* detects and measures the effects of seasonality, trends, and cycles and then adjusts the normal forecast accordingly.

Forecasts are typically classified by duration. *Short-range forecasts*, used for scheduling jobs and worker assignments, cover less than a year, and usually only three months or so. *Medium-range forecasts*—such as for sales and production planning, budgeting, and product or service line extensions—are for periods from three months to three years. *Long-range forecasts*, for decisions like new product development or major facility investments, extend more than three years.

Aggregate Planning

Aggregate planning is the process of developing, analyzing, and maintaining a preliminary, approximate schedule of the overall operations of an organization to determine what resources are necessary and what they will cost during a specified planning period (usually three to 18 months). It attempts to match the supply of and demand for a product or service by determining the appropriate quantities and timing of inputs, transformation, and outputs. In essence, the goal is to match supply and demand as economically as possible.

The aggregate plan generally contains targeted sales forecasts, production levels, inventory levels, and customer backlogs. This schedule is

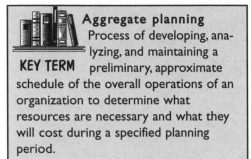

Aggregate planning Process of developing, analyzing, and maintaining a preliminary, approximate schedule of the overall operations of an organization to determine what resources are necessary and what they will cost during a specified planning period.

KEY TERM

intended to satisfy the forecast demand at a minimum cost. There are ways to influence both supply and demand by adjusting production rates, workforce levels, inventory levels, etc.

When you do it properly, aggregate planning should enable you to do the following:

- Minimize the effects of near-term, day-to-day scheduling.
- Maximize customer service.
- Minimize inventory investment.
- Minimize changes in workforce levels.
- Minimize changes in production rates.
- Maximize use of working capital and fixed assets (plant and equipment).

The operations manager should work across the organization to engage key stakeholders to actively handle fluctuations in demand by using pricing strategies and/or advertising and promotions, developing counter-cyclical products, and requesting customers to back-order or advance-order. In addition, he or she must focus on supply and capacity management, adjust the work force size through hiring or layoffs, vary labor and equipment use through overtime or idle time, build or draw from inventory, subcontract production or service operations, negotiate cooperative arrangements with other firms, and schedule backlogs, back orders, and/or stock-outs. This longer-term perspective on resource use can help minimize short-term requirements changes and reduce costs.

Aggregate planning entails all resources and requires basic information, including capacity, demand forecast covering the planning period, cost for various alternatives and resources (e.g., cost of holding inventory, cost of ordering, cost of production through various alternatives like subcontracting, back-ordering and overtime), and organizational policies regarding the usage of the above alternatives.

Aggregate planning serves as the foundation for short-range-type planning, such as production scheduling, sequencing, and loading. The master production schedule used in material requirements planning has been described as the aggregate plan "disaggregated."

Aggregate Planning Strategies

The operations manager typically has a choice of two aggregate planning strategies: a *level strategy* and a *chase strategy*. Operations managers may choose to adopt either one or opt for a strategy that combines the two.

Level Strategy for Aggregate Planning. A level aggregate planning strategy seeks to produce a comprehensive plan that maintains steady capacities (workforce levels, production schedules, output rates) and/or a steady employment level over the planning horizon. To satisfy changes in customer demand, the operations manager must raise or lower inventory levels in anticipation of forecast increases or decreases in demand. The company maintains a level workforce and a steady rate of output when demand is somewhat low, allowing it to establish higher inventory levels than currently needed. As demand increases, the company is able to continue a steady production rate/steady employment level, using the inventory surplus to meet the increase in demand.

An alternative is using a backlog or back order. A *backorder* is simply a promise to deliver the product later, when the company is able to meet demand. In essence, the back order is a way of shifting some demand, smoothing demand requirements over time.

> **Level strategy** An approach to aggregate planning that maintains stable production and workforce levels and a constant output rate by using inventory to meet increases in demand and to absorb excess output when demand decreases. **KEY TERM**

A level strategy enables a company to meet demand with constant output level and workforce level, which is better for employee relations. The level strategy typically incurs greater inventory and back-order investments, increased subcontracting or overtime costs, increased idle time, and resource use that varies over time.

Chase Strategy for Aggregate Planning. A chase strategy necessitates matching capacity (e.g., workforce levels, production schedules, output rates, etc.) over the planning horizon. These actions could result in incurring additional expenses associated with adjusting output rates and/or workforce levels and hiring or firing permanent employees or adding temporary labor. This strategy can result in uncertainty for employees and less efficient use of plant and equipment, which is not necessarily bad. It also requires the company to be very flexible.

KEY TERM **Chase strategy** An approach to aggregate planning that synchronizes production rate with demand by increasing or decreasing capacity and hiring or laying off workers as demand changes.

The major advantage of a chase strategy is that labor utilization is kept high and anticipation inventory is not required, so that inventory can be held to the lowest level possible. For some firms this means considerable savings. Most firms embracing the just-in-time production concept use a chase strategy approach to aggregate planning.

Hybrid or Mixed Strategy. Most firms find it advantageous to combine the level and chase strategies (sometimes called a hybrid or mixed strategy) to better meet organizational goals and policies and achieve lower costs than possible using either one of the strategies.

Aggregate Planning Techniques

Techniques for aggregate planning range from informal trial-and-error approaches, usually using simple tables or graphs, to more formalized and advanced mathematical techniques. Intuitive methods use management intuition, experience, and rules of thumb, frequently accompanied by graphical and/or spreadsheet analysis. The advantage of intuitive methods is that they're easier and the results are easier to explain; the disadvantage is that numerous solutions are often possible, many of which may not be optimal.

William J. Stevenson presents an informal trial-and-error process for aggregate planning in his textbook, *Production/Operations Management* (McGraw-Hill Irwin, 2004):

1. **Determine demand for each period.**
2. **Determine capacity for each period.** This capacity should match demand, which means it may require including overtime or subcontracting.
3. **Identify company, departmental, or union policies that are pertinent.** (For example, maintaining a certain safety stock level, maintaining a reasonably stable workforce, back-order policies, overtime policies, inventory level policies, nature of employment within the industry, and potential loss of goodwill and damage to image.)
4. **Determine unit costs for units produced.** These costs typically include the basic production costs (fixed and variable costs and direct and indirect labor costs) and the costs associated with making changes in capacity. Also consider the costs of holding inventory, storage, insurance, taxes, spoilage, and obsolescence. Finally, back-order costs must be computed; this generally includes expediting costs, loss of customer goodwill, and revenue loss from cancelled orders.
5. **Develop alternative plans and compute the cost for each.**
6. **If satisfactory plans emerge, select the one that best satisfies objectives.** Frequently, this is the plan with the least cost. Otherwise, return to step 5.

Mathematical Techniques. More complex aggregate planning problems can be solved optimally using *linear programming* (LP). Given the constraints on requirements, production capabilities, allowed workforce changes, overtime and subcontracting limits, and all relevant costs, LP will find an optimal solution, maximizing profit while minimizing total costs based on the availability of limited resources and certain limitations known as *constraints*.

A special type of linear programming known as the *transportation model* can be used to obtain aggregate plans that would allow balanced capacity and demand and minimization of costs. However, few real-world aggregate planning decisions are compatible with the linear assumptions of linear programming. Sunil Chopra and Peter Meindl provide an excellent example of the use of linear programming in aggregate planning in *Supply Chain Management: Strategy, Planning and Operation* (Pearson Prentice Hall, 2004).

For aggregate plans that are prepared on a product family basis, where the plan is essentially the summation of the plans for individual product lines, *mixed-integer programming* may prove useful. Mixed-integer programming can provide a method for determining the number of units to be produced in each product family.

Linear decision rule is another optimizing technique. It seeks to minimize total production costs (labor, overtime, hiring/layoff, inventory carrying cost) using a set of cost-approximating functions (three of which are quadratic) to obtain a single quadratic equation. Then, by using calculus, two linear equations can be derived from the quadratic equation, one for planning the output for each period and the other for planning the workforce for each period.

Simulation. A number of simulation models can be used for aggregate planning. Simulation allows for developing an aggregate plan and testing it under various conditions to find acceptable plans for consideration. Simulation models can also be incorporated into a decision support system, which can aid in planning and evaluating alternative control policies. These models can integrate multiple conflicting objectives by using different quantitative measures of productivity, customer service, and flexibility.

Aggregate Planning in Services. Manufacturing companies can build up inventories during periods of slack demand and then use those inventories when demand exceeds capacity. Services, on the other hand, cannot be stockpiled or inventoried. Also, since services are considered "perishable," any capacity that goes unused is essentially wasted. For example, an empty hotel room or an empty seat on a flight cannot be set aside and sold later.

Service capacity can also be very difficult to measure. When capacity is determined somewhat by machine capability, reasonably accurate measures of capacity are not extremely difficult to develop. However, services generally have variable processing requirements that make it difficult to establish a suitable measure of capacity.

Services are much more labor-intensive than manufacturing. This labor intensity can actually be an advantage, because employees can handle a variety of requirements. This degree of flexibility can make aggregate planning easier for services than for manufacturing.

Scheduling

Scheduling is the process of deciding how to allocate resources among activities. It typically involves specifying the start, duration, and end of the activities or floating as part of a sequence of events. A *schedule* is an organized list for performing activities, using resources, or allocating facilities, usually in tabular form, providing information about a series of arranged activities and particularly the times when these activities should take place.

Operations scheduling is at the heart of *Manufacturing Execution Systems (MES)*, an information system that schedules, dispatches, tracks, monitors, and controls production on the factory floor. Such systems also provide real-time linkages to material requirements planning (MRP) systems and to product and process planning, as well as to systems that extend beyond the factory, including advanced planning and scheduling systems, Enterprise Resource Planning (ERP), sales, and service management.

Typical scheduling and control functions include:

- Allocating orders, equipment, and personnel to work centers or other specified locations (essentially, short-run capacity planning).
- Determining the sequence of order performance (that is, establishing job priorities).
- Initiating performance of the scheduled work (commonly known as dispatching orders).

The objectives of work-center scheduling are to meet due dates, to minimize lead times, to minimize setup time or cost, to minimize work-in-process inventory, and to maximize machine or labor utilization. The last objective may be controversial, because simply keeping all equipment and/or employees busy may not be the most cost-effective way to manage process flow.

Sequencing

The process of determining the order in which jobs will be performed is known as *sequencing* or *priority sequencing*. Priority rules are, as you might guess, the rules used in determining the sequencing. These can be simple, requiring only that jobs be sequenced according to one piece of

---

PRINCIPLES OF WORK-CENTER SCHEDULING

1. There is a direct equivalence between work flow and cash flow.
2. The effectiveness of any shop should be measured by speed of flow through the shop.
3. Schedule jobs as a string, with process steps to the back.
4. Once started, jobs should not be interrupted.
5. Speed of flow is most efficiently achieved by focusing on bottlenecks, work centers, and jobs.
6. Reschedule every day.
7. Obtain feedback each day on jobs that are not completed at each work center.
8. Match work center input information to what workers can actually do.
9. When seeking output improvements, look for incompatibility between engineering design and process execution.
10. Certainty of standards, routings, and so forth is not possible in a shop, but always work toward achieving it.

—Richard B. Chase, Nicholas J. Aquilano, and F. Robert Jacobs, *Operations Management for Competitive Advantage* (Irwin, 2001)

---

data, such as processing time, due date, or order of arrival. Other rules may be more complex, requiring several pieces of information, typically to derive an index number, such as the least-slack rule or critical ratio rule. (These are two means of assessing the time remaining in which to finish jobs. The *least slack* simply means the job that's closest to the time by which it must be completed. The *critical ratio* is calculated as time remaining divided by work remaining.)

The following standard measures of schedule performance are used to evaluate priority rules:

- Meeting due dates of customer or downstream operations.
- Minimizing the flow time (time a job spends in the process).
- Minimizing WIP inventory.
- Minimizing idle time of machines or workers.

A method for scheduling a number of jobs on two successive work centers is *Johnson's Rule*.

The purpose is to minimize the flow time from the beginning of the first job until the finish of the last. It's a simple, iterative process:

1. List the operation time for each job on both machines.
2. Select the shortest operation time.
3. If the shortest time is for the first machine, schedule the job first; if the shortest time is for the second machine, schedule it last.
4. Repeat steps 2 and 3 for each job, prioritizing from first downward or from last upward, until the schedule is complete.

Shop floor control is a system for using data from the shop floor to maintain and communicate status information on shop orders and work centers. The major shop-floor control activities are:

- Assign priority to each shop order.
- Maintain WIP quantity information.
- Convey shop-order status information across the supply chain.
- Provide actual output data for capacity control purposes.
- Provide quantity by location by shop order for WIP inventory and accounting.
- Measure efficiency, utilization, and productivity of employees and machines.

GANTT CHARTS

TOOLS

A Gantt chart, as described in Chapter 7, is a type of bar chart that plots tasks against time. Gantt charts are effective in coordinating scheduled activities and useful for planning and scheduling projects. They can make it easier to sequence tasks according to dependencies, to estimate task durations, to decide on resource allocations, and to determine the critical path. When a job is under way, you can use Gantt charts to monitor its status and to target remedial actions to put it back on schedule, if necessary.

Managing Demand, Planning, and Scheduling Better with Bar Coding and Optical Scanning

A *bar code* (or *barcode*) is an optical machine-readable representation of data. Originally, bar codes (also known as *linear* or *1-D* bar codes) represented data in the widths of the parallel lines and the spacing. Codes now also come in patterns of squares, dots, hexagons, and other geometric patterns within images termed *2-D matrix codes*. (These 2-D codes use symbols other than bars, but we generally consider them bar codes as well.)

> ### DON'T DISREGARD DEPENDENCIES
>
> An essential concept behind project planning and critical path
> analysis is dependencies. As described in Chapter 8, these are
> four types of chronological relationships that exist between tasks:
> - Finish to start—A FS B = B starts only after A has finished
> - Finish to finish—A FF B = B finishes only after A has finished
> - Start to start—A SS B = B starts only after A starts
> - Start to finish—A SF B = B finishes only after A starts
>
> When scheduling tasks, you must consider dependencies.

We're all familiar with bar codes from their use to automate super-market checkout systems. Bar codes are used in many other areas; their various uses are generically labeled as *Automatic Identification and Data Capture (AIDC)*.

In 1998, the Uniform Code Council (now known as GS1 US) and European Article Numbering (now known as G1) jointly announced a new class of symbology to capture more data in less space—*Reduced Space Symbology (RSS)*—and has endorsed a sunrise date of 2010 for adopting RSS standards under the name of *GS1 DataBar*. This new standard of "bar coding on steroids" will combine business intelligence and technology to create rhythm and synchronicity across a closed-loop retail supply chain, thereby supporting a two-way flow of virtually integrated information that would be impossible without it—e.g., enhanced sell-through information (more granularity on size, color, packaging, source of origin, etc.), enhanced information on promotions (discounts, rebates, coupons, ads, displays, etc.), and enhanced information on inventory (aging, shelf life, product care, etc.). By accessing this information, the operations manager can help to create a closed-loop supply chain that is:

- *Agile*—able to react quickly and cost-efficiently.
- *Adaptable*—capable of customizing processes while exploiting inno-vation to reflect marketplace shifts and changes to strategies, tactics, products, and technologies.
- *Aligned*—to support collaborative planning and risk management between customers and suppliers through shared objectives, sce-nario planning, and strategic execution based on real-time trends.

The result is *improved profitability* for supply chain partners through top-line growth based on enhanced customer satisfaction and cost control through improved supply chain management.

Advanced Planning and Scheduling

Advanced Planning and Scheduling (*APS*, also known as *Advanced Manufacturing*) is a manufacturing management process that relies on integrated information to optimally allocate basic materials and production or service capacity to meet anticipated demand. APS is especially well suited to environments where simpler planning methods cannot adequately address complex trade-offs between competing priorities.

Traditional planning and scheduling systems (such as MRP) use a stepwise procedure to allocate material and production capacity. This approach is simple but cumbersome: it does not readily adapt to changes in demand, resource capacity, or material availability. Materials and capacity are planned separately, and many systems do not consider limited material availability or capacity constraints. Thus, this approach often results in plans that cannot be executed.

By linking disparate business areas, APS simultaneously plans and schedules production based on available materials, labor, and plant capacity, thereby creating the platform to operate more effectively. Production and service applications may include sales and operation planning, master planning, capacity requirements planning, material requirements planning, and various inventory management activities.

APS has commonly been applied where one or more of the following conditions are present:

- Make-to-order (as distinct from make-to-stock) manufacturing and service operations.
- Capital and/or resource-intensive production/service processes, where plant and/or service capacity is constrained.
- Multi-product or multi-service environments.
- Products or services that require a large number of components, manufacturing tasks, or activities.
- Frequent and unpredictable schedule changes.

APS software (e.g., i2, Manugistics, SAP, and Oracle Production Planning/Materials Management modules) enables manufacturing and services scheduling and advanced scheduling optimization within these environments.

Scheduling Services

In manufacturing job shops, scheduling now relies heavily on simulation to estimate the flow of work through the system to define bottlenecks and adjust job priorities. Various software packages are available to do this. In services, in contrast, the focus is typically on scheduling employees, using mathematical tools that can be used to set work schedules

SCHEDULE SMART
No matter what the scheduling situation, it's important to avoid *sub-optimization.* A schedule that works well for one part of the organization may create problems for another part of the organization—or, more important, for the customer.

to meet expected customer demand. The scheduling problem in most service organizations revolves around setting weekly, daily, and hourly personnel schedules.

Operations Manager's Checklist for Chapter 8

☑ Understand that demand management, forecasting, planning, and scheduling form an integral part of your responsibilities as operations manager.

☑ Don't rely on guesswork for forecasting, planning, and scheduling. Make sure that the sources of data from across the value chain are credible, that they are integrated, and that the processes are institutionalized through technology. Only then can you use this information to make informed decisions.

☑ Focus on demand management—understanding the demands for each of the company's products or services and satisfying those demands.

☑ Know and apply the principles of the scientific process of forecasting to provide a better basis for making decisions, planning, scheduling, and mitigating risk and uncertainty.

☑ Do aggregate planning properly and it should enable you to mini-mize the effects of near-term scheduling, maximize customer serv-ice, minimize inventory investment, minimize changes in workforce levels, minimize changes in production rates, and maximize use of working capital and fixed assets (plant and equipment).

☑ When scheduling tasks, focus on dependencies—the four types of chronological relationships that exist between tasks.

Sourcing, Procurement, Logistics, and Outsourcing:
Find It, Get It, and Keep It!

Companies now realize that relationships and processes linking them with suppliers and customers hold the keys to competitiveness. They also understand that purchasing capabilities play a pivotal role in such areas as supply base management, global sourcing, and product introduction.

Sourcing and Procurement

In this context, sourcing and purchasing have a significant opportunity to impact supply chain and business performance—but only if managers build quality supplier relationships and enable them to function by aligning sourcing and purchasing with business needs.

Sourcing and procurement typically provide many opportunities to deliver tangible bottom-line benefits. The cornerstones for the sourcing and procurement value equation are:

- Defining business requirements and demand management to ensure that procurement and sourcing efforts are in line with the business drivers.
- Strategic sourcing, to leverage spend across the business.
- Infrastructure enhancement, to ensure that benefits are sustained through channeling spend and continuous improvement.

To effect this change, operations managers will typically engage

COMPETITIVE ADVANTAGE THROUGH PROCUREMENT   SMART

"To view procurement as a cost savings activity only is to sentence one's company to complete failure. Many firms are only now recognizing that by leveraging the expertise of their supply base gains can be made that lead to a sustainable competitive advantage."   MANAGING
—Paul D. Cousins and Robert Spekman, "Strategic Supply and the Management of Inter- and Intra-Organisational Relationships," *Journal of Purchasing and Supply Management*, 9:1, January 2003, pp.19–29

sourcing and purchasing in a distributed way, rather than centralized, to manage sourcing categories (e.g., direct materials, such as steel or plastic, or indirect materials, such as office supplies or travel). In this manner, the sourcing and procurement professionals, often serving as internal business consultants or coordinators, will work across the organization to understand the business requirements while aligning those requirements with what is available in the supply market. To do that, they will:

- Profile categories to document future business requirements.
- Populate total-cost-of-ownership models to support decision-making processes.
- Develop sourcing strategies, including using alternative suppliers, renegotiating with current suppliers, changing specifications, refining processes, and enforcing compliance with specifications.
- Identify target parts and materials within categories suitable for transitioning to alternative suppliers.
- Evaluate suppliers (where appropriate with a request for information, a request for proposal, or a reverse auction).
- Support negotiations with suppliers, including supporting pricing and definition of service-level agreements.
- Support transition planning.
- Develop and improve supplier relationship management opportunities, processes, roles, and responsibilities.

A Vision for Sourcing and Procurement

The role of sourcing and procurement is threefold, as shown in Exhibit 9-1: find the money, get the money, and keep the money.

First, to find the money, the operations manager must understand where the company spends its money with third parties and prioritize the

KEY TERMS

Request for Proposal (RFP) Invitation to suppliers to submit a proposal to provide a specific product or service, through a bidding process that includes more than just price.

Request for Information (RFI) Invitation to suppliers to provide information that will support a decision as to what step to take next in the sourcing process (i.e., determining at a high level which suppliers to engage more closely).

Request for Quote (RFQ) Invitation to suppliers to bid on specific products or services, typically including very detailed specifications and structured guidelines that allow suppliers to bid on products or services that are more similar than not. RFQs typically elicit less flexible responses than RFPs and are often considered to be focused primarily on pricing, given the specificity of the quotation process.

RFx (request for anything) The acronym to use when you get tired of distinguishing among RFP, RFI, and RFQ, or when your supplier communication contains elements of multiple genres.

Reverse auction Type of auction used in industrial business-to-business procurement to obtain a well-specified product or service at the lowest price. A buyer advertises a need for a product or service and sellers compete for the right to supply what's needed by bidding the amount they would charge to do so. Generally, the lowest bidder will win the job. Also known as *procurement auction, e-auction, sourcing event, e-sourcing,* or *eRA.*

opportunities based on predetermined criteria such as size of spend, perceived lack of market competitiveness, or supply issues with current suppliers. To do this, you can:

- Optimize consumption (demand management).
- Consolidate spend (leverage suppliers).
- Optimize specifications (define requirements).

Next, to get the money (or savings), the operations manager must work with key stakeholders across the organization and source the external party spend, typically using the strategic sourcing process and category management techniques (described later in this chapter), and ensure that a process is put into place (perhaps by transitioning to a new supplier or contracting at a lower cost).

- Restructure relationships.
- Increase competition.
- Restructure and rationalize the supply base.

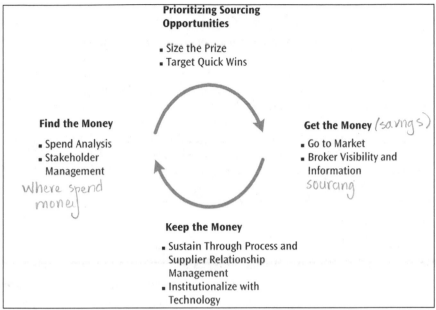

Prioritizing Sourcing
Opportunities

- Size the Prize
- Target Quick Wins

Find the Money

- Spend Analysis
- Stakeholder
  Management

Where spend money.

Get the Money *(savings)*

- Go to Market
- Broker Visibility and
  Information

sourcing

Keep the Money

- Sustain Through Process and
  Supplier Relationship
  Management
- Institutionalize with
  Technology

Exhibit 9-1. Find the money, get the money, keep the money

Finally, to keep the money, the organization institutionalizes processes and technologies that ensure compliance and a continual stream of value to the organization and to the extended enterprise.

- Optimize the organizational infrastructure.
- Institutionalize the sourcing and contract management processes.
- Reduce lifecycle/total cost of ownership.
- Optimize the sourcing technology infrastructure.

Strategic Sourcing Process

A typical sourcing and procurement approach consists of multiple phases. Exhibit 9-2 shows an example of a strategic sourcing process (SSP) consisting of seven phases:

- Determine what's required.
- Develop a sourcing strategy.
- Assess suppliers.
- Evaluate suppliers.
- Negotiate.
- Finalize tenets of agreement, develop scorecards for the supplier, review the process.

SMART

MANAGING

SOURCING SMART

When assessing potential suppliers, develop a sourcing strategy to best address the specific business requirements. While getting proposals, make sure the RFP clearly articulates your business strategy, requirements, and objectives, and identifies all services that will be subject to renegotiation through a competitive process. The RFP should contain administrative rules, technical requirements, account support requirements, key contract terms, services to be bid, and a clearly defined format for submitting prices. This RFP process may take time, so it's typically adopted only when the benefits of greater due diligence outweigh the time involved.

- Manage the supplier.

Note that the SSP process, like the operations management principles advocated throughout this book, takes a life-cycle perspective and includes both the transition to new suppliers and, more important, the ongoing management of suppliers. You only get one chance to make a first impression—and that's never truer than when you meet your next supplier. A structured sourcing process can help you be demanding but fair in your relationships with suppliers, which makes your supply chain more efficient and effective.

In this SSP approach, when making a preliminary qualitative evaluation of a firm's strategic position with regard to its supply base, we use the five forces framework developed by Michael Porter in 1979. This model helps us analyze industries and develop business strategies and industry analyses. The five forces determine the competitive intensity and therefore attractiveness of a market. Three forces come from "horizontal" competition—threat of substitute products, threat of established rivals,

SMART

MANAGING

EVALUATING PROPOSALS

Evaluate proposals from potential suppliers by doing both a financial analysis/rate comparison and a qualitative analysis (scoring) of the proposals with respect to technical and business requirements. Negotiations with suppliers may include multiple rounds of face-to-face meetings during which you should request any clarification of the proposals you need and negotiate lower prices and favorable business terms and conditions, including appropriate protections and business flexibility.

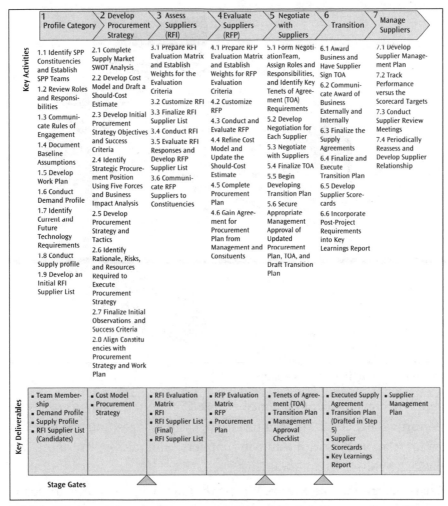

1 Profile Category	2 Develop Procurement Strategy	3 Assess Suppliers (RFI)	4 Evaluate Suppliers (RFP)	5 Negotiate with Suppliers	6 Transition	7 Manage Suppliers
Key Activities						
1.1 Identify SPP Constituencies and Establish SPP Teams	2.1 Complete Supply Market SWOT Analysis	3.1 Prepare RFI Evaluation Matrix and Establish Weights for the Evaluation Criteria	4.1 Prepare RFP Evaluation Matrix and Establish Weights for RFP Evaluation Criteria	5.1 Form Negoti-ationTeam, Assign Roles and Responsibilities, and Identify Key Tenets of Agree-ment (TOA) Requirements	6.1 Award Business and Have Supplier Sign TOA	7.1 Develop Supplier Manage-ment Plan
1.2 Review Roles and Responsi-bilities	2.2 Develop Cost Model and Draft a Should-Cost Estimate	3.2 Customize RFI	4.2 Customize RFP		6.2 Communi-cate Award of Business Externally and Internally	7.2 Track Performance versus the Scorecard Targets
1.3 Communi-cate Rules of Engagement	2.3 Develop Initial Procurement Strategy Objectives and Success Criteria	3.3 Finalize RFI Supplier List	4.3 Conduct and Evaluate RFP	5.2 Develop Negotiation for Each Supplier	6.3 Finalize the Supply Agreements	7.3 Conduct Supplier Review Meetings
1.4 Document Baseline Assumptions	2.4 Identify Strategic Procure-ment Position Using Five Forces and Business Impact Analysis	3.4 Conduct RFI	4.4 Refine Cost Model and Update the Should-Cost Estimate	5.3 Negotiate with Suppliers	6.4 Finalize and Execute Transition Plan	7.4 Periodically Reassess and Develop Supplier Relationship
1.5 Develop Work Plan		3.5 Evaluate RFI Responses and Develop RFP Supplier List	4.5 Complete Procurement Plan	5.4 Finalize TOA	6.5 Develop Supplier Score-cards	
1.6 Conduct Demand Profile	2.5 Develop Procurement Strategy and Tactics	3.6 Communi-cate RFP Suppliers to Constituencies	4.6 Gain Agree-ment for Procurement Plan from Management and Consituents	5.5 Begin Developing Transition Plan	6.6 Incorporate Post-Project Requirements into Key Learnings Report	
1.7 Identify Current and Future Technology Requirements	2.6 Identify Rationale, Risks, and Resources Required to Execute Procurement Strategy			5.6 Secure Appropriate Management Approval of Updated Procurement Plan, TOA, and Draft Transition Plan		
1.8 Conduct Supply profile	2.7 Finalize Initial Observations and Success Criteria					
1.9 Develop an Initial RFI Supplier List	2.0 Align Constitu encies with Procurement Strategy and Work Plan					
Key Deliverables						
• Team Member-ship • Demand Profile • Supply Profile • RFI Supplier List (Candidates)	• Cost Model • Procurement Strategy	• RFI Evaluation Matrix • RFI • RFI Supplier List (Final) • RFI Supplier List	• RFP Evaluation Matrix • RFP • Procurement Plan	• Tenets of Agree-ment (TOA) • Transition Plan • Management Approval Checklist	• Executed Supply Agreement • Transition Plan (Drafted in Step 5) • Supplier Scorecards • Key Learnings Report	• Supplier Management Plan

Stage Gates

Exhibit 9-2. Strategic sourcing process. Copyright © Archstone Consulting. Used with permission. All rights reserved.

and threat of new entrants—and two forces come from "vertical" compe-tition—bargaining power of suppliers and bargaining power of cus-tomers.

Dual Sourcing. If you want to reduce your number of suppliers but are wary of using only one source or even two, consider dual sourcing using the "70-30" approach. This means giving 70 percent of the volume to one supplier and 30 percent to another. Your company can obtain *economies of scale* from the major supplier, while the presence of the secondary

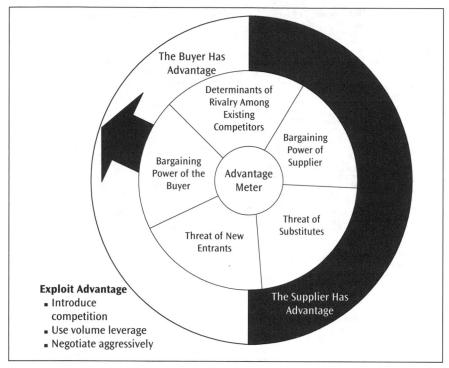

Exhibit 9-3. The five forces analysis

supplier provides competition, because if the major supplier fails to perform as expected, you can reverse the percentages. You can develop better relationships with your two suppliers, with the security of the two basic drivers—risk and reward.

Single Source vs. Sole Source. When you have a *single source*, it means you've chosen one supplier based on your sourcing strategy. When you have a *sole source*, it means you really didn't have any choice—only one supplier could adequately meet your business requirements.

Single sources require the special care and handling described in Chapter 6 for collaborative relationships. Sole sources are often a significant point of contention requiring more than their fair share of management attention. You should avoid sole sources by working to develop substitute products and/or services, but if you must have them you will need to adopt collaborative, information-based management across the board to ensure a mutually beneficial relationship.

Supplier Relationship Management

An integrated supply chain links customers and suppliers through a complex array of relationships. Managing upstream supplier relationships is a core competency of sourcing that should not be understated. Managing these relationships is challenging, largely because no two are the same. Each has at least two characteristics, stemming from the nature of the item or service, its supply market characteristics, and the buyer-supplier power differential, not to mention the personalities of the individuals it involves.

Partnerships, though widely touted as the bedrock of sourcing and purchasing, are only one of many types of relationships. Supplier relationships range from traditional, adversarial, and opportunistic to open and trust-based partnerships.

Even when partnerships are appropriate, they are sometimes poorly set up as cozy and friendly arrangements. Partnerships should be performance-based and market-driven, subject to termination if either party fails to deliver on its commitments. Risk, an inherent element of business, needs to be present in these relationships if mutual business goals are to be reached.

Open-book costing provides an example of a potentially challenging supplier management technique. While often a typical element of a partnership agreement, open-book methods require a degree of trust to implement and should be adopted only under certain conditions. Generally, these types of arrangements provide additional insight into supplier intent over time and offer a basis for continuous improvement and joint cost reduction. The fundamental premise is that moving beyond margin leads to a shared cost base that the supplier and customer can work together to reduce. The cost model makes cost drivers visible, allowing both customer and supplier to strive to better manage the cost drivers with a shared sense of urgency defined by market conditions.

Supply base reduction, though frequently misrepresented as a measure of purchasing performance, simply enables improvement of purchasing performance and particularly relationship management. Purchasing and the organization as a whole should be as concerned with managing a smaller supplier base in the right way as with meeting an arbitrary supplier reduction goal. Once the supply base is reduced, the real work of deriving value begins—in areas such as standardization and rationalization of specifications, shortening product introduction lead times, improving quality and service, and enhancing product functionality. Only within these close relationships can hackneyed phrases such as *value alignment, harmonization of interest, competence compatibility,* and *technology integration* really begin to mean something.

Dynamic Pricing. Pricing signals should be part of the procurement process in a collaborative supply network. Price is a well understood and unambiguous measure to use with electronic negotiations. Airlines and hotels are frequently masters of dynamic pricing and have good market knowledge about the dynamic state of their assets and the market, but use of the Internet and Web sites such as Orbitz and Travelocity has somewhat evened the score.

Dr. Simon Dunstall, leader of Adaptive Supply Networks for the Commonwealth Scientific and Industrial Research Organisation (Australia), suggests that linear value supply chains will move toward adaptive networks in which partners collaboratively adapt to the challenges in their shared environment ("E-Sourcing, Procurement and the Adaptive Supply Network," October 2004). He argues that procurement, sourcing, and supply chain management are "inextricably linked." Procurement through electronic means can be cost-effective and reliable, but those means must be used thoughtfully and deliberately. "Procurement processes are a major channel for demand signals and therefore should allow for rich and insightful information exchange," according to Dunstall. "In the future, supply networks will develop strong competitive advantages in efficiency and adaptability by integrating procurement and activity coordination processes."

Prompt Pay Discounts. Prompt pay discounts are a timely tool for procurement organizations, especially given the current and somewhat rare combination of historically low interest rates after multiple federal rate cuts and tight credit markets exacerbated by the mortgage crisis and the $700 billion financial bailout. The result is an environment in which prompt pay discounts provide companies an attractive alternative to otherwise low investment returns and provide suppliers necessary working capital. A company can typically generate an *additional million dollars in profit for every $100 million spent* under prompt payment discount terms. To realize these benefits, organizations must establish both prompt pay discount terms and processes to promote accelerated payment.

Organizational Alignment. Supplier relationships must deliver tangible business benefits while supporting key business processes. The intersection of sourcing and procurement with the overall business process poses a major challenge for most organizations. Sourcing deals mainly with suppliers; the business and most other functions interface with customers. The mark of effective sourcing is its ability to translate its customer and product requirements into purchasing and supplier requirements—and do so effectively and efficiently.

Even when purchasing is generating cost reductions across the entire supply base, there could be products that are highly exposed to market price erosion and are not getting the full benefit from purchasing. This problem may arise from the traditional challenge for purchasing to buy uniformly for less rather than selectively buying to meet market-defined targets.

Sourcing organizations often lack the skills, behaviors, and positioning in the wider business required to be fully effective. Also, sourcing and purchasing are still frequently treated as orphans within the organization, reporting to some other board-level function which may present inherent biases in expectations and focus. Reporting to operations will generally yield improvements in supplier quality and delivery with hard price negotiated savings. Reporting to finance emphasizes savings and working capital reductions. Reporting to product engineering provides resources focused on product introduction milestones and entry cost targets. It is easy to see that sourcing and purchasing need balanced priorities. Furthermore, it is clear that the breadth and importance of issues addressed by purchasing merit board-level representation.

Finally, measures of purchasing effectiveness have only recently begun to reflect a more balanced scorecard. Purchasing has been effective in defining measures for its suppliers in terms of cost, quality, and delivery. However, the purchasing scorecard is only now evolving to reflect the needs and expectations of its internal customers in areas such as total acquisition cost reduction, product introduction, innovation contribution, supplier development results, and others. Ultimately, it is these measures that will help to change the behavior of the purchasing professional and in turn the supplier.

Supplier Relationship Management Process

Requirements for purchased product/service are typically defined and documented by sourcing in conjunction with the users and funding is secured. Procurement is engaged to provide support and guidance in evaluating suppliers and facilitating the RFP process using the RFP template. Supplier selection will be performed in conjunction with the asset owner and according to the standard procurement process. Performance targets will be established and agreed to in the contract. Where supplier selection activities are performed, the following are some criteria for supplier selection that may be considered:

- Availability (e.g., global presence)
- Ability to supply product/service (e.g., meet requirements)
- Quality (e.g., ISO 9000 Certification)
- Competitive pricing
- Financial stability
- Product/features lifecycle

While the above will be considered, deciding factors will vary depending on group, product, or service requirements. Sourcing and purchasing activities, including contract negotiations and changes or addendums to contracts, will typically be performed by procurement, program managers, business managers, technical leads, and legal when appropriate. Contracts may include mutual non-disclosure agreements (MNDA), non-disclosure agreements (NDA), standard terms and conditions, and/or statements of work. Whenever possible, use a standardized set of contractual terms and conditions. The following are to be considered and acted upon in support of ongoing supplier management:

- Scope
- Transition from prior suppliers
- Contact names/escalation process
- Training

- Business resumption (recoverability)
- Change management
- Monitoring and evaluation

Where verification of purchased product/service occurs, the following activities are typically performed:

- Invoices, statements of work, and contracts or service level agreements (SLAs) are reviewed for accuracy (in case of products, acceptance review records may replace SLAs).
- Records (e.g., issues log, inaccurate invoices, service center tickets, etc.) of discrepancies are retained.

When discrepancies are noted, notifications of the discrepancies are submitted to individuals with budgetary responsibility or IT finance. Issues can be escalated to IT asset management if necessary. If action is taken, a record of the action (e.g., issues log, corrected invoices, etc.) will be kept in accordance with standard accounts payable procedures.

SUPPLIER METRICS
To avoid problems with suppliers, consider using the following metrics in negotiating new service contracts or renegotiating current contracts or addenda:
- Supplier report card results
- General feedback from internal staff
- Invoice accuracy rates
- Problem statistics from service center
- Service-level agreement reports produced by supplier
- Pricing
- Financial stability reviews
- Industry-wide best practices reviews (i.e., Meta, Gartner, etc.)

E-Markets: Extending the Sourcing and Procurement Benefits

When an organization has focused on strategic sourcing, developed its procurement processes, and institutionalized a culture that enables strategic procurement operations, other improvement options remain. Often, however, the lack of integrated systems in its supply chain limits its capabilities in procurement and performance management; improvement will predominantly result from enabling procurement and sourcing technologically, with the focus on refining the process and delivering a business system that will facilitate supply chain integration for its indirect and direct spend.

E-markets—markets of buyers and sellers coming together via the Internet—offer the opportunity to extend an organization's procurement transformation and increase savings. The value proposition of e-markets includes process and performance benefits that help an organization transform its procurement system. E-markets offer inherently more efficient markets by providing online market-making mechanisms to match buyers and suppliers (e.g., e-catalogues, auctions, interactive buying processes, transaction routing, etc.). They also offer access to a broader range of suppliers and buyers and improved information access, while reducing the risk of single-sourcing and maintaining volume benefits.

Outsourcing

Service delivery options are narrowing for many companies. Companies have exhausted various cost reduction, quality, and process improvement tools of the 1980s and 1990s, and the ingrained year-over-year performance requirements of the capital markets are driving companies to pursue continuous improvement. Many companies are searching for the best model to enable them to reduce costs, improve service levels, and identify new channels for growth. Decisions based on detailed strategic analysis are key to adopting the appropriate service delivery model for each organization, which includes outsourcing traditional functions and operations.

This is not a binary decision. Moving forward, companies are taking a portfolio approach, using various service delivery options to realize and sustain improvements. Outsourcing operations is a viable option for many.

Businesses outsource for a wide range of reasons, such as increasing shareholder value, reducing costs, transforming the business, improving operations, overcoming the lack of internal capabilities, keeping up with competitors, gaining competitive advantage, increasing sales, improving customer service, reducing inventory, increasing inventory velocity and turns, mitigating capital investment, improving cash flow, and turning fixed costs into variable costs. If the operations manager integrates it correctly as part of an overall operations strategy, outsourcing can be used to create a virtual corporation as a critical part of the extended enterprise.

C-Suite Perspective on Outsourcing and Offshoring

Outsourcing and offshoring are options, but not panaceas. Management, funding, investment plans, and strategy are as important as economics. Most or even all transactions can go, but chief financial officers (CFOs) remain very cautious about the general ledger, due to compliance and governance issues.

The key triggers are budget pressures, limits on technology investments, corporate restructuring, and the opportunity to "monetize" an asset through shared services. The functions most frequently offshored are information technology and finance/accounting.

It's not surprising that IT is the function most often offshored. Within business processes, it appears that finance and call centers are usually the first processes to be offshored. The finance/accounting function more often than not uses a captive model. (*Captive outsourcing* is when a company builds and operates a center in a low-cost country, rather than outsourcing to a third-party service provider when offshoring.) Call center and IT offshoring predominantly use outsourcing. Offshoring of other functions—such as HR, procurement, and engineering services—is distributed fairly evenly between the two models.

Cost reduction and competitive pressures are the strongest drivers of offshoring; functional redundancy is often less of a driver. Offshoring call center operations and IT generally saves the most money: nearly 50 percent of call center operations achieve over 40 percent savings. Improving service levels and improving processes, however, are significant drivers—which is interesting, given that they are also often the greatest risks. Other reasons cited for outsourcing operations are changing rules, including access to markets and qualified personnel, and industry practices.

> **Captive offshoring** Situation in which a company sets up a facility in another country to handle IT, business processes, back-office data processing, call center operations, or other activities. Also known as *offshore insourcing* and *offshore in-house sourcing*.
>
> **KEY TERM**

A study of offshoring by Archstone Consulting ("Does Offshoring Still Make Sense?" *Supply Chain Management Review,* January/February 2009) reported that U.S. companies are contemplating re-establishing manufacturing domestically, as costs are rising and companies are encountering strategic challenges. Also, as the report concludes, "Manufacturing or sourcing at home or closer to home . . . may also allow something more important—enabling your company to differentiate itself by tailoring products, offerings, and services to the multiple customer segments and channels you serve," a move "likely to increase revenue while decreasing cost—a powerful competitive advantage."

OUTSOURCING LESSONS LEARNED

- Regardless of experience in a given marketplace, a local partner proves invaluable.
- Gaining acceptance by clients or customers is not as easy as you may think.
- Testing must include hands-on (domestic) work shadowing, migration readiness testing, and operational readiness testing.
- Data protection and security issues require careful attention; most offshore locations do not have "safe harbor" status.
- Processes and current performance should be diligently captured and documented.
- Implementation activities often take longer in most offshore locations.
- The most successful programs consider an offshore location as simply another node on their network for global service delivery.

Logistics and Distribution

According to the Council of Supply Chain Management Professionals (CSCMP), logistics and distribution includes freight transportation, warehousing, material handling, protective packaging, inventory control, plant and warehouse site selection, order processing, marketing forecasting, and customer service. Logistics costs typically constitute 5 percent to 15 percent of the cost of goods sold. Logistics is critical to operational success. Every sourcing decision has a logistical implication, so logistics and sourcing are intimately connected. Together they form the backbone of the supply chain.

Logistics encompasses the management functions that support the complete cycle of the flows of materials, products, and information—from the purchase and internal control of production materials to the planning and control of work-in-process and to the sale, shipping, and distribution of finished products.

The focus on lean operations places a greater emphasis on delivery accuracy and reliability, with delivery windows as short as 30 minutes. Logistics now takes a more

> **Logistics management**
> "That part of supply chain management that plans, implements, and controls **KEY TERM** the efficient, effective forward and reverse flow and storage of goods, services and related information between the point of origin and the point of consumption in order to meet customers' requirements."
>
> —Council of Supply Chain Management Professionals

proactive role in getting goods from point A to point B, storing them, and even adding value along the way by performing ancillary tasks that might otherwise have been done further upstream. Logistics now incorporates comprehensive information management that reduces transportation risks and allows adding value for the customers by letting them know exactly where their goods are and when deliveries will be made (e.g., advanced shipping notices).

Modes of Transportation: Advantages and Limitations

According to *Operations Management for Competitive Advantage*, by Richard B. Chase, F. Robert Jacobs, and Nicholas J. Aquilano (10th edition, McGraw-Hill, 2004), the advantages and limitations of the primary modes of transportation include:

- *Highway (trucking)*—flexibility because items can be delivered to almost any location in a continent, good transit times, and rates usually reasonable for small quantities and over short distances.
- *Rail*—low cost, but transit times long and possibly subject to variability.
- *Water*—very high capacity and very low cost, but transit times very slow and large areas of the world not directly accessible to water carriers.
- *Pipeline*—highly specialized (limited to liquids, gases, or solids in slurry form), no packaging needed, low costs per mile, but very high initial cost to build the pipeline.
- *Air*—fast but most expensive.

Distribution and Logistics Strategy. The operations manager must ensure that he or she develops or works with partners who develop comprehensive distribution and logistics strategies aligned with company strategies, delivering capabilities to manage service levels, assets, partners (3PL/4PL), and technologies. These activities will necessarily include network design and optimization across his or her logistics and distribution of assets to achieve an optimal balance between sales and customer service requirements and manufacturing and supply chain costs. Performance-based logistics includes defining and developing leading-edge strategies and supply chain capabilities to support the provision of performance-based customer and product after-market support.

The operations manager is also responsible for transportation management, including strategy (e.g., identifying business partners and modes), operations (e.g., managing day-to-day transportation activities), and administration (e.g., monitoring, analyzing, and improving operations). A new area of emphasis for operations managers consists of developing a coherent radio-frequency identification (RFID) strategy to achieve business objectives and satisfy customer requirements while maintaining a proper balance between current investments and evolving technologies.

SMART MANAGING

THREES AND FOURS

3PLs (third-party logistics providers from outside your company) attempt to manage the key links in your supply chain by mainly focusing on primary transport, warehousing, and secondary distribution. They will typically own a good percentage of the fixed assets and manage a variety of other subcontractors. Although the emphasis is on value-added services (usually with sophisticated IT capabilities), they often have geographical boundaries and evolved into this role based on a specialized skill set of core businesses such as forwarding, trucking, or warehousing. Creating a 3PL presented a way for a commodity-service logistics provider to move into higher margin, bundled services.

4PLs (fourth-party logistics providers) operate as true business process outsourcers (BPOs) and combine process and technology to integrate and manage a portfolio of logistics services across the supply chain. As the lead logistics provider, they bring value and a reengineered approach to your needs by extending the range of services offered to address all facets of the supply chain: procurement, demand forecasting, and inventory management. A 4PL is neutral (often a consultant) and will manage the logistics process, regardless of what carriers, forwarders, or warehouses are used. The 4PL can and will even manage 3PLs that you use.

Transportation strategy typically includes decisions about freight terms, mode strategy, carrier negotiations, outsourcing, network design, vendor relationship management, quality management, transportation organization, and information technology. *Transportation operations decisions* entail managing day-to-day activities such as mode and carrier selection, shipment planning and scheduling, routing and dispatch, inbound transportation, private fleet, fleet operations and maintenance, provider communication, and pipeline visibility/event management. Finally, *transportation administration* addresses monitoring, analyzing, and improving service reporting and measurement, rate management, freight payment, claims management (e.g., OS&D—over, short, and damaged), and overall budgeting and reporting of transportation costs.

Improving transportation management can increase profitability, improve asset utilization, reduce capital commitments, and enhance service commitments. Assessing, analyzing, and incorporating logistics and distribution best practices enable world-class companies to gain these benefits, but best practices are only a tool and not a "silver bullet"

Mode Shifting	Strategic Freight Procurement	Inbound Strategies	Private Fleet Management
▪ Air to Ground ▪ LTL to TL Substance ▪ Forces to LTL ▪ TL to Intermode ▪ LTL to Pool ▪ Rail to Truck Pool ▪ Pool by Air ▪ Truck/Intermodal to Carload	▪ Core Carrier Programs ▪ Custom LTL Contracts ▪ FAK Rates ▪ Nose Load Tariffs ▪ Pul Rates, LTL Mileage, Loading Allowances ▪ Service Guarantees ▪ Standardization and Simplification ▪ Elimination of Accessories ▪ Import/Export Compliance	▪ Inbound Prepaid to Collect Conversion ▪ Inbound Consolidation ▪ Vendor Clusters ▪ Routing Guides ▪ Vendor Compliance Programs ▪ Mode Shifting ▪ DC Bypass ▪ Merge in Transit	▪ Increased Asset Utilization ▪ Reduced Maintenance Expense ▪ Improved Procurement Practices ▪ Customer Service Enhancements ▪ OBC Technology ▪ Improved Fuel Management
Typical Savings	**Typical Savings**	**Typical Savings**	**Typical Savings**
▪ Chemical Mfr 35% ▪ Mass Merchant 25% ▪ Utility Co. 74%	▪ LTL 25% ▪ TL 6% ▪ Rail 10% ▪ Parcel 25% ▪ Private Fleet 15%	▪ Utility Co. 15% ▪ Retailer 18% ▪ Pharmaceutical 12% ▪ Paper Co. 25% ▪ Computer Mfg 30%	▪ Retailer 18% ▪ Energy Co. 22% ▪ Chemical Mfg 12% ▪ Aggregate Co. 18% ▪ Telecom 19%

LTL = Less-than-truckload carrier   TL = Truckload carrier   FAK = Freight-all-kinds   DC = Distribution center
OBC = On-board-computer

Exhibit 9-4. Examples of opportunities for improving transportation management. Copyright © Archstone Consulting. Used with permission. All rights reserved.

solution; they demand stringent organizational requirements and commitments. In the final analysis, information technology is increasingly becoming crucial in optimizing transportation management processes. The Internet is progressively important to companies, providing the infrastructure to manage transportation strategies, operations, and administration.

Operations Manager's Checklist for Chapter 9

☑ Of all the facets of operations, perhaps sourcing, procurement, logistics, and outsourcing have redefined the landscape of operations the most. They've transformed a traditionally transaction-based activity into fundamental network competencies that contribute to the operations strategy across the supply chain.

☑ Sourcing and purchasing have a significant opportunity to impact supply chain and business performance—but only if managers build quality supplier relationships and enable them to function by aligning sourcing and purchasing with business needs.

☑ The ability to link suppliers, logistics and distribution providers, and outsourced partners is central to supply chain success, because the relationships and processes linking them with suppliers and customers are the key to competitiveness.

☑ Sourcing and procurement are invaluable, and it's vitally important for people in those functions to understand business requirements and facilitate internal efforts to incorporate supply chain partners into the company's competitive advantage.

☑ When you adopt outsourcing correctly as part of an overall operations strategy, it can be used to create a virtual corporation as a critical part of the extended enterprise.

☑ Logistics is critical to operational success. Every sourcing decision has a logistical implication, so logistics and sourcing are intimately connected, forming together an essential part of the connections of the supply chain.

Inventory Management:
The Good, the Bad, and the Ugly

nventory is defined, in simple terms, as a quantity of goods or materials on hand. This is inventory as *physical items*. *Inventory* can also be described as a record of goods or materials on hand. This is inventory as a *representation* of physical items.

This is the sense of "inventory" we mean when we say, "I'm going to take inventory"—unless we're expressing an intent to pilfer. To avoid embarrassing assumptions, we can say the same thing by using "inventory" as a verb— the process of taking an inventory.

> **Inventory** Quantity of goods or materials on hand or record of goods or materials on hand.
> **KEY TERM**

Types of Inventory

Five types of physical items can be considered as inventory:

- *Direct materials*—raw materials and components to be used subsequently as part of finished products.
- *Work-in-process (WIP)*—unfinished goods in production.
- *Finished goods*—products or components ready for sale (including returned goods that are salable).
- *Maintenance, repair, and operations (MRO)*—replacement parts, supplies, etc.
- *Indirect materials*—supplies used in operations.

185

Generally, when we talk about managing inventory, we're referring to raw materials, WIP, and finished goods.

What Does "Inventory" Really Mean?

Another definition of *inventory* is the value of the goods or materials on hand. Inventory actually has two values—actual and potential. This is why *inventory turnover* (how often inventory turns over per year) is so important: idle inventory has less value than inventory put to work to generate revenue, either in operations or in the marketplace.

That's the up side of inventory—it makes money. There's also a down side—money invested in inventory can be substantial, and operations managers also incur other costs when keeping inventory, as we'll discuss shortly. So you see, inventory can be good, bad, or really ugly.

Reasons for Holding Inventory

If organizations could apply the principles of lean thinking (Chapter 5) perfectly, they might be able to operate with zero inventory of materials and finished goods. And some companies endeavor to do so—by having a short manufacturing (or assembly) cycle time. Dell attempts to sell many of their computers before they ever take the inventory. However, in the real world, organizations proactively use inventories for the following reasons:

- To minimize the risk of not having sufficient products to meet sudden increases in demand—assurance of supply.
- To prepare for anticipated increases in demand in response to marketing promotions, price reductions, and seasonal buying.
- To minimize the risk of running short on materials due to supplier delays, shortages, and defects.
- To support strategic operations planning.
- To maintain stable levels of operations.
- To take advantage of prices before an announced or anticipated increase.
- To take advantage of quantity discounts from suppliers.
- To reduce administrative costs by ordering less frequently and in larger quantities (economies of scale).

- To manage a sudden decrease in demand for products.
- To reduce transport costs by shipping full loads.
- To buy larger quantities of materials items that are difficult to find or materials that are going out of production.

Reasons for Minimizing Inventory

Numerous reasons also justify keeping inventory levels as low as possible:

- To minimize the risk of obsolescence.
- To make it easier to control inventory.
- To reduce shrinkage—losses due to breakage, handling damages, pilferage, and deterioration.
- To make it easier to detect problems with inventory security and/or production inefficiencies.
- To reduce costs of labor spent accessing or storing, transporting, and keeping records.
- To minimize storage costs—company warehouses, other warehouses, insurance, and taxes.
- To reduce the cost of lost opportunities due to capital investment in inventory.

Inventory Management

For an operations manager, *inventory management* can be defined as the process of ensuring a continuous, sufficient supply of the materials, goods, and/or supplies necessary for optimal operations while minimizing the costs.

Objectives and Strategies

Inventory management requires balancing the conflicting objectives and strategies of functions within the organization. For example:

> **Inventory management**
> Process of ensuring a continuous, sufficient supply of the materials, goods, and/or supplies necessary for optimal operations while minimizing the costs.
>
> **KEY TERM**

- Sales wants an extensive inventory of goods in order to have available any item in any quantity to meet customer demand.

- Purchasing wants to be able to purchase goods whenever and in whatever quantities enable it to purchase at the lowest prices.
- Finance wants inventory to be minimal in order to minimize the investment of capital and minimize the effect of inventory on cash flow.
- Production wants an extensive inventory of materials, parts, and supplies in order to have enough to ensure operation as planned and scheduled.

Inventory management is not just about managing inventory, but also about managing the dynamics of conflicting objectives and strategies that affect inventory. As an operations manager, you must make this your mantra:

- Maximize customer service.
- Maximize the efficiency of purchasing and production.
- Minimize investment in inventory.
- Maximize profit.

Inventory System

Many computer programs can be used to manage inventory. But to use them effectively, you must know the essentials of inventory management. You must also have a good, comprehensive *inventory system*—a set of rules and procedures that you develop that encompass demand management, forecasting, planning, scheduling, sourcing, calculating inventory value and costs, reducing inventory, monitoring and maintaining inventory, keeping track of inventory, protecting inventory, measuring the use of inventory, and logistics.

Chapter 8 covered demand management, forecasting, aggregate planning, and scheduling. Chapter 9 addressed sourcing and logistics. This chapter will emphasize the other areas of inventory management.

Calculating Inventory Value and Costs

Although inventories consist of hundreds and thousands of items—and also because of that fact—operations managers use the *average aggregate inventory value*. That's the total value of all items in inventory. To find this value:

- Calculate the average number of units of each item by add the number in the beginning inventory and the number in the ending inventory and dividing that sum by two.
- Calculate the value of each item in inventory by multiplying the average number of units of that item by the value per item.
- Total the average values of all items.

Valuation and Costing

Inventory valuation represents inventories of materials, parts, supplies, of work-in-process, and of finished goods as dollars-and-cents amounts. The ultimate purpose of inventory valuation is to determine profit for the accounting period and the financial position of the company.

The balance sheet shows the financial position of the company as of a specific date. Among the assets it lists the ending (current) inventory. We need inventory valuation for this purpose and to provide the information used to calculate financial ratios that are used in assessing the financial health of the company.

The statement of income and expenses includes an item, the *cost of goods sold* (COGS), that's a calculation of the direct costs attributable to producing the goods sold by a company. This amount includes the costs of materials and direct labor used in producing the goods, but not the costs of sales and distribution. (Manufacturing companies calculate COGS. Retailers generally report the cost of purchased goods. Companies that provide services will generally report the cost of services.)

We need inventory valuation to calculate COGS. We start with the beginning inventory for the period, add the total amount of purchases made during the period, and subtract the ending inventory.

Four common methods can value inventory:

- average cost/weighted average
- first in, first out (FIFO)
- last in, first out (LIFO)
- specific cost/actual cost/specific identification

Average Cost Method (Weighted Average Method). The *Average Cost method* adds the value of all goods available for sale in the beginning inventory and the costs of purchases made during the period (the costs of purchases should include freight in and delivery charges to get the materials or goods purchased) and divides this total cost of goods available for sale by the total units available for sale to determine the average unit cost. The value of the ending inventory and the cost of goods sold are calculated based on this average unit cost. This method provides probably the most accurate measure of inventory valuation and treats all inventory in the same way thereby leveling out price fluctuations.

First In, First Out (FIFO) Method. The *FIFO method* of inventory valuation values inventory as if the first goods to be sold (cost of sales) were the first goods that were actually purchased or consumed (cost of production), regardless of the actual timing. The ending inventory consists of the goods that were added to inventory most recently. This method reflects the most recent cost of the inventory on the balance sheet, and the cost of goods sold reflects the earliest cost of purchases. The FIFO method most closely ties to actual physical flow of goods in inventory.

Last In, First Out (LIFO) Method. The *LIFO method* values inventory as if the first goods to be sold (cost of sales) were the last goods that were purchased or consumed (cost of production), regardless of the actual timing. The ending inventory consists of the goods that were added to inventory earliest. This method reflects the earliest cost of the inventory on the balance sheet, and the cost of goods sold reflects the most recent prices. The LIFO method best matches current costs with current revenues.

Specific Cost Method (Actual Cost Method, Specific Identification Method). The *Specific Cost method* requires tracking the actual cost of each individual unit of merchandise from beginning to end. This tracking obviously requires keeping comprehensive, detailed re-cords. It's generally possible only with very sophisticated computer systems and worth it only for expensive items.

PRINCIPLES OF ACCOUNTING
If you find inventory valuation confusing, read *Principles of Accounting*, Chapter 8—www.principlesofaccounting.com/chapter 8.htm. The author, Larry Walther, provides excellent explanations, complete with graphics.

TOOLS

Inventory Costs

Inventory costs, and it often costs a lot. First, there's the cost of investing capital, which can be huge—especially if it involves financing. Second, there's the cost of lost opportunity which can be significant. If a company has a 12 percent annual return on investment, then that's the cost of capital—and also the cost of the money spent to pay the inventory holding or carrying costs.

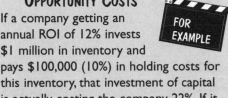

OPPORTUNITY COSTS

If a company getting an annual ROI of 12% invests $1 million in inventory and pays $100,000 (10%) in holding costs for this inventory, that investment of capital is actually costing the company 22%. If it sells an item that costs $100 to produce, the actual cost would be $122. Inventory can be very expensive!

The holding or carrying costs would include the following:

- insurance
- taxes
- transportation, material, and storage costs (including personnel, warehouse, and PP&E costs)
- inventory risk costs—
  - obsolescence
  - scrap and rework
  - cost of change orders
  - damage
  - shrinkage (including losses and theft)
  - relocation costs

Carrying costs are often estimated at 18 percent to 25 percent of the value of the inventory. APICS cites a range from 10 percent to 35 percent, depending on type of industry.

PP&E *Property, plant, and equipment*—assets that are vital to business operations but that cannot be **KEY TERM** liquidated easily. The value of PP&E assets is typically depreciated over the estimated life of the assets.

Reducing Inventory

The less inventory you hold, the less capital you have committed and the lower the carrying costs. Inventory can be reduced in several ways, but you should first try to determine the reasons for the size of the inventory. If it's the incoming inventory (i.e., materials, parts, and supplies used in operations), there may be problems with forecasting and planning and/or with purchasing. If it's the outgoing inventory (i.e., goods), problems may exist

KEY TERM **Carrying cost/Holding cost** "The cost of holding inventory, usually defined as a percentage of the dollar value of inventory per unit of time (usually a year). Carrying cost depends on the cost of capital invested as well as such costs of maintaining the inventory as taxes and insurance, obsolescence, spoilage, and space occupied."

—APICS Dictionary, 9th edition (APICS The Association for Operations Management, 1998)

APICS RESOURCES

TOOLS **APICS Dictionary.** This is the standard dictionary for terms used in operations management, produced by APICS, The Association for Operations Management (formerly known as the American Production and Inventory Control Society). First published in 1963, the dictionary currently contains more than 3,500 industry terms associated with the APICS body of knowledge.

APICS Operations Management Body of Knowledge Framework. This book establishes a structure for operations management, encompassing production, inventory, supply chain, materials management, purchasing, and logistics.

with planning and scheduling, with sales, with distribution, and/or with forecasting demand. Inventory also has a tendency to hide quality issues; many people use the analogy of inventory as a river rushing over the rocks below, which are analogous to quality problems.

By lowering the level of the water (or inventory) you can see and avoid (address) the rocks (or quality problems). Also, both incoming and outgoing inventories can be affected by the bullwhip effect, as explained in Chapter 8.

Not Too Much and Not Too Little

How much inventory is enough? For incoming inventory, answer these key questions:

- How reliable is your supply? Do alternative sources exist from which you could draw on short notice?
- Are the components produced or delivered in batches?
- Can you predict demand accurately?
- Are the prices you pay for materials, parts, and supplies steady?
- Do you get discounts for buying in bulk?

The amount of inventory you need also depends on your strategy for aggregate planning, as explained in Chapter 8—level or chase. A *level strategy* maintains stable production and workforce levels and a constant rate of output rate by using inventory to meet increases in demand and to absorb excess output when demand decreases. It requires maintaining a steady level of incoming inventory and it results in an outgoing inventory that can be very high or very low.

A *chase strategy* synchronizes production rate with demand by increasing or decreasing capacity and hiring or laying off workers as demand changes. It generally results in incoming inventories that fluctuate and low outgoing inventories.

Ways to Reduce Inventory

There are numerous ways, big and small, to reduce inventory, including the following:

- Reduce all inventories through applying lean principles, particularly just-in-time inventory management.
- Reduce incoming and WIP inventories by improving the efficiency of production operations.
- Reduce safety stock by working with suppliers to shorten cycle order fulfillment times.
- Reduce incoming inventory through material requirements planning (MRP) or tighter scheduling, which is described in more detail in Chapter 11.
- Reduce all inventories by managing the supply chain more efficiently.

Think back to the conflict of objectives and strategies mentioned in the opening pages of this chapter. Are goals and reward systems in the various functional areas at odds in terms of the whole organization and therefore suboptimizing operations?

> **INFORMATION, NOT INVENTORY**
> **SMART MANAGING**
>
> "The objective of inventory management is to replace a very expensive asset called inventory with a less expensive asset called information. In order to accomplish this objective, the information must be timely, accurate, reliable, and consistent."
>
> —J. David Viale, *Basics of Inventory Management: From Warehouse to Distribution Center* (Crisp Publications, 1997)

However, it can be risky to reduce inventory without understanding the reasons for keeping it, some of which were listed earlier in this chapter. You should focus not on reducing inventory, but rather on making improvements in operations that will then enable you to reduce inventory.

Monitoring and Maintaining Inventory

As explained in Chapter 8, two types of demand prevail—dependent and independent. *Dependent demand* for a product or service is caused by the demand for other products or services. *Independent demand* is not caused directly by another demand. Determining how much to order and when to order it is relevant and important only for independent demand, not for dependent demand.

- An inventory management system is a set of policies and controls intended to maintain proper inventory levels by monitoring them and answering the two big questions:
  - What levels of which materials and products should be maintained?
  - How much of which materials and products should be ordered and when?

The parameters for answering these questions must be reviewed continuously and revised as appropriate, since the answers to these questions depend on factors that change.

Review Systems

Two categories of control systems exist for independent-demand inventory: periodic and continuous. The *periodic review system* checks the inventory level only at fixed intervals, such as once a month. Then an order is placed of sufficient quantity to bring inventory up to a specified maximum level. The *continuous review system* (aka *perpetual inventory system*) monitors the inventory level continuously. As soon as the level falls below a specified level, an order is placed for the reorder quantity.

But how do you determine the point at which to reorder and how do you decide how much to order? You can act on instinct or you can estimate. But formulas can also help you make those decisions.

Economic Order Quantity: How Much to Order?

Order quantity is an important consideration. The optimal order quantity is called the *economic order quantity* (EOQ). The EOQ represents the lowest total cost of inventory costs, ordering costs, invoice processing costs, freight costs, etc.

Economic order quantity (EOQ) Order quantity that represents the lowest total cost of inventory costs and acquisition costs (ordering costs, invoice processing costs, payables costs, freight costs, etc.).

KEY TERMS

Ordering cost Used in calculating order quantities, the costs that increase as the number of orders placed increases. It includes costs related to the clerical work of preparing, releasing, monitoring, and receiving orders, the physical handling of goods, inspections, and setup costs, as applicable.

—*APICS Dictionary*, 9th edition (APICS The Association for Operations Management, 1998)

Ordering costs may include the cost for the purchasing agent who investigates and places the order and a share of the fixed costs of operating the purchasing department.

This is the formula for calculating EOQ:

$$EOQ = \sqrt{\frac{2AR}{P^2K}}$$

where A = total value of SKU per year, K = carrying cost, R = replenishment cost, and P = price per unit.

This formula and its variations enable you to determine:

- optimal quantity to order
- time for ordering
- total cost
- average inventory level
- maximum inventory level
- quantity to order each time

This formula is based on several assumptions:

- The demand rate is known and constant.
- The carrying cost and ordering cost are independent of the quantity ordered (i.e., no discount).

- The lead time is known and constant, so that new orders placed at the specified time arrive exactly as the inventory reaches zero.

Reorder Point: When to Order?

For each inventory item, you set a *reorder point* (ROP). This is the lowest

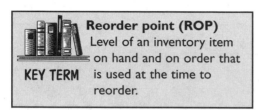

Reorder point (ROP)
Level of an inventory item on hand and on order that

KEY TERM is used at the time to reorder.

amount of that item to have on hand and on order. When your inventory drops to that point, you reorder.

A simple formula for determining ROP would be

ROP = (Usage x Lead time) + Safety stock

So, for example, if you use 600 items a month and your lead time is two weeks (25 percent of a month), then the first part of the formula gives you 300 items. That's the amount you expect to use in the two weeks it takes from making the order to getting delivery.

But what about this *safety stock*? How much extra of that item do you need beyond *cycle stock* "just in case"?

The amount of safety stock (aka *buffer stock*) you need depends on three factors:

- variation in demand
- variability in lead time
- desired level of service

Level of service is the probability that the safety stock will be sufficient to fill all customer orders placed during the lead time. This is calculated using more complicated formulas and statistical calculations. Fortunately, programs exist that can do the math for you—as long as you provide the information. And remember, "Garbage in and garbage out," so capturing the information at the source, preferably a credible source, and just as preferably, only once, is essential for the operations manager.

Keeping Track of Inventory

Before we get into the nuts and bolts of keeping track of inventory, we should consider a concept that makes it easier—or at least reduces the anxiety inherent in keeping track of hundreds or thousands of inventory items.

We've already discussed a critical distinction in inventory, between dependent demand and independent demand. Another common distinction is based on the relative importance of inventory items.

> **KEY TERMS**
>
> **Safety stock** Inventory balance that is used only if necessary. The amount of safety stock depends on three factors: variation in demand, variability in lead time, and desired level of service.
>
> **Cycle stock** Inventory that is used to meet normal demand, as opposed to *safety stock.*

Classification as Simple as ABC

"What inventory do you want to control?" You might instinctively answer, "All our inventory, of course."

That's natural, but in practical terms it makes more sense to focus your inventory control procedures where they will have the greatest impact.

In Chapter 3 we discussed the Pareto principle, the 80/20 rule, and Pareto analysis. If you "Pareto" your inventory items in terms of "value"—some critical criterion, such as dollar value, sales, dollar usage, usage rate, output, turnover—you can classify the items into three groups, generally labeled simply as A, B, and C.

Don't expect your inventory to follow the 80/20 rule. In fact, the distinctions among the A items and the B items and the C items may not be striking. The point is simply that the ABC analysis enables you to invest time and effort in areas of inventory according to their relative value (however you define that concept). You can apply rules or standards for each category. For example:

- *A items*—complete records, monitor closely, control tightly
- *B items*—good records, monitor often, control less tightly
- *C items*—adequate records, monitor periodically, control least tightly

Records

You should have an effective system for tracking inventory from the moment it arrives until the moment it leaves the facility or the moment it arrives at its destination. You need to know items and quantities (what and how much) on hand so you can plan orders more accurately. You need to keep track of costs so you have the information needed for

SMART

MANAGING

SIMPLE SYSTEM, SIMPLY SMART

ABC analysis allows you to apply the wisdom of that well-known expression, "Don't sweat the small stuff." In terms of inventory control, the expression might be revised as "Don't sweat the small stuff, pay more attention to the things that matter more, and focus most on the things that are most important." It's not as catchy, but it makes good business sense.

accounting analysis. You need to be able to reduce the necessity for physical inventory and the time and effort required.

If there's no tracking system in place, set up an inventory database to track and manage all inventory and costs. Then, do an initial check of inventory and record whatever information the system requires or can process.

Tracking Technology

We're all familiar with *stock-keeping units* (SKUs). Those identifiers make record keeping and tracking of inventory items easier and more systematic. But it would still take a lot of time and effort if not for *bar codes*. The best system is only as good as its weakest component, which is generally a human. The best of us cannot match an optical scanner for accuracy.

Inventory records can associate a wealth of information with each SKU. In addition to a description, specifications, and graphics, the record system may allow for additional inventory control information that can be easily updated, such as reorder point and economic order quantities.

We've already discussed Electronic Data Interchange (EDI) in Chapter 6, as well as newer communications technologies, such as XML and use of broadband and the Internet, for sharing data between and among companies in supply chains.

You should also be familiar with *radio-frequency identification* (RFID). This is the use of a *tag* that enables companies that produce anything tangible to mark their products so they can be tracked throughout the supply chain, from production to customers. The tag is a microchip consisting of an integrated circuit (for storing and even processing data) and an antenna that can communicate with an RFID scanner.

Let's Get Physical

To monitor inventory levels and reduce the risk of stock-outs, it's important that inventory records be accurate. As soon as any difference between the records and the physical inventory is discovered, the records should be adjusted as well as the accounting records.

It's also important to verify the accuracy of inventory records by doing a physical inventory. After all, you can't produce tangible objects out of inventory that exists only on paper or in data bytes.

To monitor accuracy, each inventory item must be counted at regular intervals. Two primary methods are typically used to count inventory: periodic and cycle.

> **SMART MANAGING**
>
> **UNDERSTAND THE ERRORS**
>
> "Counting and correcting inventory balances is not enough. The goal should be to understand the cause of the errors and correcting the processes that drove them. Well-managed cycle count programs will be used as an input to the company's continuous improvement process. The process should drive root cause analysis and process improvement."
>
> —Kate Vitasek, "Supply Chain News: Inventory Metrics, Part 2"

- *Periodic inventory counting*—implies doing one big count of all the items at the same time, usually annually.
- *Cycle inventory counting*—means doing a series of small counts of some items, every day, every other day, or every week, so that by the end of a specified period all items have been counted.

Cycle counting allows for greater flexibility. For example, A items can be scheduled for counting more frequently than B items or C items, particularly if A items are used in greater volume than B or C items. Also, counts can be scheduled for times when the items to be counted are at their lowest levels, making them easier to count.

A = B = C

As mentioned earlier, in the ABC system some inventory items are rated as more important than others. However, if the workers on the assembly line need a component, they won't care that it's "only" a C item and they won't be able to use a "more valuable" B item in its place—or even an A item. All items in inventory are uniquely important, whether A, B, or C.

Protecting Inventory

As emphasized earlier, inventory is worth a lot of money. It makes sense for you to know the risks and protect your inventories. What follows here is just a cursory discussion of what you can do.

Disasters. Earthquake. Tornado. Hurricane. Flood. Major fire. Large-scale theft. However you define "disaster," you should be prepared. You should certainly be storing data files off-site. You should certainly have a business continuation plan. And if a disaster should ever hit one of your suppliers, you should be ready to get the inventory you need from another supplier. But first, assess the risks your company and particularly your inventory face.

Obsolescence and Deterioration. Use a first-in, first-out material rotation policy. Reduce inventories to improve turnover ratio. Improve communication across the supply chain, inside the organization, and beyond. Improve your records and tracking systems.

Loss and Accidental Damage

Improve your records and tracking systems. Provide better training for employees handling inventory. Inspect and maintain handling equipment. Apply the 5S methodology (explained in Chapter 5) to storage facilities.

Theft and Pilfering

Know what you have in inventory, where it is located, and how much it is worth—and provide proper security and policies for access. Put RFID tags on at least the items that are most expensive and/or most likely to be stolen. Make sure that employees understand disciplinary policies for pilfering—and enforce them.

Keeping Score on the Use of Inventory

Considering the financial value of inventory in most companies and the operational value of inventory, it's very important to measure how it's being used. You should know the standard metrics for inventory and be using them.

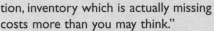

MI$$ING INVENTORY

"While most missing inventory is usually found to have been reported improperly or placed in the wrong location, inventory which is actually missing costs more than you may think."

—Kate Vitasek, "Supply Chain News: Inventory Metrics, Part 3: Shrinkage—into Thin Air"

In addition, depending on which areas of your inventory management system seem most in need of improvement, you can use more specialized metrics to evaluate, for example, the accuracy of your records, the efficiency of your storage methods, the amount of accidental breakage in handling, and so forth.

The two most important standard inventory metrics for measuring how effectively inventory is being used are *days of inventory on hand* (aka *days of supply*) and *inventory turnover ratio* (aka *inventory turns*).

Days of Inventory on Hand. This metric is easy to understand. The lower, the better—generally. Lower indicates a more productive use of inventory, but to the extreme it can be dangerous. Lean systems have failed when problems arose with their supply lines.

Days of inventory = Average aggregate inventory value/
(Annual cost of goods sold/365)

Inventory Turnover Ratio. This metric indicates how well inventory is being used. The formula calculates the dollars of sales, at cost, that are being supported by each dollar of inventory. Inventory turnover ratio is a simple measure of managerial performance. Generally, the higher the turnover ratio, the better the company is using its inventory. Turnover rate varies with the type of inventory and the type of business; you should be able to obtain average inventory turnover ratios for individual industries from trade associations.

Inventory turnover = Annual cost of goods sold/
Average aggregate inventory value for year

Other Metrics. There are many other metrics—for financial (e.g., gross margin return on inventory), for records (e.g., inventory record accuracy), for cycle time, and so on. Two important, related metrics to close this discussion are *inventory carrying rate* and *inventory carrying costs*.

interesting

Add up annual inventory costs (storage, handling, obsolescence, damage, administrative, loss, etc.) and divide the total cost by the average inventory value. To this percentage, add the percentages for opportunity cost of capital, insurance, and taxes. The sum of these percentages is your *inventory carrying rate*. Calculate your *inventory carrying costs* by multiplying your inventory carrying rate by the average inventory value.

Operations Manager's Checklist for Chapter 10

☑ Know the standard metrics for inventory and use them.

☑ Be sensitive to weaknesses in your inventory management system and use special metrics—and, of course, work to eliminate the weaknesses.

☑ Strive to ensure a continuous, sufficient supply of the materials, goods, and/or supplies necessary for optimal operations while minimizing the costs. That's the definition of *inventory management*.

☑ Remember that inventory management is not just about managing inventory, but also about managing the dynamics of conflicting objectives and strategies that affect inventory.

☑ Understand the basics of inventory valuation and costing.

☑ Push to reduce inventory. It may be listed as an asset on the balance sheet, but it can work like a liability against profitability.

☑ Monitor inventory levels and keep your records as accurate as necessary.

☑ Protect your inventory. It is a most valuable investment, whether large or small.

☑ Above all, make inventory work for you—the good—not you working for your inventory—the ugly.

Operations Technology:
Paving the Way Operations Should Work

B ob works as operations manager for a small toy factory. The employees take little plastic beads, melt them, mold them, and then bolt them together to make action figures. The figures are then painted, packaged, and shipped. He is consistently updating inventories, checking when new materials will be delivered, and making sure he has enough action figures on hand to fulfill orders from distributors and retailers. Bob gets tired of the umpteen hours he is spending every week just managing inventories and shipping orders.

But what are his choices? Fortunately, Bob can benefit from the technology revolution that has driven improvements across all facets of operations management.

Technology Overview

Operations managers now use software planning and control systems to integrate disparate information and help manage processes. Material Requirements Planning (MRP), Manufacturing Resource Planning (MRP II), and Enterprise Resource Planning (ERP) are the primary systems used to track and plan operations. Advanced Planning and Scheduling (APS) and e-procurement (electronic procurement, EP) are additional ways in which operations managers are using integrated IT capabilities to lighten the operations load. *Moore's Law*, the observation that computing power

Material Requirements Planning (MRP) System for managing manufacturing processes (primarily for products made from components) through better production planning and

KEY TERMS inventory control. A master production schedule sets out what will be built, when, and in what quantities. A bill of materials lists all the levels of raw materials, parts, components, subassemblies, and so on necessary for building a product. Materials are scheduled more closely, reducing inventories and making delivery times shorter and more predictable.

Manufacturing Resource Planning (MRP II) Method to effectively plan all resources of a manufacturing company, operationally as well as financially, including running simulations for future events.

Enterprise Resource Planning (ERP) Company-wide computer system used to manage and coordinate all the resources, information, and functions of a business.

Advanced Planning and Scheduling (APS) Manufacturing management process designed to allocate basic materials and production or service capacity optimally to meet anticipated demand.

e-Procurement Use of the Internet and other information networks to buy and sell materials and services. Sometimes known as *supplier exchange*.

INTERNET POWER

FOR EXAMPLE

"Trying to assess the true importance and function of the Net now is like asking the Wright brothers at Kitty Hawk if they were aware of the potential of American Airlines Advantage Miles."

—Brian Ferren, Executive Vice-President for Creative Technology and Research, Walt Disney Imagineering

---

doubles every 18 to 24 months, helps to explain the growth in technology solutions that support manufacturing and service operations.

However, that technology needs to be harnessed and organized. A detailed operations technology strategy and architecture can help you plan implementation, costs, and needs.

The e-Business Challenge Ahead

Computers have been connected for 40 years, but many operations managers have only recently been reluctantly dragged into the information age. Technology now seems to be at the core of every business discussion, and it's radically changing operations—in ways that we have only begun to explore.

Technology and information sharing essentially render physical distance irrelevant. If operations managers can capture and leverage the potential benefits of technology, they will achieve competitive advantage despite an era in which globalization, regulation, and constant change are making it even more difficult to increase profitability and shareholder value. E-business, as depicted in Exhibit 11-1, has the potential for creating dramatic new sources of shareholder value by enabling operations managers to:

- Understand their customers and their suppliers.
- Build customer loyalty and supplier commitment.
- Reach new, previously unattainable markets.
- Create new products and services.
- Achieve market leadership.
- Optimize and institutionalize business processes.
- Enhance human capital.
- Harness technology.
- Manage (rather than mitigate) risk and ensure compliance.

The current focus on technology by operations managers results from its potential for developing and delivering products and services faster, extending geographical reach, increasing process efficiency and effectiveness, redefining products and services and brands, and leveraging information by providing more flexible infrastructures and business models. Still, as shown by the rapid rise to industry leadership of companies such as Amazon and Dell, technology also puts some companies—typically "brick and mortar" ones—and entire industries at risk. E-business is an inherently disruptive market force. The survivors will overcome it; the visionaries will exploit it.

What should keep operations managers awake at night is the question of who will be the next Amazon, Google, or Dell—the next company that changes the rules of competition. In the E-business age, barriers to entry are diminished, opportunistic advantage rarely lasts, and the trend is to develop supply chains and work more closely with partners. The ability to ramp up or ramp down operations quickly becomes increasingly more important, and one tenet holds true: the only sustainable advantage may actually be the ability to learn faster than your competitors—even

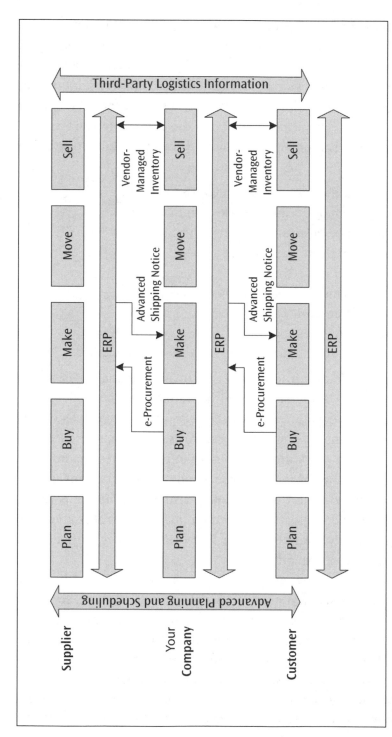

Exhibit 11-1. E-business value chain

those companies you never realized were competing with you.

Organizational learning has to work at the speed of thought, which puts added pressure on each enterprise's

> **OUT OF NOWHERE**
> The biggest threat to British Airways is not United Airlines, but rather the HP Halo system of user-friendly videoconferencing.
>
> *FOR EXAMPLE*

ability to manage knowledge effectively within and across the value chain. E-business has fundamentally redefined commerce, transformed industries, and eliminated the constraints of time and distance. The status quo is not an option.

E-Business, E-Commerce, and E-SCM

Most of the initial flurry of activity around e-business focused on the business-to-consumer (B2C) aspects of the Internet, but the real impetus for revolutionary changes affecting operations lies in the business-to-business (B2B) arena. According to Scott Hartz, former CEO of consulting for PricewaterhouseCoopers, "E-business is concerned with the impact that connectivity has on customers and suppliers. . . . Connectivity is the key, particularly as it applies to business-to-business integration."

At its most basic level, electronic supply chain management (e-SCM) addresses this notion of using information technology to conduct seamless and virtual business transactions among buyers, sellers, and trading partners to improve customer service, reduce costs, and increase shareholder value across the enterprise, in essence, streamlining and customizing the value chain buy-sell process (Exhibit 11-2). Low-cost supply chain operations suggest, in essence, zero variable-cost transactions, which enterprises must continually learn to exploit. At its core, e-SCM is concerned with providing the technologically enabled backbone B2B relationships.

Dr. Raj Veeramani, executive director of the E-Business Consortium at the University of Wisconsin-Madison, uses the term "supply web management" to describe e-SCM as "the process of coordinating and managing the interactions between businesses to meet the end customer's requirements." It deals with planning and executing the processes within an enterprise value chain so they work together to meet customers' and consumers' needs. In that context, to better plan

Plan	Buy	Make	Move	Sell
▪ Advance Planning and Scheduling ▪ Product Lifecycle Management	▪ Component and Supplier Management ▪ e-Procurement ▪ e-Sourcing ▪ EDI ▪ Telecom Expense Management	▪ MRP ▪ MRPII ▪ Computer Integrated Manufacturing ▪ Design Support	▪ Warehouse Management ▪ 3rd/4th Party Logistics Information Systems ▪ RFID	▪ Customer Relationship Management ▪ Sales Configuration Order Management ▪ Call Center ▪ Online Sales ▪ Customer Services
ERP				

Exhibit 11-2. e-SCM applications

and execute, it's essential to share information across company boundaries. Developing and using cheap and reliable communications media such as the Internet can facilitate information sharing.

To some extent, e-SCM means building the links within, between, and among organizations across the enterprise, from suppliers' suppliers to customers' customers and ultimately to consumers. Technically speaking, it involves taking processes currently functioning within businesses and moving them to networks and shared applications, as shown in Exhibit 11-2. The concept of e-SCM encompasses much of what has been called *electronic commerce*—the external channels beyond the boundaries of an organization—and includes virtually every facet of a firm's strategy and operations and the strategies and operations of its value chain partners. But, even more so, e-SCM holistically integrates and institutionalizes supply chain strategy. It goes beyond the front-end isolated projects and encourages operations to examine, and probably change, the way they perform basic enterprise-wide supply chain processes: planning, buying, making, moving, and selling.

Electronically enabled supply chain management has been built on technology. But, unlike electronic commerce, the ascendancy of e-SCM is less about technology than about business and satisfying individual customer and consumer needs. Ultimate success is about connecting value chains across the extended enterprise to enhance communications, collaboration, and customer service. It's about doing business differently while being acutely aware of a new range of options for surviving, competing, and succeeding.

The e-business-enabled value chain increases competitive advantage by linking disparate organizations to form collaborative, interactive, and proactive environments. When these concepts are embraced as fundamental supply chain philosophies across the value chain, they can engender economic success—redefining business models, changing corporate cultures, injecting intimacy into relationships with supply chain partners, and altering the competitive dynamics of entire industries.

Effective e-SCM also facilitates revolutionary business model changes. For example, it enables mass customization or one-to-one marketing. Building upon the Internet and the disruptive nature of associated technologies, e-SCM affects literally everything about the way we operate across the enterprise.

Operations Technology Review

Data traffic now exceeds voice communications across global networks, and the technologies for planning software systems, tools that enable operations and information management, and electronic procurement have fundamentally changed the operations landscape. Due to these advances over the past 20 years, an operations manager can all but automate his or her processes and keep a dashboard on the office computer to report on the health of the manufacturing or service systems. Accessing, integrating, and synthesizing this information allows the operations manager to make better informed decisions, in real time, with less risk.

Just imagine if Jessica had these tools available in her kitchen. Undoubtedly she could build a better peanut butter sandwich. . . and the world would beat a path to her door.

Radio-Frequency Identification (RFID)

Other key technologies are those that enable inventory management as well as information systems. Radio-frequency identification (RFID) chips, mentioned in Chapter 10, can improve visibility into inventories from distribution centers through to retail shelves.

Information systems for manufacturing often rely on an Enterprise Resource Planning (ERP) layer, a Manufacturing Execution System (MES) layer, and a shop floor layer. Significant amounts of shop floor data need to be introduced into production planning or supply chain management. RFID chips can play an important role in collecting, segregating, and managing such data, because they make any item on the shop floor self-identifying to the information systems. RFID devices can also be used to help distinguish among items that have a similar look and feel. For example, Bob can insert RFID tags into his indistinguishable toy parts, making them easily identifiable and thereby decreasing the manufacturing process error rate.

Material Requirements Planning (MRP)

Material requirements planning (MRP) was an early iteration of the integrated information systems vision. It was developed to simultaneously meet three objectives: to ensure production and product delivery of products; to minimize inventory; and to plan manufacturing, logistics, and procurement. This approach allowed operations managers to plan transportation and manufacturing timetables in order to know when to place an order.

The MRP process starts by inputting current or forecasted orders into a *master production schedule* (MPS), which essentially describes the amounts required and gives the dates by which specific items will be needed for each order. Planning consequently validates that the resources are available and identifies the sources across the supply chain that will be providing them. MRP then takes the end product requirements from the MPS and breaks them into their component parts and subassemblies to create a materials plan that specifies when production and purchase orders must be placed for each part so that the products can be completed on schedule.

MRP's planning functions give managers power over their domain. They let a manager look into the past to identify trends and see potential future performance. If Bob uses MRP, he will know what materials he needs and when. MRP can help Bob realize when inventory levels of certain items are low or high. He will use MRP to better estimate times for ordering new materials and planning shipments.

Manufacturing Resource Planning (MRP II)

The original MRP planned only materials, but as technology expanded commensurate with operational requirements and complexity, MRP II evolved as a way to also integrate resources. MRP II systems operate modularly and are composed of smaller systems that control the network of resource processes—order entry, scheduling, inventory control, finance, accounts payable, purchasing management, costing, and distribution—and are linked to provide their information in a useable fashion. MRP II integrates data and puts a lot of information into the manager's hands, in a manner that's easy to understand.

Unlike MRP, which focused solely on the manufacturing process, MRP II expanded to include finance and HR. Ideally, it addresses operational planning in units and financial planning in dollars and has a simulation capability to answer "what-if" questions while extending MRP.

Since humans are prone to error, paper-based or non-integrated information systems result in more errors, including missing or redundant data, incorrect calculations, and decisions based on incorrect, old, or inconsistent data. That human frailty is minimized with MRP II systems. They begin with sales forecasts that determine the raw materials demand. Like MRP, MRP II systems draw on the MPS for the breakdown of specific plans for each product on a line. While MRP helps coordinate raw materials purchasing, MRP II facilitates the development of a detailed production schedule that accounts for machine and labor capacity, scheduling the production runs according to the arrival of materials.

Integrating labor operations, financial operations, and manufacturing operations gives a manager the ability to consider some of the biggest costs in manufacturing, such as inputs, labor, and infrastructure. Just like MRP, MRPII does an excellent job determining reorder points. By knowing when the production processes will be manufacturing each product, the operations manager can establish an optimized schedule.

So what could MRP II do for Bob? Well, he definitely wouldn't worry about how to plan and schedule his production workers. Knowing his work force would enable him to streamline his energy demands and consumption—quite a feat in our energy-conscious environment. Just as with MRP, Bob would know when to order and how much to order.

Finally, MRP II would help Bob with financial planning by giving him accurate inventories, and it would reduce the amount of working capital needed. If Bob used its robust functionality, MRP II would make his life much easier.

Information Technology (IT) Strategy

An Information Technology (IT) strategy is much like any other strategy— it's an in-depth map for a given period of time. A good IT strategy focuses not only on delivering IT services to meet current and future demand, but also on delivering increased value to the company and maximum return on the IT investment. An effective IT strategy can give your operations a competitive advantage.

In our global economy, IT infrastructure is the backbone of your firm. Strategic investments in your IT systems can keep your information running at top speed. If you work with IT to improve and upgrade your technology strategy and applications on an ongoing basis, you will have technology that's better suited to your needs and, more importantly, improved operations.

An IT strategy should incorporate IT needs for short- and long-term time horizons, typically spanning three years into the future. Your company's IT strategy should include plans and budget for hardware, software, network, and services.

When forecasting IT needs, the operations manager works with IT to define its anticipated information requirements. It's critical for IT to forecast the bandwidth that the company will need in the future. In the past 10 years alone, bandwidth available to consumers has grown from 56k modems to broadband FiOS (Verizon trademark for fiber optic service) giving consumers speeds as high as 40 mbps. Certain newer technologies—such as Voice over Internet Protocol (VoIP), videoconferencing, and other data services—gobble bandwidth. These technologies will continue to drive bandwidth requirements upward over time.

As technology continues to enable operations, it becomes increasingly critical to ensure that all key facilities are enabled with appropriate network infrastructure to support the deployed systems. This means that IT strategy needs to be developed in conjunction with the operations strategy. The last thing Bob needs is a remote plant that can't upload its data to the information systems because the bandwidth of their network connection isn't good enough.

The number of end users across the enterprise determines infrastructure requirements, including how many workstations you need and what software solutions you require to fulfill those needs. When forecasting future costs, it's essential to incorporate projected increases in the size of your workforce, growth in the number of locations, and the types of systems to be implemented.

The software solutions your firm will require in the future vary according to the client-facing applications you need. If you're a graphics design firm, you will find yourself continuously buying Adobe products. If you require word processors, spreadsheets, and presentations, you'll need to purchase products from the Microsoft Office Suite. Being able to better forecast your future needs can give your purchasing department better buying and bargaining power. This can translate to lower operating costs.

Every business should have strategic plans that forecast future requirements. Advances in IT have revolutionized many facets of our lives and our businesses. Why not revolutionize your IT investment with some good planning?

Technology Implementation

Still, technology implementation can get tricky. It's up to the operations manager and his or her co-managers to determine how, when, and where as well as the speed with which to implement technology. Not only will you have to make sure to keep the costs in line, but also—and probably more important—you will have to make sure you are buying the right tools and solutions for your needs.

To ensure technology success, take some time to work

PEOPLE POTENTIAL   SMART   MANAGING

"The number-one benefit of information technology is that it empowers people to do what they want to do. It lets people be creative. It lets people be productive. It lets people learn things they didn't think they could learn before, and so in a sense it is all about the potential."

—Steve Ballmer, CEO, Microsoft, February 17, 2005

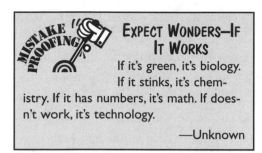

EXPECT WONDERS—IF
IT WORKS
If it's green, it's biology.
If it stinks, it's chem-
istry. If it has numbers, it's math. If does-
n't work, it's technology.

—Unknown

with your IT department to determine what you actually need. Enterprise Resource Planning (ERP) systems are great, but what if you don't need all that interconnectivity or all the options? Technology is great, but if people don't use them, your equipment and systems will be gathering dust and growing rust.

Speak with your users and make sure that they want what you're going to buy. Technology is best when it's seamless, so do what you can to make their transition smooth. User-friendly technology is attainable but only by starting from the user perspective. After all, their perspective is your reality! As employees work with new technology, help them integrate it into their daily schedules. Finally, emphasize that technology can make their work and their lives easier.

Enterprise Resource Planning (ERP)

Enterprise Resource Planning (ERP) is a business information integration system that developed after Material Requirements Planning (MRP) and Manufacturing Resource Planning (MRP II). The development of these manufacturing coordination and integration methods and tools made ERP systems possible. Both MRP and MRP II are still widely used, independently and as modules of more comprehensive ERP systems.

ERP operates companywide and integrates all systems to manage and coordinate resources, information, and business functions from shared databases. An ERP system has a service-oriented architecture with modular hardware and software units or "services" that communicate on a local area network. The modular design allows a business to add or reconfigure modules (perhaps from different vendors) while preserving data integrity in one shared database that may be centralized or distributed.

ERP systems attempt to cover all core enterprise functions. These systems can be found in non-manufacturing businesses, non-profit organizations, and governments. To be considered an ERP system, a software package must provide the function of at least two systems. For example, a software package that provides both payroll and accounting functions could technically be considered an ERP software package. ERP modules that formerly would have been stand-alone applications include product lifecycle management, supply chain management, warehouse management, customer relationship management, sales order processing, online sales, financials, human resources, and decision support systems.

Operations managers should make sure to purchase and implement only the ERP system modules that they actually need and that are technologically feasible. ERP modules typically address the applications shown in Exhibit 11-3.

In the absence of an ERP system, a large manufacturer may be using multiple software applications that cannot communicate or interface effectively with one another. ERP systems *centralize* the data in one place, which eliminates the problem of synchronizing changes and can reduce the risk of loss of sensitive data by consolidating multiple permissions and security models into a single structure.

Since ERP systems enable the software modules to communicate with each other, they can be more efficient and better regulated. Audits can be conducted easily and routinely—and oversight is incorporated, which is essential in the era of internal controls mandated by the Sarbanes-Oxley Act. This cross-communication allows for "early and often warning," thereby encouraging employees to be more aware of errant practices.

Some organizations—typically those with sufficient in-house IT skills to integrate multiple software products—choose to implement

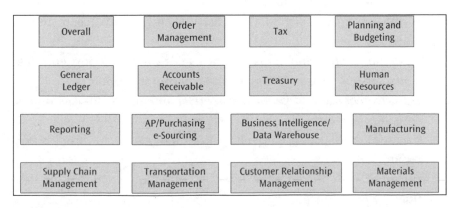

Exhibit 11-3. Typical ERP modules

only portions of an ERP system* and develop an external interface to other ERP or stand-alone systems for their other application needs. For example, managers may choose to use a human resource management system from one vendor and a purchasing management system from another and integrate the systems themselves in a "best-of-breed" approach. This is common across retailers, where even a midsize retailer will have a discrete point-of-sale product and financials application and then a series of specialized applications to handle business requirements such as warehouse management, merchandising, and logistics. Others are more interested in the inherently more integrated applications of a stated suite of ERP applications, such as SAP or Oracle.

Ideally, ERP delivers a single database that contains all data for the software modules, which include:

- *Manufacturing*—engineering, bills of material, scheduling, capacity, work flow management, quality control, cost management, manufacturing process, manufacturing projects, manufacturing flow
- *Supply chain management*—order to cash, inventory, order entry, purchasing, product configurator, supply chain planning, supplier scheduling, inspection of goods, claim processing, commission calculation
- *Financials*—general ledger, cash management, accounts payable, accounts receivable, fixed assets
- *Project management*—costing, billing, time and expense, performance units, activity management
- *Human resources*—payroll, training, time and attendance, rostering, benefits
- *Customer relationship management*—sales and marketing, commissions, service, customer contact and call center support
- *Data warehouse and various self-service interfaces*—for customers, suppliers, and employees
- *Access control*—user privilege as per authority levels for process execution
- *Customization*—to meet the extension, addition, change in process flow

10 KEYS TO ERP SUCCESS

TRICKS OF THE TRADE

1. Agree that integration is the key to business — not to the IT function.
2. Really understand and focus on the key areas.
3. Define how "global" is global and how "standard" is standard.
4. Define the benefits and how to get them.
5. Define timeline, stakeholders, and accountability.
6. Process, process, process.
7. Define your common data model and deal with the issues.
8. Always strive to balance "Are we being aspirational enough?" with "What must we get done?"
9. Develop organizational capability from day one.
10. If you feel like you are "inventing" along the way, something is probably wrong.

When implementing an ERP system, organizations can choose between customizing the software and adapting their current business processes to the "best practices" function delivered in the "out-of-the-box" version of the software. Problems with ERP systems are mainly due to inadequate investment in ongoing training for the involved IT personnel and to a lack of corporate policy protecting the integrity of the data in the ERP systems and the ways in which it is used.

The biggest hurdle is that people inherently resist change. Newton's first law of motion asserts that a body at rest will tend to remain at rest, unless an external force acts upon it. Implementing ERP is analogous to the way Einstein's theory of relativity revolutionized physics. Everyone has to go back to the drawing board just to learn how things should fit together.

ERP systems can be very complex and expensive. This has led to a new category of "ERP light" solutions. According to Thomas Wailgum ("ERP Definition and Solutions," *CIO* magazine, March 7, 2007),

> Over the last few years, however, Internet-driven changes have occurred that can drastically reduce how long it takes vendors to deliver ERP modules. These faster implementations (meaning weeks, not years) are the result of a new category of ERP software delivery referred to as on-demand or software-as-a-service (SaaS). Typically, on-demand and SaaS ERP applications (such as finance or HR packages) are hosted by a third party, and customers access the multitenant (or shared) ERP applications via a Web connection.

Because the software doesn't need to be installed as in the traditional on-premise manner, implementation times can be drastically shorter than implementing ERP applications on-premise.

Collaborative Planning and Advanced Planning and Scheduling

Collaborative planning is the redesign and implementation of planning processes across multiple enterprises using electronic business to synchronize product flow, optimize resource allocation, and reduce inventory. The key components include collaborative agreements to forecasts for standardized components among suppliers and manufacturing, real-time inventory visibility and constraint planning across the supply chain, and dynamic plant loading and rescheduling across manufacturing and supplier plants.

The goal of operations is typically to reduce inventory investments and related carrying costs, minimize inventory obsolescence, reduce order replenishment lead time, and improve manufacturing and supplier productivity. The challenge and mission of collaborative planning is to fix the information disconnects between supply chain partners across the extended enterprise. The underlying challenge is to improve the collaboration among retailers and manufacturers and among manufacturers and their suppliers through jointly managed processes and shared information.

Collaborative planning provides an environment for integrating demand- and supply-side processes to reduce inventory levels, shorten supply chain cycle times, and reduce supply chain costs. The benefits of collaborative planning include:

- Reduced inventories across the supply chain through real-time visibility of demand signals and system inventories.
- Reduced supply chain cycle time through integrated requirements planning and scheduling.
- Reduced physical asset requirements by enabling outsourcing of functions (e.g. manufacturing, assembly, etc.).
- Optimization of capacity utilization through real-time advanced planning and scheduling across multiple enterprises.
- Improved customer service through reduced order lead times and increased order fulfillment accuracy and reliability.

Advanced Planning and Scheduling (also known as *Advanced Manufacturing*) is a manufacturing management process that relies on integrated information to optimally allocate basic materials and production or service capacity to meet anticipated demand. Traditional planning and scheduling systems (such as MRP) use a stepwise procedure to allocate material and production capacity. This approach is simple but cumbersome: it does not readily adapt to changes in demand, resource capacity, or material availability. Materials and capacity are planned separately, and many systems do not consider limited material availability or capacity constraints.

APS simultaneously plans and schedules production based on available materials, labor, and plant capacity, thereby creating the platform to operate more effectively.

APS has commonly been applied where one or more of the following conditions are present:

- Make-to-order (pull) manufacturing and service operations.
- Capital- and/or resource-intensive production/service processes.
- Multi-product or multi-service environments.
- Products that require a large number of components, manufacturing tasks, or activities.
- Frequent and unpredictable schedule changes.

APS software (e.g., i2, Manugistics, SAP, and Oracle Production Planning/Materials Management modules) enables manufacturing and services scheduling and advanced scheduling optimization within these environments.

E-Procurement

E-procurement is the implementation of procurement processes among multiple enterprises using electronic business as a competitive enabler. E-procurement, as mentioned earlier, is the B2B, B2C, or business-to-government purchase and sale of products and services through the Internet as well as other information and networking systems, such as EDI and ERP.

E-procurement involves aligning electronic sourcing and purchasing with operations strategies for parts and services; purchasing commodity-based components through e-auctions or exchanges; electronically transmitting purchase orders, shipping notifications, and quality certificates; and ensuring visibility into part availability through online part catalogs and storefronts. The goal is to achieve reduced component costs (and total cost of ownership), minimized procurement processing costs, and shortened sourcing and procurement cycle times.

Typically, e-procurement enables operations to ensure procurement compliance by increasing the use of preferred suppliers, reducing off-contract spending, and reducing processing errors for more products and services at lower prices. In addition, e-procurement provides greater oversight of purchasing spend and often provides consolidated details of the actual spend with each supplier and in each product or service category, so that the full purchasing power is leveraged to negotiate increased discounts and appropriate product or service categories can be targeted for preferred supplier contracts. Finally, e-procurement reduces the administrative cost for each transaction that is shifted from paper to electronic channels, thereby reducing error rates, processing time, fax and phone usage, and on-site inventory, which enables sourcing to focus on value-added activities such as negotiating even better supplier contracts.

Most e-procurement Web sites allow qualified and registered users to identify potential buyers or sellers of relevant products and services. Subsequently, buyers or sellers may specify costs or pursue an RFx. E-procurement can also be integrated into the wider purchase-to-pay (P2P) value

---

KEY TERM

Purchase-to-pay (P2P) Label applied to business processes for requesting (requisitioning), purchasing, receiving, and paying for goods and services and accounting for those transactions. This term is most frequently used in the context of ERP purchasing and payment modules and e-procurement applications.

E-PROCUREMENT TECHNOLOGY COMPONENTS

TOOLS

- Electronic catalogue, held within the enterprise, outside, or a combination.
- Work flow for routing requisitions and catalogue updates.
- Transaction engine to record requisitions, issue POs, etc.
- ERP interface(s).
- Data warehouse for spend analysis.
- Infrastructure: PC with browser, Intranet, servers, etc.

chain with the trend toward closed-loop supply chain management.

> **Knowledge management**
> Strategy and implementation of capturing, retaining, and retrieving enterprise knowledge to increase corporate learning.
> **KEY TERM**

The new generation of e-procurement is now on-demand or delivered as software-as-a-service (SaaS). The e-procurement value chain consists of e-tendering, e-auctioning, vendor management, catalogue management, and contract management. Elements of e-procurement include Request for Information, Request for Proposal, Request for Quotation, RFx (the previous three together), eRFx (software for managing RFx projects), and, frequently, knowledge management.

E-procurement takes supply chain management to the next level, providing real-time information to the vendor on the status of a customer's needs. For example, a vendor may have an agreement with Bob to automatically ship materials when his stock level reaches a low point, so Bob doesn't need to ask for it—and risk forgetting.

Conclusion

When considering implementing any technology for operations, it's imperative to engage cross-organizational leaders as soon as possible and to encourage sponsors and leaders to review other implementations (within and outside of operations and within and outside the industry). The operations manager should think strategically, but pursue tactical benefits as needed for support—definitely not let technology or IT drive the solution. Leadership or strategic posture changes can impact plans; it's important to build stage-gates and logical stopping points into release strategy. In the final analysis, requirements and strategic imperative are two different things—and both can impact the overarching operations technology infrastructure.

Operations Manager's Checklist for Chapter 11

☑ Technology is a way of life for the operations manager; it is no longer optional.

- ☑ Address e-SCM as in integral part of your enterprise-wide philosophy. Operational requirements and the needs of the extended enterprise should drive the operations manager's use of technology.

- ☑ MRP, MRP II, and ERP have evolved to make the operations manager's life simpler in many ways; package-enabled re-engineering can help him or her get up to speed quickly by adopting best practices.

- ☑ Operations technology should be driven by business needs, not merely an IT initiative.

- ☑ Embracing operations technology and working with IT professionals can help the operations manager to optimize the technology platform necessary to institutionalize operational practices that can truly make a difference.

- ☑ Tomorrow's model for operations differs from today's; bandwidth and security will be challenges.

- ☑ Operations technology is integrative in approach, global in reach, and inclusive by nature . . . and it loves rule breakers.

Chapter
12

Corporate Social Responsibility: Saving the Planet Is Good Business

A s an operations manager, you're responsible for 95 percent of the value that's added in transforming goods or services across the extended enterprise. That naturally makes you also accountable for what happens within that enterprise, whether it affects the employees who make those goods or services, the customers who use them, or the environment.

Companies cannot ignore issues of social responsibility or environmental concerns, nor should they want to do so. Increasing government regulation and stronger public mandates for social and environmental accountability have brought these issues into the executive suite and onto strategic planning agendas—and the operations manager is in the thick of the action. Fortunately, companies are integrating their operations and supply chain processes to lower costs, better serve customers, increase diversity, and decrease risk. To address these clearly interdependent trends, companies must involve their entire operations, including the extended supply chain, to meet and even exceed the expectations of their customers, stakeholders, and governments for environmental and social responsibility.

The Basics

Corporate social responsibility (CSR)—also known as *corporate responsibility, corporate citizenship, responsible business, corporate sustainability,*

223

 **Corporate social responsibility** "Operating a business in a manner that accounts for the social and environmental impact created by the business ... a commitment to developing policies that integrate responsible practices into daily business operations."

—As You Sow (*www.asyousow.org/csr*)

corporate sustainable development, sustainable responsible business, and *corporate social performance*—serves as an integrating element for business strategy. There's no universally accepted definition for CSR. Many see it as the private sector's way of institutionalizing the economic, social, and environmental imperatives of its activities. It crosses organizational boundaries and includes functions, processes, and geographies as, ideally, a self-regulating mechanism by which enterprises proactively adhere to laws, ethical standards, and international norms.

 When implemented effectively, CSR can contribute to competitive advantage by:

- Supporting gains in operational efficiency.
- Improving risk management.
- Enhancing favorable relations with the investment community.
- Increasing access to capital.
- Improving employee relations.
- Strengthening relationships with communities.
- Improving reputation and branding.

Social Responsibilities: Making the World Better

It goes without saying that we should all accept our social responsibility and it should be good business, influencing all facets of the business model, including branding, marketing, financing, HR, and, of course, operations. Although CSR must be incorporated into the overall corporate business strategy and even organizational culture, it remains particularly incumbent on the operations manager to execute socially responsible strategies or institutionalize this socially conscious culture through his or her plans, policies, and activities. As operations manager, you do this by being aware of the effects on people and the environment from each of those processes under your direct or immediate control.

In simple terms, it's like the Boy Scout approach, in the words of the organization's founder, Robert Baden-Powell: "Try and leave this world a little better than you found it." In other words ...

- Did we ensure that our manufacturing transformation process left no by-products that would harm the environment?
- Did we add jobs in a depressed area?
- Did we contribute to the local economy?
- Did we set the example for those around us?

Social issues now affect company operations, joint ventures, licenses, franchises, and supply contracts across the entire extended value chain necessary to produce and market goods and services. In addition to these considerations, an increasing number of strategic alliances are being established to ensure corporate social accountability. A wide range of participants are engaging in private-sector initiatives at global, regional, national, and local levels. Recently, hybrid coalitions among enterprises, workers, non-governmental organizations (NGOs), investors, and others have emerged as well.

THE DIVERSE SUPPLY CHAIN   SMART

MANAGING

Supply base diversity is increasing through efforts to engage a wider range of suppliers in sourcing processes and decisions, working with businesses owned by women and members of minorities, with the prospect of making the extended enterprise more effective. In this context, according to the Institute for Supply Management™ (www.ism.ws), operations managers are endeavoring to:

- Provide socially diverse suppliers the opportunity to participate in sourcing opportunities.
- Promote inclusion of diverse suppliers in their organizations' supplier development and mentoring programs.
- Ensure long-term program sustainability through application of forward-thinking concepts beyond price.

According to As You Sow, an organization that promotes CSR, common CSR policies and practices include the following:

- Improving internal controls for more ethical accounting.
- Committing to diversity in hiring employees and barring all forms of discrimination.

- Encouraging managers to view employees as assets rather than costs.
- Integrating the ideas and suggestions of line employees into decision-making processes.
- Adopting operating policies that exceed compliance with social and environmental laws.
- Thinking of resources in more advanced ways, focusing on using natural resources in more productive, efficient, and profitable ways.
- "Taking responsibility for conditions under which goods are produced directly or by contract employees domestically or abroad."

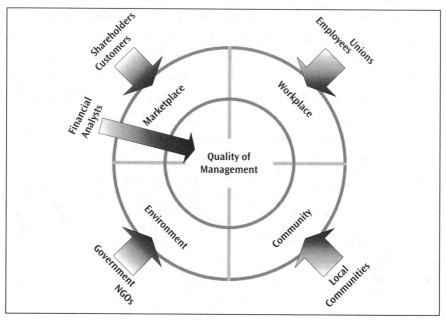

Exhibit 12-1. The business in society. Source: Mallen Baker, Development Director, Business in the Community, Business Respect, *www.businessrespect.net*

Environmental Responsibility

Environmental responsibility is a growing focus within CSR, as shown in the basic CSR cycle (Exhibit 12-2), and the area in which you as operations manager can most likely have the greatest impact.

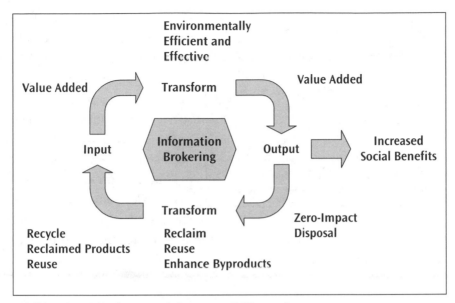

Exhibit 12-2. Corporate social responsibility cycle

Green Operations

Green operations is the execution arm of the CSR strategy. It necessarily incorporates socially responsible processes that use environmentally friendly inputs, transform these inputs with change agents whose by-products can improve or be recycled within the existing environment, and create outputs that can be either reclaimed at the end of their life cycle or disposed of without adversely affecting the environment. It sounds like a tough order to fill, having your earth and saving it, too, but the whole idea of a sustainable supply chain is to reduce costs while helping the environment.

Traditionally, many people have associated being environmentally friendly or socially responsible with increasing your costs, and on a piece part basis in isolation, they may have been correct in this assumption. But for a *sustainable* world, the thinking should be predicated on understanding the system costs using a *total cost of ownership* (TCO)

Sustainability "Meeting the needs of the present without compromising the ability of future genera- **KEY TERM** tions to meet their needs."

—World Commission on Environment and Development

KEY TERM **Total cost of ownership (TCO)** A method of cost analysis designed to determine the direct and indirect lifetime costs of acquiring, operating, transforming, and disposing of a product or service. For example, if you buy a car, the TCO might include the title, license, taxes, maintenance, insurance, fuel, repairs, and disposal (or residual value) of the car 12 years from now.

perspective for the life cycle of this product, service, or supply chain process.

Many operations managers use environmental and social issues to their advantage. They innovate with leading-edge solutions, such as "trading information for inventory" (using Electronic Data Interchange, for example) and reducing waste, that help them make operations more efficient and effective while helping the environment.

One of the bigger issues facing operations managers these days is the actions of suppliers. Companies today are being held accountable for environmental and social problems such as underage child labor used by suppliers and sub-tier suppliers throughout the extended enterprise. Unfortunately, the public and press unite to ostracize companies that deal with companies that are environmentally or socially irresponsible, especially if an adverse situation occurs, such as lead in toys or contaminated milk. Can you or your company afford that type of exposure? Many companies necessarily perform environmental or CSR audits or implement "rules of conduct" to coordinate the actions of their supply base. Others insource the activities to avoid the risk.

These companies recognize the opportunities associated with being environmentally responsible. In addition to reducing costs, complying with regulations, and appeasing shareholders, green supply chain initia-

FOR EXAMPLE **USTAINABILITY**
Sustainability can also be profitable. GE uses its *Ecomagination* program—"a business initiative to help meet customers' demand for cleaner and more energy-efficient products and to drive reliable growth for GE"—to focus on growing its revenue stream from environmentally friendly products. GE's Ecomagination division includes 80 "clean technology" products and had revenues of US$17 billion in 2008, with forecasts of US$25 billion in revenues by 2010. R&D spending within the division will rise to US$1.5 billion by 2010.

tives have the potential to boost revenues as well. Attracting incremental shoppers who are environmentally conscious is a major motivation behind the *carbon labeling* initiative. In some (albeit limited) cases, "greener" products, such as organic foods, are able to justify price premiums. With nominal extra costs, organic foods in some product categories can be priced substantially higher than non-organic foods.

> **KEY TERMS**
>
> **Carbon labeling** Marking a product with its full carbon footprint—the total amount of greenhouse gases emitted across the life cycle of the product, from production to end use and disposal.
>
> **Carbon footprint** A measure of the impact human activities have on the environment in terms of the amount of greenhouse gases produced, measured in units of carbon dioxide.

Jessica, our socially conscious mother (and family operations manager), might be inclined, like many consumers, to pay more for food grown organically and for products with lower carbon footprints. If you can develop a sustainable and socially viable supply chain, you can save significant money by not having to dispose of harmful by-products, by reducing obsolescence, and by decreasing the amount spent on scrap and the resources spent on regulatory compliance. Several companies have developed new revenue sources from the by-products they used to discard. Many companies are using sustainability as a competitive advantage to grow market share.

Going Green

So how would you start your pursuit of green operations? If you've adopted the lean principles described earlier in this book, you're well on your way. In addition, the United States Environmental Protection Agency (EPA) has produced a guide called *The Lean and Green Supply Chain: A Practical Guide for Materials Managers and Supply Chain Managers to Reduce Costs and Improve Environmental Performance* (2000, *www.epa.gov/oppt/library/pubs/archive/acct-archive/pubs/lean.pdf*). In addition to synthesizing the best practices of leading U.S. companies that have saved millions of dollars while reducing or eliminating significant environmental impacts, this guidebook provides a systematic approach to implementing a green supply chain, using a four-step decision-making process:

1. Identify environmental costs within your process or facility.
2. Determine opportunities that would yield significant cost savings and reduce environmental impact.
3. Calculate the benefits of your proposed alternatives.
4. Decide, implement, and monitor your improvement solutions.

The EPA has also produced *The Lean and Environment Toolkit* (2007, *www.epa.gov/lean/toolkit/LeanEnviroToolkit.pdf*). This book, sponsored by EPA's Lean Manufacturing and Environment Initiative, presents practical experience collected by the EPA from partner companies and organizations that tried coordinating lean implementation and environmental management.

The green supply chain management transformation roadmap (Archstone Consulting), Exhibit 12-3, charts an evolution model from awareness through discovery to sustainability. The model consists of three iterations through a four-step cycle.

Green Supply Chain Management

Going green means evaluating and managing a supply chain with environmental impact and overall resource usage as a primary concern. Green initiatives emphasize using fewer inputs and generating less waste in manufacturing and distribution processes. These initiatives include:

- Reducing packaging materials.
- Using recycled materials in products and packaging.
- Switching to renewable energy supplies and lower-emission transportation vehicles.
- Eliminating toxic materials from products.
- Reusing post-consumer products.

Green supply chain management goes beyond compliance with environmental laws and regulations. It involves re-engineering activities in the value chain. The importance of green issues has risen significantly, driven by numerous developments:

- Sharp rise in oil prices and fuel costs

EVOLUTION MODEL		① Secure Strategic Direction	② Establish Baseline and Define Metrics	③ Align with External Partners	④ Establish Internal Infra-Structure and Governance
AWARENESS	Attributes	▪ No green strategy or alignment with other initiatives ▪ Informal/ad hoc green projects	▪ Green baseline and metrics largely unknown	▪ No/minimal external collaboration	▪ Green projects are functionally siloed ▪ No ongoing resources specifically devoted to green initiatives
AWARENESS	Actions	▪ Green initiative driven by new industry requirements/regulations	▪ Requested metrics addressed as regulations dictate	▪ Initiatives focus internally	▪ Wait-and-see approach requires minimal changes to business as usual
DISCOVERY	Attributes	▪ No green strategy/goals or low priority for company and most senior officials	▪ Typically cost-driven or compliance initiatives, which dictate metrics	▪ External parties have limited input and involvement into green initiatives	▪ Limited cross-functional teams ▪ Few ongoing resources devoted to green supply chain management
DISCOVERY	Actions	▪ Green projects primarily initiated in response to regulation changes, competition, or initiatives by upstream/downstream partners	▪ Baseline established for internal impacts and perhaps major impacts (e.g., raw material from largest supplier)	▪ External discussions limited to key vendors	▪ Some formal process, goal tracking, and incentives are put in place
SUSTAINABILITY	Attributes	▪ Executive leadership driving initiative ▪ Green supply chain management one of firm's top strategic initiatives	▪ Focus of green initiative explicit (e.g., waste minimization, carbon footprint reduction, sustainability of products)	▪ Opportunities identified with upstream/downstream partners and through discussions with external organizations	▪ Organization aligned in all major departments to meet outlined green goals/objectives
SUSTAINABILITY	Actions	▪ Aspirational green goals outlined and communicated broadly	▪ Key metrics and goals defined (e.g., end product carbon footprint levels, energy usage, % sustainable inputs) ▪ Baseline measures determined for all products (both internally and externally influenced)	▪ Vendor scorecard developed (perhaps with software to document carbon footprint) ▪ Work with downstream buyers (e.g., to improve recycling) ▪ Input solicited from non-government orgs (NGOs), regulators, the scientific community, and shareholders to align efforts	▪ Initiative owners announced ▪ "Green" roles incorporated into existing positions and new positions added ▪ Tracking system and associated incentives tied to goals

Exhibit 12-3. Green supply chain management transformation roadmap. Copyright © Archstone Consulting. Used with permission. All rights reserved.

▪ New environmental regulations and legal requirements

▪ High-profile green initiatives by major retailers

▪ Increased mass media attention to product safety and industrial pollution

■ Rising consumer awareness of environmental issues and preference for "green" products

■ Shareholder proposals requiring environmental reporting

■ Increased access to information on global supply chain operations via the Internet

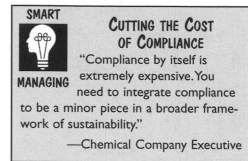

SMART MANAGING

CUTTING THE COST OF COMPLIANCE

"Compliance by itself is extremely expensive. You need to integrate compliance to be a minor piece in a broader framework of sustainability."

—Chemical Company Executive

Collaboration is critical for successful green supply chain management, which requires engagement with both traditional and nontraditional stakeholders:

■ material suppliers
■ retailers
■ consumers
■ shareholders
■ employees
■ energy and water suppliers
■ state and federal governments
■ NGOs
■ scientific community

In the final analysis, green initiatives can be applied throughout the value chain.

Green Supply Chain Planning. During planning and product design, we can replace high-carbon-footprint (high-C) materials and incorporate the concepts of reduce, recycle, reuse, and least-impact disposal in product design. It is at this point that the organization should innovate with environmentally responsible materials and processes, and ideas for minimizing waste generation. At all junctures, the materials, processes, and services should consume less energy. At this stage the organization should consider adopting environmental cost accounting to identify and assign discrete costs using life-cycle analytical and Design for Environment (DfE) techniques (e.g., Energy Star rating by the U.S. EPA).

Sourcing the Green Supply Chain. Sourcing must require environmentally responsible standards for raw materials and outsourced services by collaborating with suppliers. An effective tool is an Environmental Scorecard. Sourcing and purchasing should be reorganized to include green C-level execs reporting to the CEO who do the following:

- Trade in energy futures.
- Practice *cap and trade.*
- Certify material by accredited third parties (e.g., Green Seal, Germany's Blue Angel, Cradle-to-Cradle, LEED [Leadership in Energy and Environmental Design] for facilities, etc.).
- Audit the supply chain and their suppliers according to international standards such as ISO 14000.

Just as Jessica has already replaced the light bulbs in her house with energy-efficient bulbs, the operations manager (using those good shoes we mentioned in Chapter 1) must virtually walk through the entire supply chain to reduce energy use in processes across the extended enterprise "from cradle to grave."

> **Cap and trade** "An environmental policy tool that delivers results with a mandatory cap on emissions while providing sources flexibility in how they comply. Successful cap and trade programs reward innovation, efficiency, and early action and provide strict environmental accountability without inhibiting economic growth."
>
> **KEY TERM**
>
> —U.S. Environmental Protection Agency

Green Manufacturing. Lean manufacturing is the cornerstone for environmentally conscious manufacturing. By focusing on minimizing or eliminating waste, you save money and help save the environment. You can also insist on Environmental Health and Safety training, improved maintenance based on measured environmental impact, environmental management systems (e.g., ISO 14000), environmental facilities management, vertical integration or alliances with energy suppliers, and an inherent capability (or user-friendly access) to perform carbon offsets.

Green Logistics. Green logistics necessarily takes a systems perspective and includes delivery as well as disposal and return of goods and materi-

> **SMART**
>
> ### Bright Ideas
>
> **MANAGING**
>
> An Energy Star qualified *compact fluorescent* light (CFL) bulb uses 75% less energy than an incandescent bulb and lasts about 10 times longer. It saves $30 or more in electricity costs over its lifetime and pays for itself in about six months. And CFLs produce about 75% less heat.
>
> CFLs also reduce mercury pollution. A coal-fueled power plant produces 13.6 mg of mercury to power one 60-watt incandescent bulb, but only 3.3 mg to power an equivalent CFL. A CFL contains up to 5 mg of mercury, so using a CFL rather than an incandescent bulb reduces mercury by at least 5.3 mg.
>
> Our operations managers will be busy checking the light bulbs.
>
> Source: U.S. EPA and Department of Energy, *www.energystar.gov*

als. It emphasizes reducing packaging, using alternate fuels (e.g., biofuels, liquefied natural gas), shifting volume to rail and sea to capitalize on economies of scale, and reducing the distance in the carbon footprint of products. The return cycle necessarily incorporates reverse logistics as a closed-loop supply chain with take-back regulatory obligations and an emphasis on *remanufacturing* (i.e., cleaning, repairing, and restoring used durable products), *reuse*, and *recycling*.

Green Supply Chain Trends

European companies producing consumer packaged goods (CPG) have already responded to environmental legislation that has created new operating requirements for companies, including:

- *Product Design*—eliminating toxic chemicals from electronics products, redesigning products for ease of disposal and reuse.
- *Procurement*—participating in emissions "cap and trade" system, sourcing recycled materials, collaboration with raw material suppliers to measure total carbon footprint.
- *Transportation/Logistics*—reducing packaging materials, using alternative-fuel vehicles.
- *Manufacturing*—using renewable energy sources.
- *Reverse Logistics*—participating in credit system to offset product recycle costs.

Even without European-style legislation requiring reduction of emissions and resource usage, American CPG companies are investing in vol-

untary green supply chain programs to drive costs lower and
meet requirements of their
partners. An estimated 85 percent of companies in the CPG
industry manage active green
programs. Internal priorities
are the main driver for about
60 percent of these green initiatives, more than the influence of regulatory compliance

> **KEY TERM**
>
> **Design for Environment (DfE)** General concept encompassing various design approaches for reducing the environmental impact of a product, a service, or a process across its life cycle. Among the approaches within DfE are Design for Disassembly, Design for Recycling, Design for Energy Efficiency, Design for Remanufacture, and Design for Disposability.

and pressure from high-influence supply chain partners. Companies are
increasingly participating in broad-based supply chain initiatives:

- Incorporating Design for Environment (DfE) concept that enables "closed-loop" supply chains, ensuring that products be designed for disassembly and recyclability.
- Joining industry groups and creating supply chain collaborations to adopt and support sound business processes that strengthen the entire supply chain (e.g., EPA Green Suppliers Network).

Reducing Carbon Footprints. A *carbon footprint*, as noted earlier, is a measure of the impact of human activities on the environment in terms of the
greenhouse gases produced, measured in units of carbon dioxide. A carbon footprint consists of two parts: the direct/primary footprint and the
indirect/secondary footprint. The *direct/primary footprint* is a measure of
our direct emissions of CO_2 from burning fossil fuels, including domestic
energy consumption and transportation (e.g., cars and planes). The *indi-
rect/secondary footprint* is a measure of the indirect CO_2 emissions from
the whole life cycle of products we use, associated with their manufacture
and eventual breakdown. Exhibit 12-4 shows the components of the average person's carbon footprint.

Global Green Developments

Organizations and regulations are promoting *environmentally preferable purchasing* (EPP)—"green purchasing." A few examples follow:

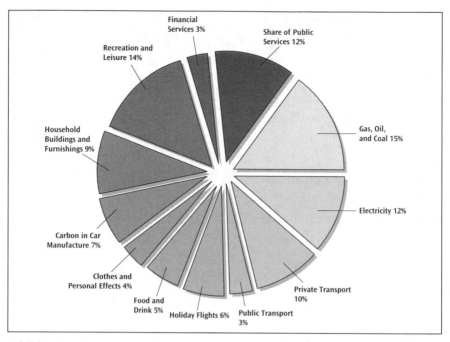

Exhibit 12-4. Breakdown of a typical person's carbon footprint in the developed world. Source: Carbon Footprint Ltd., *www.carbonfootprint.com/ carbonfootprint.html*

- The EPA developed Guidance for Environmentally Preferable Purchasing (*www.epa.gov/oppt/epp/index.htm*).
- Japan enacted the Green Purchasing Law in 2000 as national policy (*www.env.go.jp/en/laws/policy/green/1.pdf*).
- The International Green Purchasing Network was founded in April 2005 (*www.igpn.org*).
- India started the Green Purchasing Network India (*gpni.emcentre.com*).
- In the European Union (EU), companies need to take into consideration three regulatory dynamics:
  - Material content policy that includes implementation of EU restrictions on hazardous substances.
  - Product take-back policy, encompassing end-of-life policies for electronics, automobiles, and packaging (currently being re-examined for possible inclusion in a major new piece of legislation).

- Food safety laws that are becoming stricter and require investment in supply chain monitoring and information exchange.
- Regulatory directives focused on consumer products:
  - Performance requirements—Product fuel economy, energy efficiency, and emissions standards.
- U.S.'s National Energy Policy.
- EU's Directive on "eco-design" of energy-using products—
  - Impacts performance targets, labeling, and reporting requirements.
  - Focus on end-product design that affects supply chain functions: planning, sourcing, manufacturing, and marketing.
- Material mandates on environmental and human health issues concerning use of toxic and hazardous materials—
  - U.S. uses the FDA and the Consumer Product Safety Commission.
  - EU's Restriction of Hazardous Substances (RoHS), 2003.
- Carbon credit trading programs "cap and trade"—
  - Companies buy carbon allowances from other global companies to exceed their carbon emission allowances.
  - U.S. Congress is evaluating this option, which is prevalent in EU.
- Carbon tax and fees—
  - U.S. has excise taxes on ozone-depleting chemicals and tax credits for buying electric vehicles.

DON'T EXPECT REWARDS FOR RESPONSIBILITY

"To assume that the business environment has fundamentally changed and that we are entering a new world in which CSR has become critical to the success of *all* or even *most* firms is misinformed. The market has many virtues, but reconciling corporate goals and public purposes is unfortunately not among them. Managers *should* try to act more responsibly. But they should not expect the market to necessarily reward them—or punish their less responsible competitors."

—David Vogel, professor, Haas School of Business, University of California, Berkeley, and author, *The Market for Virtue: The Potential and Limits of Corporate Social Responsibility* (Brookings, 2005)

Operations Manager's Checklist for Chapter 12

☑ Corporate social responsibility is playing a continually greater role in the life of most operations managers.

☑ Be aware of the issues and regulations and take action for our environment, in order to survive and succeed in operations management.

☑ Global regulations and agencies will continue to enforce environmentally and socially responsible policies, but CSR and "green" can also be good for business. Reducing energy use and waste across the extended enterprise contributes to the bottom line, both in the near term and, more important, over the long haul.

☑ Operations managers who use lean systems approaches can develop CSR into an entrepreneurial (rather than opportunistic) competitive advantage.

The Role of the Operations Manager:

Using Science and Art to Meet the Challenges Ahead

I n its purest sense, operations is simple: First, you forecast, plan, and schedule to meet demand. Second, you source (and outsource) and procure. Third, you've got inventories to manage–raw materials or parts or components that you transform into finished goods. Fourth, you get rid of the finished goods in your inventory through logistics and distribution. Plan. Buy. Make. Move. Sell. Getting it in the right order is not so hard. Getting it right usually is.

The Challenges Ahead

Throughout this book we have suggested that operations managers must exercise a significant role in developing a firm's competitive advantage, particularly with regard to customer satisfaction, quality, and total systems cost. The strategic firm must include operations and operational considerations in its planning, development, and execution across the extended enterprise.

New concepts and techniques will further improve operations and challenge operations managers. We can't open a business periodical without reading about low-cost country sourcing, global supply descriptions, the economic crisis, mass customization, business process redesign, lean production, the learning organization, or corporate re-engineering as radical new visions for changing the direction of operations practice. At each turn, organizations are challenged by the threat of "the new competition" (Michael Best, *The New Competition*, Harvard University Press, 1990). To survive under such constraints will require different perspectives and skills. These fundamental and profound changes in business practices have significant implications for operations professionals.

The New Competition

Firms are competing in new ways. Bureaucratic and hierarchical operations are doomed whereas process excellence and operational execution will prevail. The new competition embodies global networks comprised of adaptive, learning organizations can respond quickly to marketplace changes. Micro-level concerns are of particular interest to operations.

Operations managers will need to lead efforts to break down functional silos and view functional units as interdependent parts of the supply chain. Embracing quality and lean operations will be a necessary condition but not sufficient to compete. Coordination across the extended enterprise will necessarily be most challenged in addressing the supply chain upstream and down. What must evolve is a flexible, robust network in which firms are linked together to gain sustainable strategic advantage through value-added sourcing, innovative logistics, and strategic outsourcing. The traditionally critical facets of forecasting, planning, scheduling, and inventory management will be institutionalized along process lines through user-friendly technologies. Operations managers will redefine their relationships with suppliers, customers, and even competitors as well as restructure their internal organization along lean and socially responsible lines.

In response to the global challenges and competition, more cooperative relationships between supply chain members offer potential competitive advantage. The question is not whether strategic alliances are a good idea, but rather how operations managers, by building upon the core competencies within their service operations, can best lead and leverage the extended enterprise.

The operations manager, who must broker inter-firm information sharing, becomes a critical participant in the process, guiding both the formation and implementation of strategic relationships and inter-firm supply networks. Thus, the operations professional manages information and external manufacturing and/or service operations across the extended enterprise. He or she must gather and filter relevant operations-related knowledge about products and services, processes, competition, and other factors that can affect the firm's competitive posture, and he or she must subsequently use this information to make informed decisions that put the extended enterprise first. This step-function change in thinking suggests a transformation from reactive, transaction-based operations to proactive, value-added operational execution.

At the core of this transformation is a recognition that functions must cooperate and share in the responsibility of meeting (and exceeding where necessary) customer demands by using all means at their disposal. A firm is unlikely to have an "operations problem," a "production problem," or a "service problem." Similarly, it is more likely that most supply problems transcend the operations function.

It seems a truism now that earlier partner involvement in design and operations can reduce the underlying cost structure while improving reliability and predictability. It's also important that greater (and better integrated) information sharing permits the extended enterprise to better manage its logistics and production/service scheduling, thereby also reducing the total costs of ownership and leading to greater customer satisfaction. With clear advantages in terms of time and innovation, such changes have and will continue to have a profound impact on the operations profession.

As mentioned in Chapter 1, the goal of operations is to minimize the inherent tradeoffs in making a product or delivering a service. That is, a focus on fundamental processes allows a better grasp of the basic changes that affect the firm's ability to compete and to meet the ever-changing needs in the marketplace.

For the operations manager, it is critical to understand the whole of the value chain and to appreciate the full range of activities involved in the manufacturing of a component or finished product or in developing and executing a service delivery model. Again, functional integration takes precedence over individual functions and cross-functional teams increase in importance. The question facing the operations manager is how to most effectively assemble the winning team.

Organizational Implications. To adapt to the new competition, the operations manager must influence fundamental transformations at all levels of the extended enterprise that will affect each functional area. For operations, these profound changes are critical for the future well-being of the firm. A key force for the new competition is the organization's ability to form linkages with other businesses that can provide competitive advantage. Operations can serve as the point around which both internal and external relationships are better nurtured and managed.

The Role of Operations in Creating and Sustaining Knowledge. Operations managers must engender a strong commitment to the firm's mission and goals. Managers must not only articulate the goals but also have a well-defined plan for achieving those goals. Execution is essential. Each functional unit must understand precisely its role in the process and sublimate its agenda for the greater purpose—sustained competitive advantage. For the operations manager, it requires a vision that spans the entire value chain, beginning with basic raw materials and ending with the customer. This vision must be congruent with, and in support of, the firm's mission and goals.

Additionally, operations must devote greater attention to those skills inherent in understanding and contributing to the firm's value-creating activities. Operations' contributes to controlling costs as well as to improving overall performance in quality, dependability, flexibility, and innovation. In this context, the operations manager becomes a source of knowledge regarding the processes that form the value chain. Working in conjunction with other functional managers and as part of a learning organization, the operations manager provides input for make-or-buy or strategic relationship decisions. Whatever the corporate objective, operations can influence the firm's strategic posture.

Make-or-buy decisions must be predicated on a true understanding of their relative merits. Outsourcing core operations has started the death spiral for many companies. Operations should actively contribute to the store of knowledge from which the firm defines its core competencies and decides which set of skills and activities to keep and which ones to shed. This "dis-integration" of the firm is a key component of the new competition. Non-essential activities will flow from the firm to its network, and this resultant web of firms will behave as though the work were done internally. With the operations manager's understanding of the upstream and downstream markets, he or she can help assess the leverage points that contribute to competitive advantage.

The operations manager helps protect the firm's competitive advantage, particularly as it relates to the body of corporate knowledge affected by the strategic relationships. The operations manager must help establish the parameters of information sharing and knowledge transfer between the partners. The operations manager must take care not to jeopardize the firm's core skills and capabilities by outsourcing key process or product elements and then losing that skill. The operations manager must also be watchful of partners who might use information they gain to place the firm at a competitive disadvantage, such as a buyer or supplier who could learn information that permits it to compete with you at a point further downstream.

Conclusion

Throughout this book, we have attempted to describe the new competition and present the implications it holds for the operations manager. To a large extent, this book is intended as a basic introduction, with a hidden agenda as a wake-up call.

As businesses grapple with how to make fundamental changes in how they compete, operations managers face new challenges. They must adapt to these changes and rethink the manner in which they formulate and execute operations strategy as a component of the larger corporate goals and objectives. Traditional views of operations and of other functional units are no longer valid. As functional and organizational boundaries fall, operations managers must acquire new skill sets and levels of expertise.

But the responsibility for transforming cannot come from external sources; it remains resident within operations. To lead this transformation, operations professionals must change themselves. The dynamics of competition are such that speed is essential. Lead time, time to market, and cycle time are key metrics for the successful global player.

TRANSFORMING THE OPERATIONS PROFESSIONAL

SMART MANAGING

- Manage both operations and the range of possible support services.
- Orchestrate the initial scope and nature of relationships with key stakeholders, relying on your ability to persuade and influence.
- Encourage the exchange of information within and across organizational boundaries at all levels.
- Plan, then execute—in that order. Measure twice and cut once.
- Help to develop and monitor the performance criteria on which operational effectiveness is based.
- Develop the requisite skills to nurture and sustain mutually beneficial relationships.
- Develop strategic insight and business knowledge beyond traditional operations information.
- Use technology and process to institutionalize leading-edge operations.
- Take calculated risks and explore alternatives in order to lead organization change.
- Create a mentoring culture within the firm and across the supply chain.

Even as these profound changes affect operations, the management cycle of planning, organizing, directing, motivating, controlling, and evaluating will remain fundamental to leveraging the value of operations in the organization. Undoubtedly, the inherent demands on people, processes, technology, and systems will be greater, and it will be necessary to reinvent operations management. The type of people operations managers employ and the way they plan, organize, direct, motivate, control, and evaluate operations will have to reflect the new challenges and opportunities described in this book. In the final analysis, operations managers will lead by "walking around" (both physically and virtually) the extended operations and will benefit from having good shoes and a small desk.

The challenges will be demanding, but the rewards for us and our organizations will clearly justify the sacrifices we must make.

Operations Manager's Checklist for Chapter 13

☑ Companies of all sizes and across the globe are facing a period of dramatic changes in business practices. Operations managers must adapt changes to remain strategic assets.

☑ In the "new competition," bureaucracy and hierarchy will make way for leaner, flexible, more creative management styles. Cooperation and collaboration will replace conflict within the supply chain.

☑ By effectively combining the scientific basis underpinning operations with artful application, the operations manager will be able to develop and lead the supply chain across the extended enterprise to meet these new needs.

☑ The role of the operations manager is to help nurture and manage these developing inter-company cooperation and supply chain partnerships. Operations managers should provide support to the partnerships while monitoring, controlling, and even brokering the flow of information across the supply chain.

Index